AMONG INDIAN RAJAHS AND RYOTS

AMONG INDIAN RAJAHS AND RYOTS

A CIVIL SERVANT'S RECOLLECTIONS & IMPRESSIONS OF THIRTY-SEVEN YEARS OF WORK & SPORT IN THE CENTRAL PROVINCES & BENGAL

SIR ANDREW H. L. FRASER, K.C.S.I.

GYAN

Published by

Gyan Publishing House
5, Ansari Road
Daryaganj, New Delhi-110002
Phone: 011-47034999, 9811692060
E-mail: books@gyanbooks.com

Distribution Network
gyanbooks.com
India, USA, Canada, UK, Australia, France

ISBN : 978-81-212-9765-3 (PB)
First Published, 1911

2nd Impression 2023

Printed at: Gyan Press, Delhi.

AMONG INDIAN RAJAHS AND RYOTS
Author: SIR ANDREW H. L. FRASER

AMONG INDIAN RAJAHS AND RYOTS

INDIAN IDOLS

Mahadeva ("the Great God") Siva (the Destroyer and Reproducer) and his wife Parvati riding on the Sacred Bull. This image is at the Bamra State headquarters. Parvati is also called Durga. Both the God and Goddess are usually represented as terrible, but this is the most pleasant representation of them.

AMONG INDIAN RAJAHS AND RYOTS

A CIVIL SERVANT'S RECOLLECTIONS & IMPRESSIONS OF THIRTY-SEVEN YEARS OF WORK & SPORT IN THE CENTRAL PROVINCES & BENGAL

BY

SIR ANDREW H. L. FRASER, K.C.S.I.

M.A., LL.D., LITT.D.

EX-LIEUTENANT-GOVERNOR OF BENGAL

THIRD & REVISED EDITION

WITH TWENTY-FOUR ILLUSTRATIONS & A MAP

1912

TO

MY WIFE

WHO SHARED MY WORK

FOR TWENTY-FIVE YEARS IN INDIA

CONTENTS

LIST OF ILLUSTRATIONS

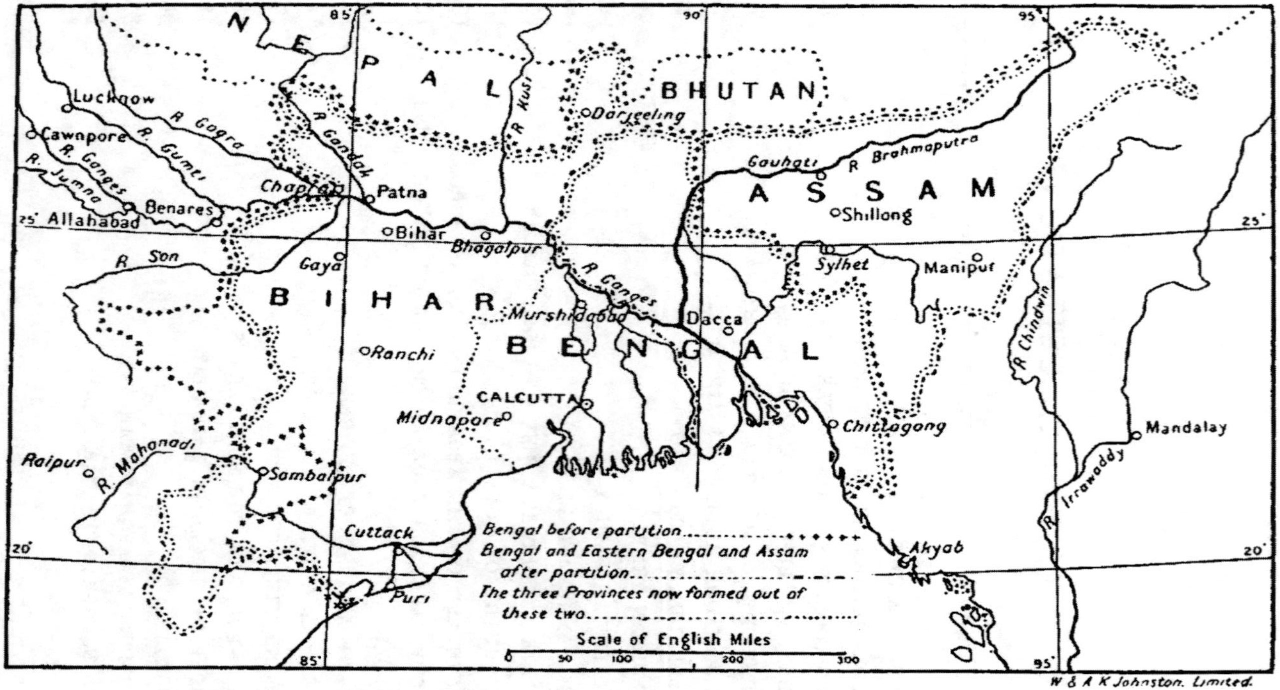

SKETCH MAP OF BENGAL BEFORE AND AFTER PARTITION AND THE EXISTING ARRANGEMENT AS ANNOUNCED BY KING GEORGE AT DELHI.

AMONG INDIAN RAJAHS AND RYOTS

CHAPTER I

EARLY DAYS

I WENT out to India impressed with the dignity of our Service, an impression derived from some of my European friends whose lives had been spent in India, from my intercourse with Indian gentlemen who were my fellow-probationers, and from reading about the life and work of those who had been employed in the making and maintenance of our Indian Empire. I found myself in a novel atmosphere and among strange and unaccustomed surroundings. I well remember the sense of loneliness which possessed me at the first. I went out at a somewhat early date so that I might spend a little time at Poona, before reporting myself for duty. I suppose it may have been due to this fact that no orders had been received in Bombay as to my destination. All that I was able to find out there was that, as I was posted to the North-West Provinces of India, I must first of all report myself at Allahabad.

Accordingly, after a short visit to Poona, I went to Allahabad, and there reported myself to the Chief Secretary. I arrived about the end of October, when Allahabad was exceedingly hot and uncomfortable. Being still unacquainted with Indian ways, I walked over from the hotel to the Secretariate at eleven o'clock. I found the Chief Secretary a most genial, courteous, and kindly man. After we had talked some time about the Service, and when I was rising to leave, he offered to call my trap. I told him that I had walked over from the hotel. He warned me seriously that at that season it was by no means a wise thing for a European to walk about in the sun, and insisted on sending for a trap for me. The trap came, and I drove in it to the Fort to visit two young officers whom I had known at home and who were stationed at Allahabad.

After I had seen them, and lunched with them, I drove to the hotel; and with some difficulty made the driver of my trap understand that I wanted to know how much I had to pay him as his fare. To my horror he told me that he was not an ordinary cab-driver, but the servant of the Chief Secretary. I had therefore the chagrin of writing a humble apology to that officer for having used his trap so long, an apology which required some care; for this entailed an explanation how his elegant conveyance had been mistaken by a miserable "griffin" for one that was for hire. A very kindly letter was received in return, informing me that I was posted to Nagpur in the Central Provinces, and asking me to dine at the Club that evening.

I proceeded the next day by train to Nagpur. This second journey took somewhat over thirty hours by rail. My knocking about and my exposure had made me feel rather indisposed; and I was huddled up in a corner of a commodious first-class carriage, such as they supply for long journeys in India, when a gentleman entered the train at Jubbulpore. He at once began to talk to me; for Europeans are still very kindly to one another in India, and were even more so then than now. He was soon in possession of the facts that I was one of the new batch of civilians, that I had already made a long journey to Allahabad, and that I was posted to the Central Provinces. I asked him about the hotel accommodation in Nagpur. He told me that there was no hotel, but that there was a Dak (or Travellers') Bungalow.

It was thus that I became acquainted with Mr. J. W. Chisholm, who, though considerably my senior, has been my friend throughout my service, and is my friend to this day. He told me that he was the District Magistrate of Jubbulpore, and had just been appointed to take up the newly-created Excise Commissionership. He said that he was going to stay with Mr. J. W. Neill, the Chief Secretary, that he would probably be at the station to meet him, and that he was sure that I should not be allowed to go to the Dak Bungalow. So it turned out; for Mr. Neill took me into his house, offered me the choice of my first District, and, finding that I knew nothing about the Central Provinces, advised me to ask for the District of Jubbulpore. The officiating Chief Commissioner, Col. Keatinge, posted me to Jubbulpore accordingly; and, after a few pleasant days spent with Mr. Neill, I had another journey of twenty-four hours back to that station.

It was in the beautiful station of Jubbulpore that I began my long Indian career. It has had much variety of experience and of interest, and has afforded me unique opportunities of becoming acquainted with India and its peoples. I served the Crown for thirty-seven years, of which over a quarter of a century was spent in the Central Provinces, of which I have (perhaps on that account only) the most pleasant memories. I spent a whole year in visiting every province in India and almost every important Native State, as a member of the Commission appointed to inquire into the use and abuse of intoxicating drugs, of which my friend, Sir Mackworth Young, was the President. After that I served with the Government of India as Secretary in the Home Department. Then after a few years as Chief Commissioner of my old Province, I was appointed by Lord Curzon's Government to be President of the Police Commission, which again took me to every Province in India. On the conclusion of the labours of that Commission, I was appointed Lieutenant-Governor of Bengal, and gave the last five years of my service to that province.

To return to the old days, the somewhat lofty ideas that I held regarding the Service which I had joined were dissipated to a certain extent when I found myself gazetted as a magistrate of the third class, the greater part of my work being to try cases of assault and petty theft. I was also informed that I had still examinations to pass in languages, in criminal, civil, and revenue law and procedure, and in the practice of the treasury and accounts. I was fortunately placed under a District Magistrate or Deputy Commissioner who took considerable interest in his subordinates. Mr. Girdleston, of the Political Department, had been appointed to be Deputy Commissioner of Jubbulpore; and when he was transferred to be resident at the Court of Nepal, he was succeeded by Col. Saurin Brooke; and these two were my superiors during my first year of service.

Mr. Girdleston was animated by the highest traditions of the Civil Service, and was especially anxious to train me in frank and friendly relations with the people, and to impress on me the necessity for passing my examinations in the higher standard with the least possible delay, so that I might soon be qualified for full work as a member of the Service. Col. Saurin Brooke was devoted to municipal and local work; and it was a pleasure to him to take me round and show me the working of the Jubbulpore Municipality, and of the District Councils in the interior. Nothing could have been better for me than the training which these officers gave me. I had also among my fellow-assistants two men who were very anxious to do all they could to help me to acquire a knowledge of my profession. The one was an Englishman, Mr. W. A. Nedham, a man of considerable Indian experience and of the kindliest disposition and manners. He advised and assisted me in many ways, both in the preparation for my examination and also in the work that was given me to do. The other was Aulad Hussain, a Muhammadan officer, who was afterwards made a Khan Bahadur and a C.I.E. for his excellent services. He was senior to me in the Commission, and took great delight in helping me in my work, and in endeavouring to show me how best to understand the people, and to find my way to their hearts. To all these men, and to many such as they among the officers of the Central Provinces, I owe a great debt of gratitude. Throughout my service, I believe, it was the remembrance of what I owe to them that made me anxious to attend to the training of young civilians on their first arrival in India.

I very soon began to have friends among the people. I remember well the dignified and courteous old Rajah of Saugor, who was then living as a pensioner in Jubbulpore, and became a constant visitor at my house, from whom I learned a great deal about the people. I remember Baijanath Pande, an influential Brahman malguzar (or land-holder) in Bijeraghogarh, a Parganah of the Murwara Tahsil (subdivision), with whom I was brought into contact in connection with inquiries into a local scarcity in that part of the Jubbulpore District. My intimacy with these and many others gave me opportunities of talking in the vernacular to men of good position, and of acquiring those niceties of courtesy in speech which characterize the communications between natives of India of high class, and the ignorance of which on the part of some European officers tends to uncomfortable relations with some of the best disposed Indians.

One thing was above all others impressed on my mind by my kindly advisers, and my own experience proved it, namely, that almost the worst thing that a European officer can do in his intercourse with Indians with whom he is brought into contact is to lose his temper. They are extremely sensitive in regard to the manner in which they are treated; and an officer who loses his temper and acquires the reputation of being sometimes violent in his language creates a complete and practically impassable barrier between himself and the people of the country. They do not know at what time an irascible officer may use language to them which may expose them to the ridicule of their fellow-countrymen, whether they be their equals or their inferiors. An important lesson for a young officer in India to learn is, that courtesy, always desirable in the communications of life, is much more than desirable—it is absolutely essential—in communications with Indians.

In my early days the cases which I had to try—the small assault and petty theft cases—were generally conducted by police prosecutors and junior members of the Bar, who in those days, in the Central Provinces at least, did not profess a knowledge of English. Some of them, indeed, knew English well enough to understand ordinary remarks made to them in that tongue; but they did not know it well enough to speak the language in court; and they were certainly not encouraged by the Central Provinces officers of those days to do so. The British officers were determined, in accordance with the fine traditions of the Service, and especially on account of their constant association with the people in Revenue, Settlement and other departments of executive work, to conduct their court work in the vernacular. It is now far too common to see work in court conducted entirely in the English language; but there is practically still no part of India where this can be done without grave disadvantage, except perhaps in the Provincial High Courts. The great mass of the people do not know English; and it is not fair to the parties or to the witnesses that their cases should be conducted in a language which they do not understand. The judge should himself be able to understand what any ordinary witness before him is saying, and to ask such a witness in his own vernacular questions which will elucidate his statement.

The great majority of the cases which I had to try when I first joined the Service in Jubbulpore had to be tried in a small room, where I sat at a table, without even the dignity of a daïs, and had in front of me the parties, the witnesses, and the counsel, all talking in the vernacular. I admit that I have a painful recollection of the length of time that it took me in the earlier of these cases to understand all that was said to me, and to make counsel and witnesses understand all that was in my mind. But the training was invaluable; and the patience of the people and courtesy of the Bar made a deep impression on my mind. It is really much to be regretted that the progress of the knowledge of English among the learned professions, and their desire to conduct their cases in that language, have released the young civilian of the present day from the necessity of submitting to these somewhat trying, but exceedingly valuable, experiences.

The prevalence of English in our courts is undoubtedly due in part to the pressure of work, and to the not unnatural desire of officers, not well acquainted with the vernacular, to get through their cases more easily and more quickly; but it is also undoubtedly due to the reluctance of members of the Bar to address the court in the vernacular. There are, indeed, many practitioners at the Bar now, who frankly declare their incapacity to deliver an address in the vernacular. This is greatly to be regretted. It is not just to the people to have court business conducted in a foreign language; and it is deplorable in its effect on the members of the Service; for there is no qualification in an officer which will wholly compensate for want of knowledge of the vernacular.

In my very early days I broke down utterly, and had to take leave within eighteen months of my arrival in India. This was entirely due to want of knowledge, and want of advice, regarding the dangers to which the European is exposed in India from climate and from insanitary conditions. It has often seemed to me most deplorable that young men should be allowed to start life in that country without the necessary advice and warning. Lady Wilson, the wife of Sir James Wilson, of the Punjab Service, has published an excellent little pamphlet of advice to young men setting out on an Indian career; and Surgeon-General Sir Charles Lukis, the present Director-General of the Indian Medical Department, when he was Principal of the Medical College in Calcutta, wrote at my request another most useful pamphlet, containing practical hints for the preservation of health in India. These two little works should, I think, be placed by the India Office in the hands of young men joining the Indian Services. They might save many a breakdown, and so obviate much trouble and anxiety to officers and much expense to Government.

In my early London days the probationers for the Indian Civil Service were grossly neglected. We had, indeed, very clear instructions given to us as to the lines of study which we should follow; and in that respect our training was excellent.

I think that, in one or two respects, it was better than the training now given to probationers. In the first place, it was a two years' course of probation instead of only one, as at present. This was of great advantage to us in two respects. It gave us a better opportunity of grounding ourselves in the language and literature of the East than probationers now have; and, as it is very difficult in India to secure good scientific tuition in the vernaculars, it was a great benefit to have secured this at home. There is no doubt that, when we reached India, we had a great deal to learn of the colloquial use of the vernaculars, of correct pronunciation, and of adaptation of our speech to the varying circumstances and dialects of the people among whom we had to work; but we had a far better basis than the present system gives, on which to build up a useful knowledge of the Eastern languages current among the people of the Provinces to which we were sent.

In the second place, there is no doubt that our two years' training was far more useful to us in respect of the history of India, the principles of political economy, and our knowledge of law. As regards the last, we had not only to study law books, and to pass examinations on them; but we were compelled, also, to attend police courts for criminal law, county courts for civil law, and the higher courts for both; to report cases to the Commissioners; and to write intelligent notes on the practice of the courts, and the principles of the law of evidence as illustrated in these cases. That practical work in the English courts gave us a conception of the methods used in our courts, and a respect for the administration of justice there, which it is difficult to believe the young civilians of the present day can acquire without such training. This portion of our work was of special interest to us, and was, I think, also of much value. It is greatly to be regretted that this part of the training of civilians should have been abandoned.

There is no doubt a difficulty, now that the age for entrance into the service has been raised, in giving a two years' course of probation; but I am very far from thinking that the raising of the age for the Competitive Examination, and the reduction of the period of probation, have secured a better class of men, from the point of view of the interests of India, than the system under which I entered the Service. In my time the maximum age was twenty-one. Every candidate was bound to be over nineteen and under twenty-one when he appeared for the Competitive Examination. That left it possible for men to complete a University education and take a degree before appearing for examination, though it must be admitted that a large number of those who did appear had sacrificed their University training for special preparation for the Competitive Examination. At the same time, the men who came up for the Competitive Examination then differed from those who appear for it now in that, being somewhat younger, their ideas were not so completely set, and they were more capable of adapting themselves to the circumstances and requirements of the career which they had selected.

They entered on that career without having acquired certain tastes and habits of life which, while thoroughly suitable to a scholarly career at home, and even to the general life of this country, are not such as make a man very ready to adapt himself to the circumstances of a new country, and to enter easily and without effort into co-operation with his fellow-subjects of different race, and in many respects of different character. I am sure that there are many advantages in having men thoroughly well educated, and possessed of high University qualifications before they enter on any career of life; but I am not sure that the training and life of an English University are easily exchanged by the man who has settled down to them for the peculiar life which the civilian has to lead in India. In any case, to secure the advantages which the present system is believed to give, the efficient and adequate training of the probationers is to a great extent sacrificed.

The great defect of the old system was undoubtedly this, that the probationers for the Service were practically compelled to come and live in London, without any supervision or control over their lives. It is true that men were permitted to conduct their studies where they liked; some actually did pass their probationary period in Edinburgh or Dublin, or some other centre of British University life; and they were allowed to report Scottish or Irish as well as English cases. At the same time, the facilities for tuition in the subjects prescribed for the study of the probationers, and for the further examinations, were much greater in London than elsewhere. Study in London was undoubtedly the best training then available; and, had there been any attempt to guide the young men, and to save them from the temptations and dangers of life in the great capital, the system would not practically have been open to criticism. But that so many of the probationers passed without stain through the period of probation, was due far more to their own good fortune or good sense than to any influence exercised over them by the authorities. One or two cases there were of young men who threw away their opportunities, and sacrificed all the expense and trouble involved in their education, by the follies of their life in London; and one can only say in their defence that the fault lay as much with those who ought to have made better provision for the supervision and regulation of their life in town, as with the young men themselves.

In my time there was a good number of men who devoted themselves to the study of law at one or other of the Inns of Court; and there were certain barristers who gave themselves to teaching young civilians with special reference to Indian Law, and the circumstances of Indian practice and service. This was an enormous advantage. The personal acquaintance with an honourable, upright and able member of the Bar, the private intercourse with him, the acquisition of his ways of looking at questions involving the principles of law and justice, and the communication by him of the high traditions of the English Bar, were of very great advantage.

Directly and pecuniarily, the legal training which I received in London may not manifestly have been of much use to me in my Indian career. It is true that I was posted to a Non-regulation Province, in which the distinction between Executive and Judicial functions had not then been made, and that I therefore had Judicial work not only as a magistrate in the earlier part of my career, when Assistant Commissioner and Deputy Commissioner, but also later on as a Sessions Judge, when Commissioner; but I did not belong at any part of my career to the Judicial Department. All the same, my legal training was of great advantage to me. Some such training is necessary for all civilians, for in every branch of the Service they have to apply the principles of law, and to be animated by the impartial spirit of the English judges.

It is, of course, particularly for the Judicial Department that special legal training is now clearly and undoubtedly essential; where that is not given fully in the probationary period of service, it ought to be supplemented by careful and expert tuition at later periods; and for this the Government of India ought to make, and are now beginning to make, some provision. Even in my own case, the legal training that I had, and the position which I held in India, as a member of the English Bar, was of no little advantage. Legal practitioners in India sometimes showed more consideration in their treatment of me, and were more willing to pay respect to my views, and to my decisions, when they knew that I was a member of what is in India the highest branch of the legal profession. In one particular case, where I was Commissioner and Sessions Judge, the local Bar appointed me to be the Honorary President of the Bar Association, and accepted my assistance and co-operation in helping them to get rid of certain abuses. I have therefore had no reason whatever to regret the time that I spent at the Middle Temple, and my call to the Bar.

CHAPTER II

EUROPEAN OFFICERS OF MY PROVINCE

When I joined the Central Provinces, that part of India was officered largely by men belonging to what was then known as the Staff Corps, consisting of officers of the Indian Army who had elected for Staff employment. The greater number of the Districts were in the hands of these officers, along with a sprinkling of members of the Indian Civil Service; but the Commissionerships and Secretariate appointments were practically in the hands of the Civil Service. The men who held these high appointments were men from other Provinces, whose services had been specially asked for by Sir Richard Temple, who was the real founder of the Province, and Sir John Morris, who was the first Chief Commissioner after Sir Richard to hold the Province for any length of time. Both these officers were well known to be unusually happy in the selection of their subordinates; and some of the Commissioners and heads of departments serving in the Province when I joined were men of great distinction, such as Sir Alfred Lyall, Sir Charles Bernard, and Sir Charles Elliott.

Among the military officers employed in Districts, and occasionally in Commissionerships, there were a few men of really exceptional ability, who commanded the respect of all who came into contact with them, and especially of those who served under them; but there were others—and they were, I think, the majority—who never could have claimed to be men of any special ability, or to be well trained in law and the principles of administration. Yet they were thoroughly sensible men, and well suited for the work of a new and backward Province. They would have found themselves very much out of their element, and probably not infrequently in hot water, had they served in a Province such as Bengal, with its teeming Bar, and the crowd of critics rather inclined to a hostile attitude; but in the Central Provinces they ruled happily over a happy people. The distinguishing characteristic of these men was that they knew the Province. They had learned it in the work they had done in the different grades of the Settlement Department, and in the constant camp life which was the tradition of the Province in those early days; and they were for the most part, not only sensible men, but men animated by justice and by kindliness.

Some of these men showed their good sense by a clear understanding of their own limitations. I remember serving under one as his assistant when I joined the District as a somewhat junior officer. He asked me to come and see him and talk over the division of the work. He told me that he felt that he knew a great deal about forest work, about local works, which were ordinarily in the charge of the Municipal Committees and District Council, and also about police work. He said that he would retain these matters in his own charge, in addition to the court work, which, as District Magistrate, he was bound to do; but he would be very glad, with a view to my own training, to let me see as much of the work in connection with them as I found time to examine.

He added that he understood that I was a University man and also a barrister-at-law, and that he would therefore like me to take full charge of education and kindred matters, and also to prepare for him the records in the revision and appellate work of his court. I found my time with him most valuable as a training. I devoted myself with diligence to the departments which he had allotted to me; and, as I was able to assist him considerably in his judicial appellate and revision work, I found him very willing to assist me and instruct me in regard to the departments which he had retained under his own control and in the miscellaneous work of the District; and he discussed freely all questions of any interest connected with the administration of the District.

I think that this was a very typical case. The "Military Deputy Commissioner," as we used to call him, knew very well what he himself was fit for, and he recognized the qualifications of the specially trained civilian for certain work which he did not think he was altogether as well qualified to perform. The result was that, though the more highly trained civilians sometimes thought a little lightly of some of these men, the administration of the Province was on the whole well conducted by them.

I remember an officer whom I had not had the pleasure of meeting before I entered the Secretariate. He was a District Magistrate in another part of the Province from that in which I had been serving. He was in charge of an important District, and had an excellent reputation as a sensible and efficient officer. In the Secretariate I found that his reports were clear and interesting; that his answers to matters referred to him, as well as to other local officers, were often especially useful; and that he succeeded, apparently, in getting through a surprising amount of work. I thought of him as an able and, perhaps, even brilliant man.

I accompanied the Chief Commissioner on tour, the Secretary in the Public Works being also with us. We came to the District of which this Magistrate was in charge. After a day or two with him, I found that he was distinctly not brilliant, and that he could hardly be called able. In the course of conversation I mentioned to the Secretary in the Public Works what my impression had been, and that I was somewhat disappointed, on personal acquaintance, with the officer of whom I had formed so high an opinion. My colleague, who knew him well, replied: "There are two classes of men who deal with business in two different ways. A man of the one class, when he has a difficult piece of work to do, scratches his head thoughtfully, and says to himself, 'How on earth am I to do this?' A man of the other class, under similar circumstances, also scratches his head thoughtfully, but says, 'Who on earth am I to get to do this?' Our friend is of the second class. He is not a very able man; but he has a qualification which compensates fully for the lack of personal ability, namely, a capacity for choosing the subordinate best fitted to do any particular work for him."

There is no doubt that one of the most valuable characteristics of an officer in a responsible position is the good sense which enables him to know whom to trust, and whom to select for any particular piece of work. After all, what we want is to have the work well done, and it is less important who it is that does it. It is as useless as it is unwise for any man who has a heavy charge, and who is supplied with a good staff, to try to do everything for himself. It is decidedly of advantage that he should be able to do things well for himself, when it is desirable that he should do them at all; and it is necessary that he should be able to know whether the work of his subordinates is good or not; but it is also essential to efficient work that he should be ready to give a reasonably full share of the work to his subordinates, so as to leave himself time for initiation and general supervision, without an undue burden of details.

I have often found a thoroughly able man administering a charge with less success than many officers inferior in capacity to himself, because of the want of the power to call upon his colleagues and his subordinates for loyal and hearty co-operation. This is sometimes due merely to a blundering desire to push forward, no matter how high the pressure, with any piece of work that happens to come into one's hand. It is sometimes, however, due to a characteristic which is, I think, in India regarded with very special dislike and contempt—I mean the suspicion of subordinates. An officer undoubtedly ought to exercise close and keen supervision to prevent mistakes and carelessness, and to obviate the possibility of dishonesty; but he ought quickly to know whom he can trust; and he ought never to show suspicion of an officer who has won his way into a position of trust unless such suspicion has very serious justification. It is wonderful how general throughout the Services is the honourable feeling of confidence on the part of superiors, and loyalty on the part of subordinates; but there are some men whose characters are so framed that they are full of suspicion on every side. I do not think that there is any class of officers more unfit for the delicate and responsible positions into which men are called in the Executive Service in India.

On one occasion I was walking around Pachmarhi with my old chief, Sir John Morris; and there was with us another officer of the Province, a civilian of great ability, who afterwards rose to very high distinction. This officer was pressing on Sir John Morris the desirability of getting rid, gradually no doubt but as speedily as possible, of the military element in the Commission. He was urging that the time had come when they should be relegated to the military service for general duty, or placed on pension, so as to make way for more fully trained men belonging to the Civil Service. He was insisting on the view that these men were not really fit for their appointments; that many of them might commit serious mistakes unless they were carefully watched; and that they should therefore be removed.

Sir John Morris took up two positions in regard to these men. The one was that they were of more value than their previous training might have led one to expect, owing to their real knowledge of the country, and the kindly and sympathetic relations which had grown up between them and the people; the other, that it was essential to maintain good faith with every class of officers, if the Government was to continue to receive the confidence of its subordinates and to secure loyal and efficient service. He was therefore opposed to any drastic measure of change. At the close of the argument he made use of an expression which was entirely typical of the character of his administration. He said, "It would no doubt be easy to administer a Province, if every officer were thoroughly well qualified for the post which he holds; but it is a better test of administrative capacity to be able to secure really good all-round service from a somewhat inferior staff."

This was a principle which lay at the very root of Sir John's administration. He kept his eyes and ears open wherever he went; he discussed matters in the fullest and frankest way with all officers whom he met, and especially with those who were nearest to himself in position; and he strongly advised the Commissioners of Division and the heads of departments to travel about throughout their charges and discuss all questions freely and frankly with their subordinates. The result of this was twofold. In the first place, it secured an administration throughout the Province that was really measured in efficiency by the possibilities of the best men and not of the worst; and in the second place, it secured those kindly and confidential relations between officers which led officers from other Provinces to describe the Central Provinces Administration as "a happy family." I have often heard men from other parts of India speak in the strongest terms of this characteristic, which remains an effective tradition in the Province to this day.

It is wonderful how little capacity some thoroughly practical men have of conveying to others the information of which they are full. I remember the Provincial head of one of our important departments, who knew more about the details of his department than almost any officer I ever met. He was devoted to his work, full of knowledge and full of energy; but it was very difficult to get him to reply to official references or to submit in writing a report at all worthy of himself. On one occasion when I was Secretary there were some dozen or score of important references from the Secretariate pending in his office. The Government was at its hill station. This officer, in the course of a tour, visited the place. He was at once told that he must not leave until all these cases had been disposed of. He telegraphed for the necessary papers and sat down with me and went into all the questions one by one. I never saw a man so full of valuable information, when one set to work to pump him systematically. And in a few days we had entirely disposed of the whole budget of arrears and taken the orders of the Head of the Government on every case. This officer afterwards served under a less sensible and considerate Chief than we then had, and his heart was nearly broken by the harshness of the communications which he received.

On one occasion I was taking up to another of the Chiefs under whom I served a draft in which I had clearly stated the facts of a case in which one of the officers of the Province had seriously blundered. My draft was full and clear, and, on the whole, just, except that it took no cognizance of the fact that the officer in question was a conscientious, hard-working officer, who was highly esteemed by the people of his District. The tone of the letter was therefore too severe. My Chief was Mr. W. B. Jones, C.S.I., a Central Provinces officer who had, some time before, gone for a time into the Political Department as Resident at Hyderabad (Deccan), and had just returned to his old Province as its Chief. He talked the draft over with me, and, while acknowledging the completeness and accuracy of the statement of the case, pointed out the undue severity of tone. With great courtesy he made it clear to me that a censure couched in considerate language was, in the case at least of a loyal and conscientious officer, at least as effective as one that was harsh in tone. It was a good lesson to learn, and well worth being carefully taught. I never forgot it, though I daresay I did not always act fully in accordance with it.

Another incident lives in my memory. I was a very young officer, and Under (then called "Assistant") Secretary to the Chief Commissioner. The roof of my room required repairs, and I had to sit for a few days at another table in the same room with the Chief Secretary, Mr. Lindsay Neill. This was one of the hardest working officers I ever met. He could work all day long without rest or recreation for weeks on end; and he loved his work. His principal defect seemed to me to be that he did far too much with his own hand. I have often known him to refuse help in the mere clerical drudgery of a case he was dealing with: he liked to deal wholly with a case "from start to finish."

One day an officer of a somewhat nervous character, but very capable, came driving up to the door. Mr. Neill could see from where he sat who it was that was driving up. Immediately a drawer was pulled open and a yellow-backed novel taken out; and up went Mr. Neill's legs on a corner of the open drawer, as he lay back in his chair. The officer was announced, and came forward, saying, "Are you busy?" Mr. Neill replied, "No," laid the yellow-back face downwards on the table, and placed his feet on the floor. The officer said all he had to say, got all the advice he wanted, and went away. I ventured to ask Mr. Neill the meaning of the production of the yellow-back, which I was confident he never read. He replied, "There are one or two good men who are horribly nervous if they think they are interrupting a busy man: they never can state their case in a hurry. The statement of such a man is less effective, and takes ever so much more time, unless you put him at his ease and make him believe that he has caught you at a slack hour." This was quite like Mr. Neill, who was a keen observer of men and very considerate. I have never slavishly imitated his plan of having an unreadable novel at hand for the purpose; but I have often adopted his wise habit of letting men state their case in their own way, and, as far as possible, letting them take their own time in the statement.

I recall another incident of a somewhat touching character in connection with Mr. Neill, which was to some extent indicative, not only of the kindliness of his own disposition, but also of the simple and kindly relations that existed in those days between the people and even very senior officers. After some time spent in district and departmental work away from the Secretariate, I was called on to take over charge of the office of Chief Secretary from Mr. Neill. In giving over charge he told me that there were two helpless old men, to each of whom he made from his own purse a regular allowance of one rupee a week. They received their allowances on two different days near the Secretariate. They were both men who had lost their reason through civil litigation. Neither of them understood our system; each believed that the Civil Courts had done him grievous wrong, and had too much of the old Oriental notions to understand that the highest authority in the land could not interfere on his behalf. So he had petitioned the Chief Commissioner. Mr. Neill had seen them both, ascertained that nothing could be done, gauged the gentle and inoffensive mental weakness, and made up his mind not to pass orders which might extinguish hope.

So every week each of these two old men was told that no order had yet been passed, and that he must come up again next week, but that one rupee had been allowed as "khurak."* They lived quietly in Nagpur city, and their neighbours have told me how they would talk about the justice of the Chief Commissioner. These neighbours guessed what the old men did not know, that the kindly Chief Secretary was making their sad lives a little brighter by an ingenious method of extending help which would otherwise have been refused. This device, at small cost to the thoughtful and sympathetic officer, enabled these two old men to live, peacefully, and without much sense of bitterness, until their sad lives ended at God's behest. I do not belittle the action of my friend when I add that it was not wholly exceptional in those days, but rather characteristic of the relations between many of the officers of my old Province and the people among whom they lived.

I once heard an Indian friend of my own speak with intense enthusiasm of the action of an officer, then a young man though now holding a position of some importance. There was cholera prevalent in the District where Mr. Napier was serving, and he was out in camp with his tents. News reached him that Mr. Chatterjee, the District Forest Officer, who was in camp some miles off, was down with cholera. Mr. Chatterjee was a fine man, straight, upright, and capable. Mr. Napier knew him a little then, and they became great friends afterwards. On receipt

* Subsistence allowance or diet money.

of this news, Mr. Napier galloped off at once to Mr. Chatterjee's camp, found him desperately ill, far from help and with no one near him who had any idea of what to do in such an emergency. He settled down determinedly, as he would have done for his own brother or old friend, and nursed him over the crisis and back to health. It was well to have been ready to seize such an opportunity: such an act of recognition of our common humanity and its obligations is of immense value. Mr. Chatterjee, like many Indians, was liberal in the use of his means: he delighted in founding scholarships and giving gifts to dispensaries, schools, and libraries: a good number of these benefactions were afterwards made by him in the name of his devoted brother officer of another race. Mr. Chatterjee was one of my friends in the Central Provinces; and many an opportunity he gave me of knowing his inmost thoughts. It was with great regret that I heard of his death after years of excellent service for which the prompt action of Mr. Napier was the means of sparing him.

This incident reminds me of an occasion when, at the very beginning of my service, I was sent out to deal with the most appalling outbreak of cholera which I have heard of during all my life in India. I had to take with me a staff of police and vaccinators who were deputed for sanitary work in connection with that terrible epidemic. We found that blind panic had seized the villagers, causing them to desert their houses and property and take to flight into the jungle with a ruthless disregard of the sick and the dying. These were often locked up in their cottages and left, with nothing but a jar of water, to meet their fate.

As I was starting on this expedition I telegraphed to my friend, Dr. Joseph Barter, who was then acting as Sanitary Commissioner, to send me as soon as he could any brief directions which might suggest themselves to him as of possible service to me. He sent me some papers regarding the treatment of epidemics; and with them he sent a sensible letter, containing a few practical suggestions. Some of these were purely medical and need not be recorded; for sanitary science has certainly made great strides of late years in India. Others were the sage counsels of a kindly Irishman who had lived much among the people and understood them well. Among these was a recommendation that I should myself smoke, and also permit my subordinates to smoke if they desired. As regards myself, he said that some thought tobacco a disinfectant, and that in any case smoking was a cheery habit. As regards my subordinates, to understand the meaning of his instruction it is necessary to remember that although many of the natives of that part of India use tobacco freely, yet, as a rule, the native does not consider it correct to smoke in the presence of his superior. But it appeared to my adviser that for me distinctly to inform my men that they might smoke without regard to this sentiment, would produce a feeling of *camaraderie*, and an atmosphere of geniality and intimacy, in which the sense of danger would be minimized, and most effective work would be done.

His second piece of advice was equally useful. It was that I should never enter on work in an infected village while hungry, nor allow my subordinates to do so. He urged me to carry with me a good supply of provisions for the whole camp, and to select, at some distance from the village we might be visiting, a spot where there was least risk of infection, and there partake myself, and insist on my staff partaking, of a hearty meal. In this way, he said, the body is fitted to resist infection, and there is a vigour and cheerfulness about work which is very important under the circumstances of an epidemic.

His third piece of advice was that of a courageous Irish gentleman. It was that I should myself work with the men, and let the men work with me, and that I should never send them to any place where I was unwilling to go myself, nor call on them to do any work which I was unwilling to do. If disinfecting had to be done, if the sick had to be tended, if bodies of the dead had to be removed and burned, I was to be with the men in all such operations. I found the advice valuable at the time; and it was with intense gratitude to my adviser that I returned, at the close of our work, with a complete staff, not one of my men having taken the disease during our operations. The advice, valuable on this occasion, was never forgotten under similar circumstances, and my respect for my adviser, who still lives in an honourable retirement at home, and will long live in the memory of many simple people throughout the Districts of the Central Provinces, has remained undiminished through all our years of friendship.

CHAPTER III

MORE ABOUT CENTRAL PROVINCES OFFICERS

I HAVE perhaps sufficiently indicated that one important feature of official life in the Central Provinces in the old days was the importance attached to the training of young officers. I have the liveliest recollection of the great kindness almost invariably shown to me in my early service by the officers of all grades under whom I had the privilege of serving. This made life more pleasant, and was therefore worthy of commendation from the point of view of our common humanity. It was also praiseworthy from the official point of view. It made work not only smoother, but far more efficient.

We were taught from the very first to take an interest in our work, and were encouraged to do our very best to discharge our duties honestly and efficiently. We talked frankly about our work to our superiors. When we made mistakes these were pointed out to us with clearness and precision, but, as a rule, with kindness also. It was only the man who deliberately scamped his work, or who showed "zid"* in his work, that got into really hot water. When work was good, it received commendation which was all the more frank that it was entirely unofficial.

It is impossible to overestimate the effect of kindly and wise treatment of young officers by those who have had much experience, and occupy comparatively high positions. The memory of what I owed to many of my superiors has, I think,

* "*Zid*" is a well-known word in India; it indicates an implacable persecuting spirit of personal spite.

influenced me in my treatment of young officers since I attained to the higher offices in the Service. My wife and I made it a practice to receive newly joined civilians at Government House, Nagpur, when I was Chief Commissioner of the Central Provinces, and at Belvedere, when I was Lieutenant-Governor of Bengal. They spent their first few days with us.

This enabled my wife to talk to them freely about their life in India, and to give them many hints which not a few of them have spoken of as of great value. It also enabled me to get some knowledge of them, and to give them hints about their work in a more effective way than by mere circular orders. It had another good effect. These young officers realised that the head of the province desired to be on friendly terms with them, and that they had not settled down entirely among strangers who were indifferent to their welfare, and inclined to ignore them and their work. My wife and I have had many kindly intimations, sometimes after several years, of how much the young men appreciated this treatment.

My chief officers and I used to consider with anxious care to what District each of these young officers should be sent. The District was selected from various considerations, of which the healthiness of the climate was one. It is wasteful, as well as cruel, to send an officer to an unhealthy station unless the interests of the Service demand it. These interests rarely, if ever, require that a young man, who is under training, should be sent to any particular place: the place for him is the place where he can best prepare himself for the work of his life. Another consideration was the kind of work which was being carried on in the different Districts. We tried to choose a District the work of which afforded the best chances of a sound training. But perhaps the most important consideration of all was the character of the officers who were in charge of the most likely Districts. We wanted to send the young officer to be under a District officer who was a sound and sensible workman, who cared for the people, who was likely to take an interest in his young subordinate, and who would devote himself to training him in the manner best fitted to make him a useful officer in his turn.

When we had selected the District to which a young officer was to be sent, I wrote privately to the officer under whom he was to serve. I happen to have a copy of one of the letters which I issued. It may be quoted here as indicating both what my experience had been as a young officer, and what I thought might be done for men in similar circumstances. The letter is marked "Confidential," and runs as follows.

"I am sending to you A. B. from among the civilians who have just passed their examinations and come out from home posted to this province. It is because I think that your influence over him will be good, that you will be kind to him, and that you will assist him in preparing for his future career, that I send him to you.

"I should like you very carefully and earnestly to advise him to give his best efforts to passing his examinations. You know how important it is for men to become qualified at once to take their place in district administration. Until he passes, he is very much less useful to Government; and his position is not a pleasant one for himself. The sooner he gets rid of the burden of examinations, and acquires the knowledge which examinations are intended to test, the better for him and for the service.

"A. B. should be employed in assisting you in any way that you think right, subject to this limitation, that he should not ordinarily be called upon to do more work than is required to give him some experimental knowledge of work and so assist him in his examinations and in acquiring fitness for the duties of an Assistant. I shall not reduce your staff at all in consequence of his being sent to you, so that it may be possible for you to utilise his services only so far as will be of advantage to him in his training. My idea is that he should be regarded as an extra man, so that he may have plenty of time for study for his examinations; and I look to you not to allow him to forget the necessity for passing them quickly.

A DARBAR PANDAL

A "pandal" prepared at a district headquarters for a reception to the Lieutenant-Governor by the Indian gentlemen of the district

"A. B. should be stationed at the head-quarters of your district. If you think fit to take him into camp, you should be careful that this is not allowed to interfere with his studies and other work, and that he is not allowed to fall into the erroneous notion that a tour in the interior of a district is undertaken merely for sport and recreation. While he is under training, he should be required to visit the various institutions which are available for him (schools, pounds, police posts, dispensaries, municipalities, roads and buildings, the various Government offices and the like), so that he may become acquainted with the general administration of the district; and, of course, he ought to be placed some time during his training, as the rules require, in joint charge of the Treasury, so that he may learn Treasury work.

"As soon as you think him fit, he may be nominated a member of the head-quarters Municipal Committee or of the District Board, so that he may acquire a knowledge of the manner in which the members transact business, and get into the way of courteous discussion and co-operation with them. He ought also to look into sanitation and local works and make special inquiries and reports for you. I think it essential that in everything which the young civilian is called upon to do, he should be made to realise that a Government officer has serious responsibility resting upon him. If he is the member, for example, of a local body, he ought to realise that he is not only nominally a member, that he is bound to take his share in the work, and that he is bound to keep the District Officer thoroughly acquainted with all that is going on. He should be shown the best means of making himself useful; and the District Officer ought to be able to judge, from the reports which he receives from him, and from conversation with him, whether he is making the best use of his opportunities.

"I would ask you from the very first earnestly to impress upon A. B. the duty of kindly, sympathetic and courteous treatment of Indians of all classes, and of working cordially with Indian gentlemen. Everything depends upon how a young officer begins in this respect. Let him understand from the first that firmness commands the true respect of the ordinary Indian only when accompanied by real kindness, and that the one thing above all which the ordinary Indian desires is to be heard. If he is heard and realises that his case has been fully considered, there is seldom any discontent with the order finally passed, no matter what that order may be.

"Impress on A. B. also the necessity for treating Indian gentlemen as gentlemen. There is no one that is more sensitive, nor more observant, in regard to courtesy and gentlemanly treatment than the Indian gentleman. Keep A. B. in mind that an Indian gentleman ought to be treated as a European gentleman should be treated. Courtesy in receiving him and in intercourse with him is very important. To keep him waiting without real necessity, or to let him wait in an unsuitable place, is a galling, but unfortunately not an unusual, discourtesy; and harshness and rudeness of speech are as much to be avoided with the Indian as with the European. The use of the proper forms of address to the Indian gentleman is a mark both of breeding and of sound education in the vernacular.

"In regard to his intercourse with the common people, let A. B. remember that they are to be treated as a gentleman treats common people at home. If he is animated towards them by kindliness and sympathy, returns their salutations, and shows an interest in their affairs, he will do well. For this purpose you should encourage him to acquire a thorough knowledge of Indian customs and of the vernacular. This will help him in his dealings with Indians of all classes. It is the tradition of our service that the officers of the Indian Civil Service, on the whole, treat the Indians well. This is due to the fact that they know and understand them at least as well as any body of men in the country. I earnestly trust that the young men who are now coming out will be trained to regard this as one of the very highest traditions of the service.

"You will see also that A. B. understands the discipline

of the service and the usual marks of respect which ought to be shown to senior officers. The service is stronger and more efficient if discipline is well maintained. Let him also understand that courtesy and heartiness in co-operation must always characterise his relations with officers of other departments. Ill-manners which tend to friction are a great defect in a Government servant.

"I would also ask you to keep your eye on A. B. in regard to his friends, and try to prevent his being on too intimate terms with undesirable persons. You know as well as I do, that there are in Bengal special dangers in this respect, and that it is very necessary that a young officer should be kept out of familiar intercourse with undesirable society and especially out of any undesirable matrimonial entanglement. I have ventured to speak to A. B. about the special danger that exists in India, in taking alcohol when it is by no means required. He is a thoroughly temperate man; and I hope that this will continue to be his character.

"One other matter remains, namely, the matter of health. I certainly do not wish any of our young civilians to become nervous about his health and to be constantly thinking about it. But you know the dangers that arise from ignorance amongst our young men. I daresay that, like me, you have had experience of cases of men who have lost much in having to take early leave in their service, and also one or two cases of early death, due only to ignorance of danger and disregard of symptoms which ought to have been immediately attended to. A. B. should be warned to consult the doctor at once in regard to any derangement of his digestive system and in regard to fever. In this connection I would express the hope that he will also show himself a good physical man, and join in the athletic recreations of the station.

"I hope that you will not think that I am unduly inclined to lecture; but I want you to understand my object in specially selecting you to start A. B. in his career."

It is curious how little some men who have been long in India realise the importance of courtesy to the common people in town or country. The Indian has a special faculty of recognising a gentleman. Some men fail to realise this. I remember about seventeen years ago driving around Lahore with a very senior officer. He was dilating on the change of attitude towards Europeans which was, he said, coming over the people of the town. He especially complained that, though they all knew him, hardly any Indian saluted him. I told him that if I were an Indian I should not salute him, because I had observed that he did not return salutations. He replied that he thought that the people did not expect an officer to do so! As a fact, an Indian regards the failure to return his salute not only as a discourtesy, but also very often as an ill omen. It is both discourteous and unkind. The European who treats the Indian of any rank without due courtesy separates himself from them, and tends to prejudice their relations with all the members of his own race.

In the old days in the Central Provinces our officers had a good habit of doing much of their work in friendly consultation, instead of leaving all discussion to be carried on in writing. This did not at all interfere with the direct responsibility of the local officer. An officer, who had come from another Province and had taken over charge of one of our Divisions as a Commissioner, once said to me, "The office of Commissioner here is altogether different in character from that of a Commissioner in my old Province. There the Commissioner merely supervises the work of his District officer. Here I find myself less a Commissioner and rather the Collector or Deputy Commissioner of five Districts." I endeavoured to show him that he had failed to understand the genius and traditions of the Province. The Commissioner was expected frequently to visit, and to be constantly in touch with, his District officers; but he was not to do their work. He was to know all that they were doing, and to give his advice freely. When questions of importance were under discussion, the discussion should not be allowed to continue too long a mere matter of writing, but should at the right point terminate in a frank and exhaustive consultation, the final results of which should be reduced to writing either by the District officer or by the Commissioner, to form part of the Record.

Sometimes such a discussion might be between the Commissioner and one Deputy Commissioner regarding a matter concerning one District only. The Deputy Commissioner would state his case in writing. The Commissioner would give a written statement of his views on it, as then advised. This secured at the initial stage that accuracy which careful perusal of documents and the restraint of writing ordinarily tend to produce. But it would be absurd to go on for weeks with a written discussion which was apt to develop into controversy, So, if the Deputy Commissioner still had difficulties, these would be discussed at an early meeting with the Commissioner. The whole subject would be talked over in a frank and friendly spirit. And then, in the great majority of cases the Deputy Commissioner would write a letter beginning with a reference to the last letter on the subject, "and our subsequent consultation," and put the whole matter on record with all his proposals in detail as now agreed on. A brief letter from the Commissioner expressing his concurrence closed the correspondence. The Deputy Commissioner was responsible throughout: he had to do the work, and he did it; but he had in the doing of it the best advice and the intelligent concurrence and support of his Commissioner.

I learned that style of work from my old Chief, Sir John Morris. When I took up the appointment of Chief Secretary to his Administration, he had been long enough in the Province to know every District and almost every question likely to arise. In certain cases he had to give time and labour of his own to the papers. But in the great majority of cases, I used to study the files, take notes of points on which I was uncertain or thought that his orders were necessary. We would discuss these cases from my notes, perhaps, as we took an early walk together in Pachmarhi, or from camp to camp on tour, or during the hour appointed for bringing up papers in his office. After such a discussion I went home and set to work at once to write out the conclusions we had arrived at in the form of a note. In the great majority of cases he merely appended his initials, with perhaps the words "I concur." If any man looking at old files, and seeing the words "I concur. J. H. M." on many of them, thinks that my old Chief was perfunctory in his work, he makes a great mistake. Nothing could be further from the truth. It was Sir John that really made the Central Provinces what they are, by his Settlement work and his long tenure of the office of Chief Commissioner; he ruled the Province effectively and wisely; and I doubt whether his name will ever be forgotten. It is over a quarter of a century since he retired; and I do not think there is any name more widely known and respected to this day.

This habit of frank and friendly consultation was not limited to questions between two officers only. When I was appointed Commissioner of Chhattisgarh, I at once saw how important it would be to have the officers of different Districts meet for discussion and consultation regarding many questions which more or less affect the administration of all Districts.

The last Saturday of the month was an office holiday, if the state of business allowed. All the Deputy Commissioners used to come up, as soon as railway facilities made that possible, to spend that day and the Sunday following with me, as regularly as circumstances would allow.

We sometimes had special questions marked for discussion, in regard to which local difficulties had been experienced, or advice had been asked for by the Chief Commissioner. For a District officer to obtain on such questions the light of experience not only of the Commissioner, but also of every other Deputy Commissioner, was felt to be of great importance. The relief from the monotony and loneliness of District work and the sense of the solidarity of the work of the Division were also much appreciated. Many officers have spoken to me of the great advantage of such opportunities of conference. To me they were always deeply interesting and of inestimable value.

When I became Chief Commissioner, I extended the system by introducing annual conferences during the hot weather for two or three weeks at Pachmarhi, the provincial sanitorium. Men were not at that season of the year too much occupied locally to be able to come up to Pachmarhi, where, of course, they could do their routine work ; and they were glad to come. All the Commissioners of Division were invited ; and when they met in conference, the heads of the departments concerned, and the Secretaries interested, in the questions under discussion were also present. Many questions, regarding which written opinions had been given during the year, were threshed out and settled in conference. The saving of time was enormous ; and it was most surprising to find how often decisions were arrived at which commended themselves to the unanimous judgment of all the officers present. The spirit of mutual understanding and confidence which these conferences produced between the Head of the Province and his colleagues in all departments and Divisions, as well as amongst these officers themselves, was universally recognised.

When I was touring through Bengal, as President of the Police Commission, one of the Commissioners of that Province, who has since been promoted to higher office, asked me about these conferences, and expressed a great desire to see them introduced there. At that time there was no thought of my going to Bengal as Lieutenant-Governor. But when, a year later, I was sent to that office, one of the first communications I got was a letter asking me to introduce the system. I did so, and our experience was that it was a great success. In course of time it was expanded to this extent that, in the discussion of certain questions, we secured the presence of European and Indian non-officials whose assistance we found of much value. These conferences are more valuable to those taking part in them, and in some respects to the administration generally, than even the Legislative Councils ; because they are confidential, and absolutely frank and friendly. But, of course, they cannot in any way take the place of the Legislative Councils in respect of questions, the discussion of which must be public. The two ought to coexist, each in its own sphere.

It seems to me that the true theory of government in the East is to be found in a system which combines decentralisation in work, with thorough understanding and confidence between superior and inferior authority. The centre of District administration is the District Magistrate: the people should know him as the man who does the work and is responsible for it. The Commissioner should know what the District officer is doing: he should give him the best advice, and help him to avoid mistakes; but he should regard it as essential to avoid, as far as possible, pushing himself to the front, or weakening the authority of the District officer in his District.

Precisely in the same way, the responsibility for the work of a Division or of a department should be recognised as resting on the Commissioner, or head of the department. The Local Government should know clearly what is going on, and be in constant touch with these high officers, but ought, as far as possible, to avoid weakening their authority or interfering with their work. A practice of sending me confidential "demi-official" letters twice a month was loyally carried out by all Commissioners and heads of departments in Bengal, and was spoken of as of great value to them: it certainly was so to me. And again, the head of the Province ought to be always recognised before the people as the responsible authority in provincial work: undue interference with him by the Government of India cannot but be disastrous.

With all respect, and with some diffidence, as one that judges the matter not from personal knowledge of the relations in question, but from the effect produced by certain impressions regarding these relations on outsiders and the people generally, I should say that the same is true of the relations between the Secretary of State in Council and the Government of India. Government in India ought to be recognised as vested in H.E. the Viceroy in Council. The Secretary of State in Council must supervise, and, when necessary, control the work of the Government of India. This he does under his responsibility to Parliament, which, after all, is the supreme authority in the Empire. And he ought to be in constant touch with the Government of India, and in a position to understand, and, when necessary, to explain and justify its action. But he ought not unduly to interfere with that Government, or weaken its authority. To transfer the seat of government in India to London seems to me not only contrary to the traditions of our rule, but necessarily unwise and even disastrous.

CHAPTER IV

INDIAN OFFICERS OF MY PROVINCE

It was in the early days of the Central Provinces that I joined the Service; and at that time a good number of the Indian officers employed there, men who were doing the work of Assistant Magistrates and Deputy Collectors, were undoubtedly suspected of susceptibility to inducements to deviate from honest and righteous action. In these early days, when these men were appointed to the Service, the Province was young, and there was a greater demand for officers than the supply could well meet. A good number of them were, consequently, either ill-trained and sometimes even ill-conditioned natives of the Province itself, or men who had been obtained from other Province, and were sometimes far from being good bargains.

We had certainly some excellent local men, of good position, and trained in the few local institutions we then had which were capable of training men well. But these were not the majority. The majority were men of inferior training and social position, often recruited from the ministerial ranks. Similarly there were one or two Provinces that undoubtedly "shot their rubbish" into the Central Provinces; but there was one Province that treated us exceptionally well, the Presidency of Bombay. A man happened to be in a high position there, who took a great interest in the future of his deserving subordinates; and, as the Central Provinces offered a fine field for good work and quick promotion for deserving men, he sent us some of his very best. The names of men like Bapu Rao

Patwardhan, Rhambhaji Rao, and others, occur to me as amongst the very best Indian officers that I have ever met in the whole course of my service. They were men loyal to the Government, and devoted to their work and to the interests of the people, who talked freely and frankly to us about any matter which they thought ought to be brought to our notice, whether it was immediately within their own department of work or not, and who were therefore most valuable advisers in regard to the interests and feelings of the people.

There was a man who served with me, as Assistant Magistrate and Deputy Collector, in the first District I ever held for any length of time. He was a Brahman from the Konkana, but had been educated in Poona. I was struck with the fact that he talked English with a slight Scottish accent, and discovered that he had been educated in a Scottish Missionary Institution. He took an early opportunity of telling me that the people of India had a great regard for religion, and did not understand how religious spirit could exist apart from religious observance. So he always regretted to see any professedly Christian officer living without some public profession of his religion. At the headquarters of the District in which we were serving there was no chaplain, though there was a church; and he urged that some arrangement might be made that the professedly Christian community might meet on their sacred day. It was interesting to hear this good old Brahman pressing this out of regard for his old missionary teachers and for the religion which they had taught him to respect, though he had not embraced it. He was a very straightforward man, and did not hesitate to bring abuses to my notice, and to offer me frank advice.

On one occasion he mentioned to me that unusually excellent services rendered by a Brahman of Orissa had not been adequately recognised. I asked him what business it was of his. His reply was, "None whatever. I have never met the man; and he is, of course, not of my caste. But your Government is always just when it is fully informed; and I do not like to hear men speaking of a case that does not seem to show that spirit of justice. I know also that the matter does not directly concern you; but you might bring it to the notice of the Chief Commissioner." A solitary incident like that might have been capable of some special explanation; but it was so characteristic of my friend that there was no explanation possible except that he was loyal and upright.

A comparatively young Indian had just been appointed to the Judicial Service, and posted to a District where he was for a time very much overworked. He was a Brahman from Bombay. A petition was filed against him before one of the appellate courts, stating that he had publicly given a decision orally for the plaintiff in a case, that he had refused for a long time to give any copy of his judgment, and that at last, after a month or so had elapsed, he had allowed a copy to be obtained, when it was found that the judgment was in favour of the defendant. It was urged that this was undoubtedly due to the fact that he had awaited illegal gratification, and that when he had received it he had given judgment in favour of the person who had tendered it.

His defence was that he had been very much overwhelmed with work, and had got into arrears; that he kept an office box in which he put cases for the writing of judgments at home; that, unfortunately, he never turned the box upside down, and had consequently only reached this case when all his arrears were worked off, which was not until a month after the case had been heard. He admitted that inquiry from the court officials disclosed the fact that his oral decision had been in favour of the plaintiff; but he denied that there had been any cause, except forgetfulness, for his giving his final decision in favour of the defendant. I knew the man, and was sent down to conduct a final inquiry on behalf of the Chief Commissioner.

There was no doubt whatever left in my mind as to the straightforwardness of the defence; and the case in which the mistake had occurred was one in which, dealing at all events with the record alone, without seeing the parties and the witnesses, there was every ground for doubt as to which side ought to win. My young friend Bhargo Rao, however, fell more or less under the general suspicion with which Indian officers of the Provincial Service were then regarded; and it was therefore less easy to persuade his superiors to take my view of the case. They did so, however, and his future career justified their decision. He rose to the very top of the Provincial Service, was trusted on all hands, received from the Government the high title of Rao Bahadur, and retired from the Service full of honour.

On the other hand, there were men about whom there was always the gravest suspicion, and there was always a desire on the part of litigants and others to have some other officer to deal with their cases. At a very early stage in my service I was sent urgently to a somewhat remote district to report myself to the District officer. As soon as I arrived I was ordered to take charge of all the official papers belonging to an Indian officer of the District staff. He was suspended and ultimately punished for corruption. It was an exceedingly trying but useful experience.

There were certain Districts where senior officers were less watchful than elsewhere; and in some of these corruption was undoubtedly very common. On one occasion, thirty-five years ago, when, as Under Secretary, I was travelling with the Chief Commissioner, a man of high position and good character as a landlord offered me a very considerable bribe to induce me to place before my Chief a certain view of a pending case. It was a view very much to the benefit of the landlord in question, but not likely to inflict direct injury of any kind on any one else. It was, in fact, the view which I had been inclined to take. I related the circumstances to my Chief, and asked his advice as to how I should act. He decided not to prosecute the man, who had borne a good character, but to take other steps to mark our sense of the gross impropriety of his conduct. The man felt very much the position in which he had placed himself, and recognised that he might have been the subject of a criminal prosecution. He made no defence, except that he was "an ignorant rustic." But an Indian officer of high character, who knew the District well, said that the man's action had been due to the prevalence of corruption among prominent officials in that District.

It was not only in regard to the bad tradition prevailing in some quarters about the acceptance of illegal gratifications that some of the Indian officers were distrusted in those days. Some of them also showed themselves prejudiced and unjust towards members of certain sections of the community. There were men like Khan Bahadur Aulad Husain, Rao Bahadur Bapu Rao Patwardhan, Rambhaji Rao, and others who were able to hold the balance justly between men of different race, caste or creed, in a way that won the respect and admiration alike of Europeans and Indians. But there were others who were well known to be unfair and often hostile to those of different caste or creed from themselves. One of these was a Kayasth, whose hatred of Muhammadans was well known, and led in one case to one of the saddest incidents that I can recall in my service, the assassination of a popular officer who threw himself too much into the hands of his Assistant.

He was assassinated by a fanatic Muhammadan, whose intention was to take the life of the Kayasth Assistant for having used the stones of an old mosque in the construction of a bathing *ghat* (flight of steps) on the river. The assassin fired on the District Magistrate when the latter stepped forward to interfere. He then fled, threatening with his revolver any who should attempt his arrest. He was seized by a native, a brave foreman of railway (coolie) labourers, who held him until help came, though he was himself fatally wounded and died almost immediately. It is marvellous how, among the natives of India, courage and devotion are found where one would hardly think of looking for such qualities.

One more reminiscence concerning the Indian officer is worthy of record. During my early days in the Province there was one battle which we were constantly fighting: that was the fight against the tendency of Indians to surround themselves with men of their own caste or community. The offices were constantly being packed with men of one class. Thus, for example, if a Chitpawan Brahman from Bombay became head of an office as Clerk of Court, his tendency was within a surprisingly short period to have every post of any importance in that office filled with people of his own caste. Those of other castes had generally their lives made so uncomfortable to them that they applied for transfer. Failing to turn out men in this way, the head of the office would patiently wait until vacancies occurred and then fill them with men of his own class. It became absolutely essential to control constantly and vigorously the appointment of men to office. Perhaps certain castes like the Poona Brahmans were more addicted to this than others; but I am not sure that this can be said. The tendency is human and especially Oriental.

This indicates one of the difficulties which arise in administration from the employment of Indians. We have now, indeed, many Indians who have by their training acquired a much more impartial way of doing business; but the difficulty has not yet nearly passed away; and there is no doubt that the simpler natives of India generally prefer to have in places of authority men who are free from this tendency, and from any connection with local castes and races. Of course, it must be borne in mind that, in some cases at least, this tendency on the part of Indian officers was due to the fact that they had more confidence in their own caste-fellows than in other Indians; and I have known some few Europeans who seem to think that no one is to be trusted except a European. This is a frame of mind, in Indian and European alike, which is altogether inconsistent with the sound administration of the country.

In the early days of my service in the Central Provinces any officer of experience who was asked what was the character of the Indians in the Service would probably have said: "Aulad Husain and Bapu Rao Patwardhan and one or two others may be trusted in every way; but the great majority are corrupt and untrustworthy." If the same question were asked now, the answer would probably be: "A and B and one or two more are certainly open to suspicion; but the vast majority may be implicitly trusted." Several causes have undoubtedly contributed to this most remarkable change. Education has greatly advanced in the Central Provinces; and it has been possible, much more generally than formerly, to employ local officers. There is no doubt that this is a great advantage. We have had among our very best officers in the Central Provinces some men from other Provinces; but this is undoubtedly not the rule. Indians do not, as a rule, care to leave the Province to which they belong and work among strangers; and the voluntary immigration of men from other Provinces is therefore generally confined to men who have not the capacity to make a good position for themselves nearer home. In only a few cases we have examples of youthful energy and enterprise which have given us some of our very best men. At the same time it has been a comparatively rare experience to find another Local Government willing to send to our help any other than its somewhat inferior or at least mediocre officers.

Another cause of the change has been that very much greater care has recently been taken in the selection of the Indian officers for the Judicial and Executive appointments of the Provincial Service. Such greater care has become possible, as the diffusion of education has made the field of selection wider. The Service has also been made much more attractive. The officers have begun to realise more that they are the comrades and coadjutors of the European officers with whom they work; and their sense of the dignity of their position is in some respects increased. Their salaries have also been raised; and much higher offices are now open to Indians than at the time when I joined the Service.

I have no doubt whatever that in the Central Provinces the remarkable change which has taken place in the character of our officers is also due in great measure to the excellent teachers whom we have had in our colleges. One of the most influential colleges in the Central Provinces is the Nagpur Hislop College, manned by Scottish missionaries of high character and of sound education. For these men their students have always had the highest respect, and many of them, even while they do not embrace Christianity, have imbibed the moral principles of their teachers. I have already referred to the interesting fact that some of our best officers in the Central Provinces had something of a Scottish accent. I attribute this to the fact that some of them came from Bombay, where they had been educated (as I ascertained) by Scottish missionaries in Bombay and Poona. Others were educated in the Missionary College at Nagpur; and a few more had had a considerable part of their training from a Scottish teacher, who, for a long time, was the head of the only other college in the Central Provinces, that at Jubbulpore; and my experience is that these men who talked with a Scottish accent had received an education which included training in high principles.

I remember the Honourable Sir Asutosh Mukerji, now Judge of the High Court and Vice-Chancellor of the Calcutta University, speaking in the Viceroy's Council in the strongest terms of the injury which education in Bengal had received from the substitution of cheaper and inferior professors for the fine men who used to come from our own country; and I am persuaded that University education might have produced very much higher results in India if men of sound home training and good common sense had been more generally employed in our colleges. The injury which has resulted from false economy on the one hand, and carelessness in the selection of professors on the other, cannot be calculated.

It is not education alone, however, that has effected the change to which I refer. It is the opening out of a more dignified career to Indian officers of the Provincial Services. This has been steadily kept in view. It has been a constant policy based on the desire to fulfil a noble promise. In his admirable address on "The Place of India in the Empire," delivered before the Edinburgh Philosophical Institution in October, 1909, Lord Curzon referred to the scope for participation of Indians themselves in the government of their country. He laid before his audience certain facts and incidents of a very illuminative character. He said, for example, "The Englishman proceeding to India may expect to see his own countrymen everywhere, and above all in the offices and buildings of Government, in the Law Courts, and on the Magisterial Bench. As a matter of fact, except in the great cities, he will rarely come across an Englishman at all. I once visited a city of eighty thousand people, in which there were only two official Englishmen, both of whom happened to be away." A fact like this would deeply impress a man of keen observation and thoughtful mind. The influence of England in India is now, one may say, for the most part exercised locally through Indian officers.

Lord Curzon proceeded to give important figures. He said, "When we assumed the Government of India, the Native Agency was so injuriously inefficient and corrupt that the British were obliged to take control of all branches of the administration. But ever since there has been a progressive reduction of the European and increase of the Native element, until Indians now fill by far the greater number of the Executive, Magisterial and Judicial posts, entire classes of appointments being reserved for them, either by definite rule, or by unbroken practice. Figures were published when I was in India which showed that out of twenty-eight thousand three hundred Government servants drawing more than £60 a year—a high salary in India—eleven thousand eight hundred were Indian or Eurasian inhabitants of the country. Below that figure the Indians practically sweep the board; and I have seen the total number of Government employees in India given as one million five hundred thousand Indians to ten thousand Europeans."

These figures are no doubt very noteworthy, but they do not bring into prominence the real point in the question of the employment of Indians, as contemplated and discussed by the educated and ambitious classes in India. These classes aim at the appointment of Indians, as largely as possible, to the higher posts in the Executive Service of Government. Lord Curzon, indeed, refers to this, and states a principle which has been, to the honour of our Government in India, recognised by the Government of India, and by Local Governments ever since Her Majesty the late Queen Victoria, on behalf of the British nation, took over the government of that great dependency from the old East India Company. Lord Curzon's words are these: "No one would impose or defend a merely racial bar. The question at issue is rather not what is the maximum number of offices that can safely be given to Indians, but what is the minimum number that must of necessity be reserved for Europeans." Lord Curzon did not go on to say how that principle has been applied in the past; and this is after all the crucial question in regard to this matter.

Judicial appointments are not much prized by the educated classes, or, I ought to say, by the Congress party, or the Nationalists among these educated classes. It is in respect of the higher Executive appointments that there has been the strongest agitation. It is power that is desired; and power is in the Executive officer. The record of the Government policy and action in regard to this matter is one of which the Government may well be proud. That record does not in any way require to be kept in the background, but really indicates a high-principled and determined effort to meet the just claims of the people of the country. I shall refer to this in fuller detail in dealing with recent unrest. I mention it here as one of the causes which have led to the great improvement among our Indian officers.

Better training has fitted Indians for higher office, and the throwing open of higher and more responsible offices has made Indians more proud of their service, and more anxious to discharge their duties in an honourable and worthy way. There are no finer men now than some of the Indians of the old days; but the Provincial Service, as a whole, is immeasurably improved.

CHAPTER V

JUDICIAL AND EXECUTIVE FUNCTIONS OF OUR OFFICERS

These reminiscences of officers serving in my old Province recall to my mind what I saw there of the introduction of a more elaborate system of administration. When I joined the Province there was no demarcation between Executive and Judicial functions at all, except in regard to the heads of the two departments. The Chief Commissioner was the head of the Local Government generally, and the head of the Executive Service in particular. The Judicial Commissioner was the head of the Judicial department. The latter was subordinate to the Chief Commissioner in one respect only, that is, that he had to report on his work and the administration of his department to the Chief Commissioner, and that the latter was theoretically, at least, entitled to express either satisfaction or dissatisfaction with the work. But there was no appeal from the Judicial Commissioner in any civil or criminal case; nor had the Chief Commissioner any power of direct interference in the work of the Judicial Commissioner except such as may be held to be involved in the exercise of the royal prerogative of mercy. The Judicial Commissioner sat alone as a High Court, the highest court in the Province in both civil and criminal cases, exercising in both classes of cases the powers of revision and appeal. From his decision in any criminal case no appeal lay; but in civil cases there was, under certain limitations, an appeal to the Privy Council.

The original civil and criminal work was done by the Commissioners (each in charge of a Division), the Deputy Commissioners (each in charge of a District), and the Tahsildars (each in charge of a Subdivision of a District), and by assistants to some of these officers, and by Honorary Magistrates. The Commissioners, Deputy Commissioners and Tahsildars were responsible for Executive and Judicial (both civil and criminal) work within their respective charges, and had, of course, powers according to their position. This was all very well in the early days of the Province, when the work was not heavy, when cases were not intricate, and when the people found, under the kindly common sense of their new rulers, a considerable improvement on anything that they had hitherto experienced; but such a system could not last. It was manifest that the work of the Civil Courts could not be done by officers charged with the Executive administration.

There were indeed advantages attached to the trial of civil cases by Executive officers which are of very considerable importance in India. The knowledge of the people which the Executive officers possessed, and the custom of fixing civil cases very often to be tried on the spot, were very considerable advantages in the old system; and there are many thoughtful and sensible Indians who are found to deplore the absence of these two advantages under the present system. It does not seem to be a necessary feature of the present system that the judges should be ignorant of the people, or even that they should entirely abandon local inquiries; but it is undoubtedly very commonly characteristic of it.

There were admittedly, on the other hand, grave disadvantages in having civil cases tried by Executive officers. These have been very much enlarged on by some of the best Anglo-Indian officers, who struggled for what they then called the separation of the Judicial and Executive functions. Perhaps one of the worst features of the old system was this, that Executive work, on the efficiency of which depends in large measure the happiness of the great mass of the community, was sacrificed to civil Judicial work. This was only natural. Civil cases very soon began to be more and more a burden on the officers of the Province. They had to be tried regularly and punctually. If parties and witnesses were called up from great distances to attend the court, it was intolerable that they should be turned away and compelled to come back another day, because the officer presiding in the court had urgent Executive work to do. A sense of the great inconvenience involved in making these people take long journeys in vain led officers to give civil judicial work the first place in the day's routine; and this tendency was emphasised by the fact that the Judicial Commissioner scrutinised most carefully the returns of civil judicial work, and was inclined to be somewhat unsparing in his censure when cases were delayed.

The consequence of this was that, when such cases occupied a longer portion of the day than had been anticipated, other work was pushed aside, and the Executive duties of these officers were often neglected or perfunctorily performed. The Executive Government, seeing this, began to appoint separate officers for the trial of civil cases. Naib (assistant) Tahsildars were appointed to relieve the Indian Revenue officer in charge of the Subdivision of his Judicial work, so that he might be free to travel all round his Tahsil and keep himself in touch with the people. The same principal had to be extended to the District officer and to the Commissioner; and I well recall the great satisfaction with which, as a Commissioner of Division, I handed over the trial of civil cases to an officer specially appointed to this work. These cases had often been very interesting; but the extent to which they interfered with the efficient discharge of Executive work was altogether incalculable.

As things developed further in the Province, as the Province itself advanced in wealth and in civilisation, the work continued to increase, and the staff of officers had to be considerably reinforced. Gradually it became necessary to give District Magistrates assistance in the trial of criminal cases; and a natural desire for that efficiency which springs from the division of labour led to the appointing of special officers to take the great bulk of the criminal case work of the Districts into their hands. At the same time the Commissioners, whose work had greatly increased, were relieved of the trial of sessions cases, and of the hearing of criminal appeals from Magistrates, and these cases were given over to men who were known as "Additional Commissioners," and who developed into the Divisional and Sessions Judges of the present day. Here, also, there was undoubtedly a great improvement in administration. Practice and training produced a more efficient performance of court work. At the same time the District Magistrate, though relieved of the drudgery of the trial of cases, many of which occupied days together, and prevented him from exercising that constant supervision over all the interests of the District which is absolutely necessary, was still left responsible for the peace of his District. To my mind this is at the present time an essential feature of sound Indian administration.

There is on the part of the "National Congress" a demand constantly reiterated for what they call "the separation of Executive and Judicial functions." They quote the utterances of some of the finest men, the ablest officers that India has seen, either ignorant of, or distinctly and deliberately misrepresenting, the real facts. The utterances that they quote refer to the separation of Executive functions from the trial of civil cases. The men from whom they quote never dreamed of the entire separation of Executive functions from the criminal administration of a District, for which the "National Congress" clamours. I do not profess that the present system which exists all over India must never be altered; but I am clearly of opinion that it ought not to be altered out of deference to garbled or misapplied quotations from the utterances of great men, for whose judgment it is right that the highest respect should be shown, but who were dealing with a question altogether different from that which is now under consideration. Above all, it ought not to be altered without carefully considering the effect which any alteration may have on the responsibility of the District officer for the peace of his District, and on the possibility of the efficient discharge of that responsibility.

There is one argument which is frequently used in favour of taking from the District officer all magisterial work, and all responsibility for the Judicial criminal work of his District. It has been thus expressed: "There is an unconscious bias in favour of conviction entertained by the Magistrate who is responsible for the peace of the District, or by the Magistrate who is subordinate to the District Magistrate, and sees with his eyes." This seems to me a most mischievous statement. It is an exaggerated statement, and constitutes a libel upon a distinguished body of men, the Magistrates of our Districts, who belong both to the Indian Civil Service and to the Provincial Service. It is surely also contrary to the evidence of statistics to say that unduly severe sentences and convictions on inadequate evidence arise from any bias on the part of the Magistrates; for it is found that, even in cases which have involved police inquiry beforehand, the proportion of convictions is under sixty per cent.

On the other hand, it ought to be emphasised that there are no courts in India which have aimed, as the magisterial courts have done, at unearthing and punishing false cases. There is no public feeling in favour of punishing false evidence and of putting down false cases. In the civil courts it is often found difficult to persuade judges, even when the falsity of a case has been established, to revise their original decision, or to take steps against the fabricator of false evidence. With the Bar, and with those who frequent the courts, any attempt to punish false evidence is undoubtedly met too generally by more or less active opposition. False evidence is too often practically regarded by the people generally as a natural and suitable weapon when one comes to court. It is a matter of simple experience in the interior that the magistrates alone make any real effort towards putting down this terrible abuse, whereby the courts are to a large extent losing the confidence of the people of the country.

Besides, it must be borne in mind that one of the most frequent forms of the miscarriage of justice is the discharge or acquittal of the guilty. This is often a serious danger to the public peace. It is too customary in India to speak as though an acquittal must be regarded as always absolutely innocuous, if not really meritorious. It would be a very serious thing if such a view came to be accepted by the High Courts and by the Government. There is in India a natural tendency to acquit (*a*) from aversion to give pain; (*b*) from aversion to take the trouble to solve a doubt: the accused is often "given the benefit of a doubt" which ought to have been faced and settled, and (*c*) from a desire to avoid appeal. This tendency would be greatly strengthened if the salutary control over the subordinate courts by the District Magistrate were removed; for that officer realises his responsibility for the peace of his District, and is compelled, by a sense of that responsibility, to take the necessary trouble to inquire effectively into such cases.

Another argument used is that, although blunders arising from "unconscious bias" do not frequently occur, they give rise amongst an advanced people, of whom the educated are expert in law and ready to assert their rights, "to a general distrust in the impartiality of the Magistrates." I am bound to admit that there is on the part of many educated men in certain parts of India, and especially in the legal profession, a great jealousy, though not, I believe, any distrust of the District Magistrates. I have no doubt that this is in large measure due to the great care taken by so many of these officers in really getting at the facts of the case, and preventing the poorer people from being oppressed by processes of law. It is not true that there is any real distrust of the magistracy as a body among the people generally. It is the rarest thing possible to meet with any such feeling. Pleaders sometimes make such allegations to their clients and to the superior courts. This is only in the way of their business, as they understand it.

I know, however, and expression has been given to this fact by many of the most experienced and thoughtful of our Indian fellow-subjects, that there are not many villages in which the civil courts are known, where the people do not often discuss them in terms of strong condemnation and distrust. The reason for this is, that under the present system the civil judges are too often out of touch with the people, and are occupied only in the consideration of what is laid before them and of what takes place within the four walls of the courts. Their slavery to technicality and legal formalities leads frequently to injustice with which dissatisfaction is often strongly expressed, and which, were it not for the fatalistic disposition of the people, would often have added very much to the discontent and violent resistance to the action of these courts of which we have had unfortunately too much experience.

The argument connected with the theory of a bias on the part of the Magistrate is also to a lerge extent the survival of the memory of former times, when the Magistrate had not only to exercise magisterial functions, but was also the actual head of the police, the true prosecutor in the case, a state of things which has long since passed away.

Besides this, it is a matter of personal knowledge that not even in England does any man like to go to court, either as the accused in a criminal case or as the defendant in a civil case. There is no doubt that this natural feeling has been interpreted by some as indicating the belief in a bias on the part of the presiding Magistrate or Judge. It is inconsistent with this alleged distrust of the District Magistrate, and it is a very wonderful and satisfactory experience of life in India, to find that everywhere the District Magistrate is regarded as the friend of the weak and the oppressed. They come to him on every occasion in criminal matters; and they do not often come to him in vain. In civil cases they find him unable to give help of any kind; and they do not understand it. It would be very dangerous to make him equally helpless in criminal cases. We should be handing the weak over entirely to the tender mercies of the strong.

FUNCTIONS OF OUR OFFICERS

Another reason for the strong desire to separate Executive and Judicial functions is the idea that these functions are entirely separate in England, and that their union is only appropriate to a comparatively primitive stage of civilization. It is forgotten that in England, Executive (or, as they are sometimes called, "Administrative") and Judicial functions are actually united in the same officers. Justices of the Peace have large powers of both kinds. In their Judicial capacity they sit to try indictable offences at quarter sessions, and exercise their summary jurisdiction in their petty sessional divisions. In the exercise of their administrative powers they issue warrants and summonses, hold preliminary examinations in the case of indictable offences, take surety of the peace and good behaviour, or dispose of the police and other power at their command for the suppression of unlawful assemblies and riots. Thus the same dual system exists in principle in England as exists in India. Surely it cannot be urged that a system in force in England is too primitive and backward for India. As a mere matter of fact it is, in the opinion of the vast majority of all classes of officers, and of all those with any stake in the country, who were consulted on the subject some years ago, absolutely essential in India.

The Government of India took up this question during Lord Curzon's administration, in connection with a very misleading but influentially signed memorial on the subject. The memorial was misleading, in the first place, because it quoted in this connection certain utterances of distinguished men on the question of the removal of the trial of cases involving civil rights from the hands of the officers entrusted with Executive functions and the criminal administration of their charges. These utterances were, as I have already shown, entirely irrelevant to the present question. It was also misleading, because it referred to about a score of cases in which an alleged failure of justice had taken place, without pointing out, on the one hand, that these cases extended over about twenty years, and were not more numerous than those which are pilloried in a single issue of *Truth*; nor, on the other hand, that most of them had been set right on appeal or on revision. The Government of India consulted Local Governments and their officers, including not only the Executive officers, but also the highest Judicial authorities. The preponderance of opinion among both was decidedly against any change; and it might well have been hoped that the matter would have been set at rest for at all events a considerable number of years. It is distinctly unfortunate that it should have been revived.

Reference is sometimes made to the views of a certain section of educated opinion. It is most important that such a reference should be carefully tested. I shall show, in dealing with the matter of political unrest, how very small a proportion of the population of India are entitled to be regarded as educated; and it will not do to attach too much importance to their opinion in regard to a matter which affects far more the interests of those who are not educated. It is also necessary to inquire what proportion of that small educated section of the community holds the views which are quoted.

I had occasion within two or three days of my finally leaving India to meet a conference regarding a certain question which was at the time attracting considerable attention. At that conference a non-official Indian of high standing declared that the movement in favour of the separation of Judicial and Executive functions, to which reference happened casually to be made, was engineered by lawyers; that they were largely animated by self-interest; and that they practically coerced many men characterised by weakness or inertia to advocate, if not to accept, their views. He was supported in this statement by all the Indian gentlemen present; and there is no doubt that some allowance has to be made for the facts, both that there are many educated Indians who strongly oppose this scheme of the separation of Executive and Judicial functions, and that the main supporters of the scheme are the lawyers. I have received strong pronouncements against the scheme by the leading and most influential Muhammadan and Hindu noblemen and gentry, the planters of Behar, the Anglo-Indian Association, and the District Magistrates who are responsible for the preservation of the public peace.

The most serious result of the proposed separation would be the loss of the control exercised at present by the District Magistrate over the criminal administration, through his inspection of courts and his supervision of their work. It is notorious that in the civil courts cases are sometimes carelessly disposed of, that great inconvenience is caused to parties and witnesses, that unfair advantage is gained by the party with the long purse, and that injustice is too often done, merely from the want of inspection by an officer with real knowledge of, and interest in, the circumstances of the District. Removed from the control of the District Magistrate, the criminal courts might well become the instruments of more frequent and more serious injustice and oppression than the civil courts. The latter must at least come to a definite finding on the issues between the parties; but a lazy or unscrupulous magistrate can discharge or acquit an accused person on vague grounds of dissatisfaction with the evidence for the prosecution. The fate of whole villages may hang on the successful prosecution of an oppressive bravo or a brutal landlord; and length of purse may prevent success before an unsupervised and Vakil-ridden magistrate.

One matter which really lies at the bottom of this agitation, at least in some parts of India, is this, that the criminal courts do not make a distinction between the *Bhadralog** and the poor. It is undoubtedly a current opinion with certain sections of the community who can make their voices heard, that a well-to-do man should be allowed to compromise even such offences as dacoity or branding. This is a fact which shows how little real advancement in true sentiment there is among many of the so-called ceducated lasses in certain parts of India. The controlling authority must be strong, and in touch with the circumstances of the locality to prevent such compromises.

This view of the agitation is, of course, closely associated with

* Middle class, literally respectable people.

the cognate explanation, namely, the desire to advance the pleaders and to make the Judicial department all-powerful. No one doubts that the pleaders are at the bottom of the agitation; and they themselves clearly state that what they desire to see is the criminal courts made the same as the civil. The reason for this is that the *Munsif* (local civil judge) is out of touch with the district, and is confined to what he hears within the four walls of his court, so that the pleaders on the one side or the other have it all their own way. There is no particular check over the judge, so long as his record reads correctly. Now this is a matter which requires serious consideration. It is the Bar and the Bar "Libraries" or Associations which have been clamouring for this change. They all speak from the theoretical rather than from the practical point of view. Many of them also speak from a purely selfish view of the case. They want a change which will increase their power. It is not a change required nor desired by people generally.

Throughout the country there is a growing distrust of what is called the "Vakil Raj" (the rule of the lawyers). This power of the Bar is regarded by the people generally as a power which undermines the prestige and diminishes the beneficence of British rule. Loyal men fear it; and many, who, without being very enthusiastically loyal, have a stake in the country, resent it exceedingly. The "Vakil Raj" has been advanced, according to the Indians who think in this way, by several of the measures of Government. One of these is our Civil Procedure, with its technicalities and its abounding lawyers. The whole power in the civil courts rests with *munsifs*, subordinate judges, and others who belong to the legal profession and have been trained merely as lawyers, who are generally out of touch with the people, educated in the city law colleges, full of little else than technicalities, and absolutely without sympathy. The only voice that is heard within the courts is the voice of the lawyer. No one who comes into court without a lawyer feels that he has the slightest chance of getting justice; and all that many lawyers (though there are distinguished exceptions) care about is the fees they win and whatever will make for the winning of the particular case in which they are at the time engaged. This is a somewhat harsh description of what prevails over the whole country; but I do not give it as my own. It is a description which would be given by most non-professional Indians who discuss the matter in the interior.

Besides this, the lawyers have had a disastrously undue influence given to them in the unsuitable local self-government franchise prevailing in many parts of India. They have taken into their hands, wherever the elective principle has been introduced, virtually the whole conduct of local affairs. The Honourable the Maharajah Bahadur of Darbhanga, the wealthiest and one of the most influential nobles of Bengal, said to me one day, when I was urging him to state his opinion on a certain matter publicly and boldly, "It is your policy which is to blame for the unwillingness of the Zamindars to take their place and state their opinions publicly. You have thrown all the power into the hands of the pleaders. They rule the courts; they have all the power of the local bodies; and they have a practical monopoly of the Legislative Councils. We cannot oppose them." These considerations present a very serious view of the state of affairs; and if the separation of the Executive and Judicial functions in respect of the criminal administration of our Districts is carried out, whatever advantages theoretically or practically may be secured, there is no doubt of this, that it will extend this system and increase the power of the lawyers, which is far too great already. For one ordinary Indian who honestly holds any view in favour of the separation of Executive and Judicial functions, there are ten who merely wish to see the courts and the office of the magistrate in the hands of the "vakil" (lawyer). There never was a more purely class agitation.

To anyone who knows India and the necessity for safeguarding in India the interests of the weak, the "Vakil Raj" constitutes a real danger; and the separation of Executive and Judicial functions calls for serious consideration and hesitation.

This is especially the case at the present time. The effect of the measure, no matter what may be plausibly said to the contrary, would necessarily be to reduce to some extent the proper authority and power for good of the Executive, as represented by the District officer; and the power of the Executive ought not to be reduced at the present time. There are foolish sneers about "the prestige" of the District Magistrate, as though the District Magistrate desired prestige merely in his own personal interest or for his own selfish satisfaction and pride. The prestige of the District officer means his power to maintain the interests of the weak against the strong, and to carry out the administration of his District in the interests of all parties alike.

If there ever was a time when it was necessary to strengthen the Executive rather than to weaken it, it is the present time; and this measure, of more than doubtful expediency at any time, is specially inopportune now. The Maharajah Sir Prodyot Tagore well said, "Executive authority should, under existing circumstances, be strengthened and not weakened; and means ought to be taken to increase its prestige and not to diminish it." I have allowed myself to deal at some length with this subject because it is one the discussion of which touches many aspects of life in India, and the decision of which cannot fail to be fraught with grave consequences to the administration of the country.

CHAPTER VI

SOME INDIAN FRIENDS

INDIAN Society in Nagpur when I was first posted there, in the beginning of 1877, was not of a very high type. It was only a few years after the Bhonsla Dynasty had been set aside by Lord Dalhousie, owing to the failure of the Rajah of Nagpur to adopt an heir. The Nagpur territories had been added to the British Crown; and the adopted son of the widowed Rani had been made a political pensioner, very much, I fancy, in the best interests of the territories themselves and of the people. There were still a number of the old hangers-on of the court, none the better for their enforced idleness, and the influence which they exercised in Nagpur Society was certainly not of the best. There were one or two distinguished exceptions. One of these was Madho Rao Chitnavis, whom I first knew as a dignified and courteous Maratha gentleman who was on friendly terms with the Local Government officers, and engaged earnestly in municipal work, to which he was attracted by his great interest in the welfare of the town. He was much esteemed among the people, especially amongst the better classes, and also regarded with respect and confidence by the Government. He was a man of very attractive manners, though of somewhat blunt speech.

I became acquainted with him first in 1874-6, when I was a young Assistant Commissioner in Bhandara, forty miles east of Nagpur, where he had large estates. He was a good landlord; and his relations with his tenants were most cordial. He very often visited Bhandara, and hardly ever came there without coming to see me. Sometimes when I was touring among his villages he was with me for days together. We struck up a real friendship, though there was a great disparity in our years. I cannot help thinking that he was very anxious that I should enter into such kindly relations with the people as might influence my treatment of them during the whole of my service. He had two sons, both of whom were educated in Nagpur, and sent in due time to the Bombay University to complete their education. His anxious and wise provision for their training was a striking indication of his character.

After some years the Government of India gave to the Central Provinces two appointments in the Statutory Service, which had been devised by Lord Lytton. This service was intended to be composed of Indians of good social position, high character, and sound education, who would hold offices hitherto reserved for members of the Indian Civil Service. The then Chief Commissioner, Mr. W. B. Jones, C.S.I., determined to give the two appointments—one to a Muhammadan, a son of Khan Bahadur Aulad Hussain, and the other to a Hindu, the younger of the two sons of Madho Rao Chitnavis.

A day or two after this decision had been arrived at, and before it had been publicly announced, I received an urgent message from my kind old friend, telling me that he believed his end was drawing near, and that he desired to see me once once before he died. I drove down to the city; and on the way I called in at the old Government House (or as it was then called, in memory of the political days of the late Bhonsla rule, "the Residency") and asked Mr. Jones whether he would permit me to tell my friend what had been decided about his second son. Mr. Jones willingly agreed, and sent by me a kind message to Madho Rao.

When I reached his house I found my friend very ill indeed. His two sons were present with him; and after talking to me for a few minutes in the kindly, thoughtful way which had always characterized him, he told me that one of his objects in sending for me was to ask me to be a friend to his sons, as I had been his friend. He took my hands and laid them on his sons' heads in the old Oriental patriarchal way. I told him that, while his eldest son would succeed him in the management of the great family estates, the younger son was destined to hold office under the Crown as a member of the Statutory Civil Service; and I promised that, so long as they permitted it, I should be their friend and should endeavour to do for them what he would have done, so far as a stranger can discharge a father's part. He expressed his deep gratitude to the Chief Commissioner for his kind thought of his second son and thanked me for the promise I had given; and so we parted. Soon after he breathed his last; and from that time his two sons have been amongst the most intimate of my Indian friends.

Sir Gangadhar Madho Chitnavis, K.C.I.E., the elder son, has served the Government and the people well, as President of the Nagpur Municipality, as chairman of the District Council, and as member of the Legislative Council of His Excellency the Viceroy. He is now a member of the enlarged Council. Shankar Madho Chitnavis, the second son, is now Deputy Commissioner and District Magistrate of one of the Districts of the Chhattisgarh Division of the Central Provinces, and has acted as Commissioner. He has carried one District through a grievous famine and another through a severe visitation of the plague. He served on the Labour Commission appointed by the Government of India, and he has throughout maintained a high character and earned the respect of all who know him. They are both of them worthy men; and it is my firm belief, which I trust is not a delusion, that I have understood them well and have been on really intimate terms with them for over a quarter of a century.

In the very beginning of the sixth year of my service, I was called to Nagpur early in 1877, as Under Secretary to the Chief Commissioner. There I very soon made the acquaintance of Babu (now Sir) Bipin Krishna Bose, a Bengali, who had come to practise at the Nagpur Bar. I made his acquaintance first in a Literary Society attended by both Europeans and Indians. He read a very able paper on "Utilitarianism"; and I made a full criticism of the paper, differing greatly from him in his principles and conclusions. This was the beginning of a friendship between us, just as it might have been the beginning of a friendship between two men of Western birth. His is a very beautiful character. If it has a defect it is an excess of gentleness; but he is very far from being a weak man. He is a man of sound ability, of thorough uprightness, and of great public spirit. He has been a member of the Viceroy's Legislative Council; and after long and honourable service as Government Advocate in Nagpur he is now a judge of the local High Court, as "Additional Judicial Commissioner."

We had opportunities of doing much work together in Nagpur in the old days, and in Calcutta since; and we have seen much of each other during the many years of our friendship. He has come to me often to talk over the most private concerns of his life; and I have obtained from him friendly advice and assistance in many cases of difficulty. I do not know how to speak of my friendship for him in language other than I should use in speaking of my friendship for a friend in the West; and I believe that we know and understand each other well. I attribute much of any knowledge that I have of the people, and of any good work that I have been able to do among them, to my intimate friendship with Sir Bipin Krishna Bose. His affectionate sympathy in certain times of trial, his hearty congratulation in respect of anything that might be regarded as good fortune, and at the end the kindliness of his farewell when I left India, can never be forgotten.

To one other friend I must make reference. When I went to Bengal in 1903 as Lieutenant-Governor, I found that the young Maharajadhiraja Bahadur Bijay Chand Mahtab, having completed his twenty-first year, had just been installed as Zamindar of Burdwan, to which position he had succeeded to his adoptive father while still a minor. This young man had been well educated in his own home. His own father had brought him up and had inculcated in his mind lessons of wisdom and of loyalty to the Government. He was intensely desirous to take his proper place, and discharge the duties of his station. He wished to be a good landlord and to do what he could to advance the interests of the people of India generally and of his own people in particular. I very soon became acquainted with him; and, despite the difference in our years, our acquaintance rapidly developed into sincere friendship. I do not think that there is any man on the earth, either in the East or in the West, who has spoken to me so freely about matters of vital concern and interest to him; for he has treated me almost as his father; and it has been the greatest delight to me to see him more and more take his place as a wise and strong leader of the people in progress and in good works. He is the senior Hindu nobleman of Bengal, having the highest hereditary dignity and titles, though not the greatest wealth, amongst these noblemen.

He was a member of the Council of Bengal while I was Lieutenant-Governor; and under the new regulations he has recently, since I left India, been elected by the Zamindars of Bengal to the enlarged Legislative Councils, both of the Viceroy and of the Lieutenant-Governor. His Maharani, like the wife of my friend Mr. Shankar Madho Chitnavis, has with quiet dignity emerged from behind the *parda*, to take her place alongside of her husband in great social functions, and to assist him, as a good wife can, in the great work of his life. Everywhere she is received with respect and cordiality; and the relations which exist, in public as well as in private, between these two, are indicative of the excellent character of both, and are honourable to the Indian people.

There was one incident which occurred just before I left India which gave him a unique opportunity of proving the devotion of his friendship. On the 7th of November, 1908, just about a month before I left India for good, an attempt was made on my life, which is described in detail in the chapter dealing with "Unrest in India: its limitations." There the Maharajadhiraja Bahadur bravely placed himself between me and the pistol of a would-be assassin, and offered his own life to save mine. It is miserable to think of the fatuous folly and wicked crime into which the wretched student who attempted my life was led by the advice of some whose voices are still heard in India. It was pleasant, however, to see how utterly out of sympathy he was with the public generally; and it is a thing never to be forgotten that this brave young nobleman deliberately offered his life to save the life of his Lieutenant-Governor and friend. If he had done it for his own father it would have been an act of signal filial devotion; that he did it for me constitutes an act which it is impossible for me adequately to describe, and which will form an indissoluble bond of friendship between us for ever.

There are some among the Indian friends whom I have learned to love as we love our friends at home. There are others whom I could name, some of them perhaps not quite of the same high character as some of these—for in all countries our friends are human and have their own weaknesses or defects—but all of them men whom it has been a privilege to call friends, and in my friendship with whom I have found that, in the East as in the West, "as iron sharpeneth iron so the face of a man his friend."

It is to the experiences which I have been describing that I owe my opinions of the relations between Europeans and Indians. There is a very interesting and instructive book by Mr. Meredith Townsend, entitled "Asia and Europe," which contains a great deal of valuable matter regarding the East and its connection and relations with the West. But there is one chapter in that book entitled "The Mental Seclusion of India" which contains what seems to me erroneous and even mischievous teaching. I regard much of the teaching of it as erroneous; because it seems to me to be contrary to my own experience and that of many Anglo-Indians whom I have known. I regard it as mischievous, because it authoritatively states views and recites so-called facts which, if accepted, would certainly not make it easier for the East and the West to work together. As the book is undoubtedly one which is much sought after by young men going to India, and as this particular teaching is not such as can render their work either easier or more worthy, I deeply regret to find it in the volume.

It is not easy to understand precisely how it is that Mr. Meredith Townsend has acquired the experience on which he bases his statements. I have not been able to ascertain how extensive his knowledge of India really is, and how far it is limited to the town of Calcutta. My impression, however, is that he knew little of India outside the capital. Now it is perfectly clear that this knowledge of India is very defective. India as a whole is a land of agriculturists dwelling in small villages and hamlets. A great city where the three prevailing interests and modes of life are Government Secretariates, law courts and merchants' offices, and where the most important and influential sections of the community are largely either Asiatic or European foreigners, can hardly be said to represent India at all. I have heard it said, and I am inclined to regard the statement as true, that there is no one who knows less of India than the man whose experience is confined to Calcutta.

There is another point also which must be borne in mind, namely, that in Calcutta we have sharp Indian business men meeting smart Europeans in rivalry and competition; that their interests conflict one with another; that they inhabit different sections of the capital; and that they have, until quite recently, shown little disposition to co-operate or to cultivate friendship with one another. I have never in all my experience of India seen anything to compare with the aloofness between Europeans and Indians which I found when I went some years ago to take up my residence in Calcutta. Perhaps, also, it may be strongly said that there have for many years been influences at work in Calcutta which have not tended to the promotion of kindly feeling between the races; that the Europeans have not laid themselves out to understand the Indians, and that the Indians have been, in a strangely sensitive manner, jealous of Europeans.

Mr. Meredith Townsend makes the following statement: "That Europeans are, with personal exceptions, by nature and the will of God stupid, is the single broad idea which has ever clearly emerged from the sea of the native mind." I have heard a statement like this made by a very astute Indian; but it was, I believe, even intended to be a compliment. It was to the effect that Europeans are stupidly frank, and blurt out too freely what is on their minds. My own experience is, however, that the truest wisdom lies in being always straightforward and outspoken with the people, and never attempting, under any circumstances, to meet guile with guile. The great majority of good Indians believe this to be invariably the soundest course. If taken literally, however, Mr. Townsend's statement appears extraordinary, in view of the eagerness with which practically all sections of the community desire to have European Executive officers in preference to Indians, the readiness with which they accept, even on Mr. Meredith Townsend's own saying, the principles which animate Europeans in the government and administration of the country, and the devotion and loyalty with which Indians will follow Europeans to danger or death. I am persuaded that there is no one who has had to do with the people of India generally, and especially of the interior, who will not regard this statement, which might have been made by the most superficial of Anglo-Indian novelists, as quite unworthy of the generally thoughtful character of Mr. Meredith Townsend's book.

It cannot be pretended that the mere understanding of the people who are governed leads to successful government, and Mr. Meredith Townsend is right when he says that the fact that the "great Civilian" has understood "justice, toleration, mercy and the use of firmness, and has applied those principles steadily, fearlessly and with a certain respect for logic, seldom displayed by his own caste in Europe," is the best explanation of his success as a governor. At the same time, he seems to me to be quite mistaken when he says that it is impossible for the European to understand the Asiatic; and his teaching in this respect is mischievous, for the duty which the "great Civilian" impresses most earnestly on his subordinates is to use every endeavour to arrive at such an understanding.

SOME INDIAN FRIENDS

Mr. Meredith Townsend says: "The Civilian or adventurer does not reside among the Indian people at all, but only on the spot where the Indian people also abide—a very different thing. There he is and there are they; but they are fenced off from each other by an invisible, impalpable, but impassable wall, as rigid and as inexplicable as that which divides the master from his dog, the worshipping coach-dog from the worshipped horse, the friendly spaniel from the acquiescent cat. The wall is not as we believe difference of manners or of habits or of means of association, for those difficulties have been conquered by officers, travellers, missionaries and others, in places like China, where the external difference is so much greater. They have, indeed, been conquered by individuals even in India itself, where many men, especially missionaries, who are not feared, do live in as friendly and as frequent intercourse with Indians as they would with their own people at home. The wall is less material than that, and is raised mainly by the Indian himself who, whatever his profession or grade or occupation, deliberately secludes his mind from the European with a jealous, minute, and persistent care of which no man not gifted with an insight like that of Thackeray could succeed in giving even a remote idea."

There is no doubt a considerable amount of truth in this statement; but it is very far from being the whole truth; and the measure of truth which it contains hardly renders it less mischievous, but does perhaps render it more difficult to controvert. It is undoubtedly true that there are many Europeans who live in juxtaposition to the Indians not only without understanding them, but without knowing anything about them. It is also true that the Indian has a great capacity for keeping the mere acquaintance, with whom he has no confidential relations, quite out of touch with himself, and of secluding from him his thoughts and feelings. I have known Orientals who were quite unintelligible to me: their minds and feelings were a sealed book to me. Without any discourtesy they kept me outside.

The Oriental has great reserve and can easily, when he

chooses to do so, refrain from unlocking his mind, revealing his real thoughts and manifesting his true character. It would be a strange thing if the Englishman, whose habitual reserve is proverbial, failed to understand this characteristic. It was an Oriental philosopher—Semitic, however, not Aryan—who said that, "the heart knoweth its own bitterness, and the stranger doth not intermeddle with its joy." To admit this, however, is not the same thing as to say that the Western cannot understand the Eastern, and that their hearts and minds cannot come into touch. It is altogether contrary to the experience of some of us to say that the Eastern and the Western are divided from one another by such a wall as divides the master from his dog, the coach-dog from the horse, or the spaniel from the cat.

It is no cant sentiment with men who have spent their lives among Eastern peoples, that "God has made of one blood all nations of men to dwell on all the face of the earth." Human hearts, human needs, human sentiments are much the same in the East and in the West. Circumstances, traditions, and environments are different; but, when these have been taken into account and have had due allowance made for them, it is found that human nature remains. Hearts therefore can come together in the East just as they can in the West. It is true that the history of India supplies an explanation of the tendency of the Indian to keep the stranger, especially if he be a representative of the governing body, out of his confidence. This undoubtedly makes it more difficult to overcome the shyness and seclusiveness which is to be found more or less in every man; but though there may be difficulties, the task is possible and well worth performing.

When I went to the Central Provinces in 1871 I found myself the youngest officer in a Commission, almost all the senior officers of which had been engaged in Settlement work. There is no work like this for bringing the European officers into intimate contact with the people of the country. The Settlement Officer went out into camp for about six or eight months of the year. All that time he wandered about from village to

THE GOLA (GRANARY) AT BANKIPUR IN THE PATNA DISTRICT

This was erected as part of a general plan ordered by the Governor General in Council in 1784 for the prevention of famine. It was to be filled from above: hence the footway to the top. It was never used, but remains "the monument of a mistake." It has a wonderful reverberating echo, which can carry a whisper round the walls, and can at one point in the middle produce from a whisper the impression of many voices.

FAMINE COOLIES STARTING WORK

village with his tents, his camels, his horses, and his cattle. He lived not only alongside of the people, but also among them. He pitched his tent for several days at a time at a particular village, and learned all that he could about it. He met the people in groups in their fields, and discussed with them the capacity of the soil and the character of the crops which were grown on it. He talked with them familiarly round the camp fire at night, when the day's work was over. Perhaps he may have begun by thinking that the people were distinguished above all the people of the earth that he had known for falsehood and fraud; but he very soon changed his mind. The village people were very different from the litigants and witnesses in court. He found that, when he got alongside of them in their own homes, and talked to them in front of their own people, they were wonderfully truthful; and it was surprisingly easy to arrive at right conclusions with regard to the important matters about which he was inquiring. He found rich and poor alike inclined to be frank and friendly.

He soon began to understand that the people, when dragged to the courts by litigation, felt that they were entering upon a struggle with their enemies, that all things were fair in war, and that if one can circumvent his enemy even by false statements, he must be a somewhat silly person not to do so. There is a good deal of the same sort of spirit among litigants everywhere. It is perhaps, however, especially characteristic of the Oriental to believe that anything which secures victory over an enemy is permissible and desirable; and that, where power seems to give advantage on one side, deceit may well be practised on the other. This is in accordance with the traditions and history of India. It is quite otherwise when the people are visited in their own hamlets, and their affairs are discussed in front of their friends and neighbours. It is one of the first lessons which a well-trained civilian learns, from his valuable experience in camp, that the one way to arrive with some definite assurance at the truth is to make an inquiry on the spot.

The Settlement Officer, however, learned far more than this.

He got alongside of the people in respect of the interests that most vitally concerned them; he spoke to them frankly and plainly about these things; and the common humanity of the Eastern mind responded, as a rule, to his frankness. There were, no doubt, many who did their best to conceal the truth; but the people as a whole were honest and open in their dealings with him, as he was frank with them. Their frankness was not confined to business. If he were, as he could hardly fail to become, a sympathetic man, he very soon became acquainted with the private history and concerns of a great number of the people with whom he was brought into contact. He had private talks with them; he knew their family concerns, the little hopes that buoyed them up in life, and the cares and worries that depressed them; he found simple and kindly ways, such as he had associated more with the Western peoples whom he had up to this time known so much better, but which he was glad to recognise as existing in those whom he was now making his new friends. The sentiments he had entertained regarding the Indian peoples from a mere knowledge of them in the law courts and offices of the head-quarters station, very speedily gave way to a broad human way of regarding those who were after all men of like passions with himself.

There is perhaps nothing in India that brings men more into touch with the people of the country than such work as Settlement;* there is nothing that enables a man more to understand them; and there is nothing that produces better relations between European Officers and the people, or tends to the better government of the country. The tone of the officers of the Central Provinces Commission, when I joined the Province, was the result of having been engaged in such work for years. At the head of the Province was Mr. (now Sir John) Morris, himself an old Settlement Officer and Settlement Commissioner;

* The Settlement Officer is the officer who, subject to appeal to and revision by higher authority, records the rights of the different members and classes of the village community, and settles the conditions and terms under which they hold their lands. The settlement is made after careful public inquiry on the spot.

Facing p. 78.

The names beneath the lower photographs should be reversed, for "Rao Bahadur Bhargo Rao" *read* "Khan Bahadur Aulad Husain, C.I.E.," and for "Khan Bahadur Aulad Husain, C.I.E." *read* "Rao Bahadur Bhargo Rao."

THE HON. SIR BIPIN KRISHNA BOSE
overnment Advocate, Nagpur, Central Provinces

THE HON. MR. GANGADHAR MADHO CHITNAWIS, C.I.E.
Representative of the Central Provinces in the Legislative Council of the Viceroy.

RAO BAHADUR BHARGO RAO
Judge of the Small Cause Court at Nagpur.

KHAN BAHADUR AULAD HUSAIN, C.I.E.
Long a Settlement Officer in the Central Provinces.

and under him were working in every district men who had been trained under his kindly and sympathetic example in the same kind of work and with the same regard for the people. The Settlement that had been made was a lenient, judicious, and righteous Settlement; and the Province advanced by leaps and bounds during the succeeding years under its influence.

What I am concerned with at present, however, is the spirit which animated the men whose training had been effected in the course of this work of Settlement. They were not all distinguished officers. Some of them were very ordinary men. A large number of them were military officers who had joined the old "Staff Corps," and entered civil employ in what was called a "Non-regulation Province"; but with few exceptions they were men imbued with a strong sense of duty, a great knowledge of the country, and a deep sympathy with the people in all their most vital concerns. It is this spirit which the best Anglo-Indian officers, the "great Civilians" of whom Meredith Townsend speaks, desire to see reproduced in the succeeding race of Government officers. These men found no difficulty, after their long experience among the people, in understanding them, in knowing the men whom they might trust, and in selecting from among them some to whom they accorded indeed no partial or unfair treatment in their relations with the Government, but whom they regarded undoubtedly as their friends.

Among my most intimate friends in the earlier part of my service were some of these officers. Sir John Morris himself, Sir Charles Bernard, Sir Charles Crosthwaite, Mr. J. W. Neill, Mr. J. W. Chisholm, Col. Henry Ward, and others were among them. These men gave me the advantage of their own experience among the people. With these men I had the privilege to serve. I was several seasons, early in my service, in camp on the Staff of Sir John Morris, the Chief Commissioner; and later I became his Chief Secretary. I shared the same bungalow at different times for several months together, first with Sir Charles Bernard, and then with Sir Charles Crosthwaite, when their wives were at home. I served for years under

Mr. Neill and Mr. Chisholm in the Secretariate, and under Col. Ward as his assistant in District work. From all of them I learned to regard the Indians as fellow-men, and not as a different kind of animal altogether, and to see in them the attractive qualities which have called forth the most devoted work and warmest feelings of generations of British officers. I also had among my friends kindly and devoted missionaries such as the Rev. John and Mrs. Cooper of Nagpur, who knew the people and loved them, and had the greatest delight in telling me all that they could about them.

Not less valuable to me at that time were some of the friendships which I formed amongst Indians. One of my best friends at the very beginning of my service was the late Khan Bahadur Aulad Hussain, C.I.E. When I went to Jubbulpore, which was the first station to which I was posted, he was Senior Assistant Commissioner there. He and I struck up an acquaintance very soon; and he took great delight in teaching me my work. I had from the very first a great admiration for him. He could read English; but he spoke little of it. He was of the old school, a scholarly man in Persian and Arabic, and a devout Muhammadan. He did all his work in the vernacular, and strongly urged on me the importance of acquiring a knowledge of the vernacular languages, so that I might be able to have free intercourse with the people. He helped me very materially in important duties, which were somewhat early thrust upon me, owing to the exigencies of the service and the inadequate supply of officers. His high religious character, the great reputation for probity and justice which he had amongst all classes of the people, the great confidence reposed in him by the Government, and his own singularly attractive manners and great strength of character, won my heartiest esteem.

He soon became my friend; and there was scarcely a subject at all which we did not discuss freely with one another. I knew all the details of his family life, was introduced to every member of his family, and saw as much of them as the customs of the country allowed. I was in camp with him alone, sometimes for weeks, and I acquired as intimate knowledge of his character as I have ever had in respect of a Western friend. I can only express my relations with the Khan Bahadur in such language as I should use in speaking of the best and most esteemed and most intimate of my Western friends. It cannot be wondered at that, with such an early education and training, I should feel deep regret at the particular sentiments which I have quoted from Meredith Townsend's otherwise valuable book.

CHAPTER VII

THE INDIAN PEOPLES

It is not altogether easy for an Indian officer, who has been accustomed to deal only with Indian questions in India, to convey an accurate impression of his views to people at home, because of certain ways of looking at India which he has acquired from experience, and which have from habit become to him a second nature. He has a tendency to forget both his first impressions and also the course of experience and discipline by which these were displaced by a fuller knowledge of India and its peoples. In one of his excellent papers, collected and published under the title of "Twenty-one days in India," Aberigh Mackay suggests the following conundrum: "*Q.* What is it that the travelling M.P. treasures up and the Anglo-Indian hastens to throw away? *A.* Erroneous, hazy, distorted first impressions." There is a great deal of truth in this, and it is a common subject of ridicule in India that men, who visit the country for a few days, consider themselves qualified to pronounce opinions about the most difficult questions of Indian administration and life. At the same time, crude first impressions are worth remembering, if for nothing else than for this purpose, that they may enable an Anglo-Indian to understand the mental attitude of one who does not know the country. Without some such understanding, it is difficult to communicate information.

One of the difficulties in understanding Indian questions undoubtedly arises from the enormous area of the peninsula and the vast and varied populations which it contains. India is not one country; and there is no "Indian nation." This is generally admitted and so far recognised at home; but it is difficult for one who has looked at Indian questions from afar, and does not know India itself, to realise how vast the peninsula is, and how varied are its peoples. One even hears such a question as this, "I hear you have come from Lahore, which is, I believe, in India. Do you know my friend Mr. Jones who is in business in Madras?" Well, over a thousand miles of space lie between the two places as the crow flies; and there is little communication in the way of business between the Punjab, of which Lahore is the capital, and the Presidency of Madras. Yet, your friend is disappointed that you should not have met Mr. Jones. One might almost as well say, "I hear you have come from Edinburgh. Do you know my friend, who is employed in a bank in Paris?"

The vastness of the Indian Empire may be understood more or less by anyone who grasps this simple fact, that its area is almost, and its population is just, equal to the area and the population of Europe without Russia. As to its peoples, they are diverse in almost every respect in which one people can be separated from another. They have languages not only differing as much as the Latin tongues differ among themselves, but also differing in family as the language of Germany differs from that of France. There are the Aryan languages of the north of India and the Dravidian languages of the south, as well as a large number of dialects and languages used by the aboriginal tribes and races in Central India. As the languages differ, so do the manners and modes of thought. It is of great importance to remember that the Bengalis do not differ from the Marathas of Bombay less than the Italians differ from the French; nor the men of Agra and Oudh from the Madrasis less than the Germans from either of these two Latin races.

The races of India differ in physique, as for example the powerful and martial Punjabi from the feebler inhabitants of the malarious districts of Bengal. They differ in history, as in the case of the north-country Muhammadan or the Bombay Brahman who looks back on a past full of memories and traditions of power, and the great majority of the peoples of the south and the east, whose history was rather that of subjection and oppression. They differ in religion. This difference is not only between Muhammadans and Hindus, but also, for example, between those who worship Shiva and Kali and the votaries of Vishnu and Krishna, or between both these forms of Hinduism and the Fetish worship of many of the aboriginal tribes. Even races calling themselves Hindus are often not really of the same religion; for while Hinduism cannot receive the individual into its bosom on account of the impossibility of finding him a place in any of its castes, it can receive, and has often received, a whole tribe as a separate caste, requiring not the renunciation of the old gods, but only the recognition of the special privileges and sanctity of the Brahmans.

If one were able to read what he sees in the first day spent in Bombay, in the light of the knowledge that comes to him in later years, he would understand at a glance how distinct are the races and peoples of India. He sees men in varied costume with diverse head-dresses; and he lumps them all up together into a very great nation of strange manners and costumes. He has to learn that these different dresses and manners indicate different races and nations, representatives of which are to be found gathered together for commerce and business in Bombay, but which belong to different parts of the country and are divided from one another by all that divides nations anywhere.

Very soon, too, the man who arrives in India, to begin the work of his life, is made acquainted with the fact that India is a land of far distances. I had to take a thirty hours' journey by rail from Bombay to Allahabad, and was then sent thirty hours from Allahabad to Nagpur, and back again twenty-four hours to Jubbulpore before I settled in my first station. I had thus early begun to realise the great distances that one has to travel; but it was not until I was appointed, in 1893, to the Hemp Drugs Commission, and travelled over the whole of India during that Commission's full year of work, visiting every

A Suburban Temple

A beautiful suburban temple, showing the usual tank and ghats. The ghat is the flight of steps leading down to the water's edge: it is an act of piety to construct a temple ghat.

Province and several of the Native States, that I realised the differences that exist among the peoples of India, and the enormous area of the peninsula itself. That experience and my experience nine years later as President of the Police Commission, which also took me all over India to all Provinces and to one or two Native States, was valuable to me as giving me opportunities of seeing India, which, I suppose, are quite unique.

When one is listening to a man who professes to speak from personal knowledge on any Indian subject, he ought first of all to endeavour to ascertain where the speaker has obtained his experience, and what qualifications he has for speaking on the subject under consideration. If the subject is one concerning only a part of India, and if the speaker's experience belongs wholly to another part, it may be at least very doubtful whether he is entitled to speak with authority at all. No length of residence in Bengal will entitle a man to speak, with the authority of one who has seen things for himself, in regard to any question affecting Bombay. Study of books and papers or information given by friends and acquaintances may enable a man to speak usefully about that which he has not seen; but his claim to be heard depends in that case on the trustworthiness of the source from which he has received his information, and does not depend on his own experience or observation. This distinction is most necessary to bear in mind in regard to India and its interests; and it arises from the differences between Provinces and races which I have endeavoured to make clear.

In this connection it may be observed that there is nothing more misleading than to accept as authoritative the statements about India and its peoples, which are made by those who base their claim to be heard on a long residence in Calcutta, or any other Presidency town. It should be borne in mind that India, with all the differences that exist between different parts of the country, has this common feature throughout, that it is an agricultural country, consisting mainly of villages, smaller or greater, scattered over its hills and plains. In the Presidency towns one sees, no doubt, many Indians gathered together; but they have separated themselves, either recently or at a more remote period of their family history, from the great occupations and interests of the people of India. They have come together, some of them, for the acquisition of Western learning which the great mass of their countrymen do not value and are inclined to think as little suited to an Indian as the peacock's feathers to the jackdaw of the fable.

Some of them have come for the study and practice of law, of which the great mass of their fellow-countrymen are ignorant and suspicious; some of them for the sake of commerce, in which the great mass of their countrymen have no intelligent interest or direct concern. Their habits of life in the town are altogether different from the habits of the country; and there is no tie that binds the professional and commercial classes of the capital cities to the people of the country generally. The former do not understand the latter; and the latter, while they may, where necessity compels them, utilise the services of the former, are by no means as a rule in frank and intelligent sympathy with them.

It is a common saying among people in Bengal that there is no one more ignorant of the people of the interior and of their affairs than the man whose training and career are confined to Calcutta; and I dare say the statement is true. The man who lives a town life in Great Britain is not the best authority on rural affairs, though he generally keeps up some connection with the country. He pays periodical visits and tries to live the country life and get into touch with the country people and their concerns; he spends there many of his weekends and sometimes weeks at a time; and when there he throws himself deliberately into the life of the country, and lives as if himself of its people. On the other hand, the man whose life-work is done in the Indian Presidency town, ordinarily goes to the country far too little; and, even when he does go there, he lives apart from the people in the aloofness which his sense of educational superiority and want of community of interest lead him to adopt. He has not, and does not care to have, much sympathy with, or knowledge of, the country and the country people.

When this great barrier between the people of the town and the people of the country is taken into consideration, as well as the great differences of race and religion that exist throughout India, one begins to realise something of the difficulty of dealing with Indian questions. The sources of information to the man who does not travel about and live among the people of the country, who, as a rule, are silent and invisible to those who do not make an effort to hear and see them, are the newspapers and orators of the great cities. These men write and talk as freely and as fully in regard to matters of which they are entirely ignorant as in regard to matters with which they may claim some acquaintance.

I remember hearing a missionary in a public meeting in Scotland setting himself to correct what he stated to be a popular fallacy in regard to Indian temples. He said that people coming from India spoke of the beauty and picturesqueness of Indian temples; and on the authority of his own long residence in India he assured his audience that this was pure sentiment or misrepresentation. He had seen many temples; and they were nothing but squalid shrines. I found that his experience was limited to Calcutta; and I was able to make some allowance for his statement. But there rose before my mind pictures of many temples which I had seen in many parts of India, beautiful for situation and capable, so far as their outward appearance went, of being the joy of the whole land. I recalled the reaches of the sacred Narbada, beautified by the temples and shrines which the piety of many generations of simple people had erected on its banks, or temples with fair walls and battlements on the tops of hills and even mountains, to which the piety of simple pilgrims lead them for quiet and secluded worship.

I have heard men tell of the state of feeling in India, of the jealousy of the people in respect of the British Government and its officers; and I have found that they have been simply quoting the utterances of some of the carping and even seditious native papers of Calcutta. Not only do these newspapers themselves mistake "the cackle of their bourg for the great wave that murmurs round the world"; but there are many also who are deceived by the arrogant and authoritative tone of these papers into accepting their ebullitions as the expression of the feelings of the great mass of the people. A friend of mine, who is rightly regarded as competent to speak on many Indian questions, said to me, when I was appointed Lieutenant-Governor of Bengal, that it was no use attempting to get into touch with the people of that Province. "For," he said, "to put it in a word, we have lost Bengal." He explained that in his opinion we had lost all touch with the people of that Province; that their affections had become alienated from us; and that we could not rely on their goodwill.

It was not many weeks after this, when, in the course of a tour in the Province, I was passing through a railway station in the interior. My special train arrived there about 6 a.m., and halted for a few minutes. In accordance with my old Central Provinces custom, I had risen early and was fully dressed. I stepped out of the train to enjoy the cool morning air, a man altogether unknown to anyone on the platform. None of my staff even looked out of their windows. The police who lined the platform judged that I must be connected with the Lieutenant-Governor, and stood at attention; but they did not present arms, as they would have done had they recognised me. I saw a large crowd at one end of the platform, near an over-bridge which crossed the line. Some of the crowd had come up the steps of the over-bridge, as far as the point where another flight of steps from the platform joined it; but they did not attempt to enter the station, and stood looking at the scene from the position they had taken up. I went up to the over-bridge and began to talk to those who were in front of the crowd. I could not speak Bengali; but I talked to them in Hindustani, which seemed to be known to many.

In the course of our conversation I asked them what they had come for; and they said they had come to see the Lieutenant-Governor (or as they called him, the "Lord Sahib") passing. In reply to my inquiry whether they expected to see the Lieutenant-Governor, they said that they did not, as the hour was so early; but they liked all the same, they said, to see his train and to think that he was in it. I talked to them about their affairs, about the season and the crops, the municipal administration of the town, and the like. After we had talked for some time, and when the train was about to move on, I said, "Would you not like to see the Lieutenant-Governor?" An intelligent old grey-beard, who seemed to have some position among the crowd, promptly said, "Are you the new Lieutenant-Governor?" When I replied in the affirmative, he at once shouted the announcement to the crowd; and I received as hearty an ovation as I should have received perhaps in any part of India.

The experience of that morning was corroborated by all my subsequent experience in Bengal. It is not true that "we have lost Bengal." We have certainly not the same opportunities of getting into touch with the people that we have in the temporarily settled* districts of other Provinces, where the agricultural interests of the people are largely identical with those of the Government, and where this community of interest binds the Government and the people together; but, if we make the effort, we can get into touch and have sympathy with the people of Bengal to a very great extent, if not quite as fully as in the rest of India. Everywhere I found the people friendly and pleased to find me accessible to them.

The people all over the country are anxious to know the officers who govern them; and it is too often the fault of our officers themselves if they are not on good terms with the people. It is true that mischievous relations may very easily

* In other Provinces the land revenue payments to the Government are periodically revised; in the greater part of Bengal they were permanently fixed by Lord Cornwallis.

be produced between the people and the Government by misrepresentation. The people are ignorant and superstitious; and appeals to their ignorance and superstition find them excitable. They can be misled, and they have, in certain localities and at certain times, been misled, to their own loss and to the injury of the administration; but as a whole they are loyal to those who rule, and affectionate in their loyalty to the rulers who show themselves friendly. There is no general antipathy to, or jealousy of, the British Government or its officers. The contrary is the case. The Government is regarded with loyalty; and British officers are often asked for as District Officers; and when they visit any locality they receive a most hearty welcome.

It is pitiable, in view of all one's experience in India, to see how the expressions of a certain section of the comparatively educated classes are received as though they constituted the voice of the peoples of India, or, as it is called, "the national voice." I recall an unfortunate incident which occurred in the course of a confidential conference at which I was presiding. The conference consisted of a number of Government officers, some representatives of the Hindu and Muhammadan communities, some feudatory chiefs, noblemen, and landowners, and some European and Indian business and professional men, as representative a gathering as could be got together at the time. We sat down to discuss the matter before us. Just opposite me was seated a Bengali, an old member of what is called "the National Congress"; and beside me was seated a Chief of much influence and high character. The gentleman opposite, in some remark he made, used the expression "the national opinion." The Chief asked what he meant by "the national opinion." "Is it your own opinion," he said, "or mine, which differs from yours?" More or less apologetically the man opposite said, "Everybody knows what I mean. I mean the congress view." The matter dropped. Again a little later the same man used the same expression. The Chief somewhat lost his temper at this persistence, and demanded, "What do you mean by the national opinion? Do you not know that there is no Indian nation, that, if the British authority were removed, some of the races of India might be at your throats at once, and that the rule and authority of Bengalis would not be tolerated out of Bengal ?"

The man opposite sank back in his chair, not a little unsettled by this ebullition of temper. I intervened, and pointed out to the Chief that this was scarcely language to be used in a friendly and confidential conference, and that the matter to which he referred was scarcely relevant to the question which we were considering. The Chief frankly concurred and apologised. The fact remains that there was some truth in what he had said. There is no Indian nation. What may be in the future none can tell. Our own history shows the possibility of welding different races into one nation, but only when they live together within the same area, eat together, work together, and intermarry. It is not so in India; and at present, at least, there is no Indian nation. Indian races are not in sympathy with one another; and British rule is necessary for the maintenance of peace and for the progress of the country. If we ever have anything like full self-government in India, it is as likely to be self-government of separate Provinces as that of the whole of the vast and varied Peninsula.

It must specially be remembered and realised that India is not a country of great cities. Scarcely one-tenth of the population live in cities or even in small towns or large villages with more than six thousand inhabitants. In England we have one-third of the population gathered together in crowded cities of not less than one hundred thousand inhabitants; but over the whole of the vast Peninsula of India we have only twenty-eight such cities, with a total city population of only seven millions out of the three hundred millions of its inhabitants. It is worth while to remember that it is almost exclusively in the large cities that we have anything of unrest, except where, by the progagation of false statements, temporary disturbances have been created among the villagers.

There is a great distinction between town life and country life in India. There is a great distinction between town and country everywhere; but in India it is very much more marked and more important than in any country with which I am at all acquainted. The city life of India, in such cities, I mean, as Bombay or Calcutta, where there is great commercial activity, is altogether different from the life of the interior. Such cities are only Indian in the sense that they are in India. The life of the vast peninsula is, as a whole, village or rural life. The people in their own homes are still, despite railways and post offices and many of the agencies of Western civilisation, very much the same as they were centuries ago. The standard of comfort has no doubt risen to a certain extent. A number of the people in the villages have seen things of which their fathers had no conception; but their life and their modes of thought are still essentially the same. The foreigners in India are after all comparatively few, and their influence except in respect that it has made for peace and stability, has not very materially affected the lives of the people. The city life is a foreign life. There are proportionately far more foreigners working in the city; and the people who are working with them are far more affected by foreign influence. As I have already said, they are, to an extent which we in the West cannot easily understand, out of touch with their own countrymen in the interior.

There are large tracts in India about which one may travel day after day and see even still the simple Arcadian life that the old classical Indian books very beautifully portray. Nothing is more delightful than such work as this, to march for a month or two on end through the villages of a District or Division or Province, bringing the Government into contact with the people in respect of the matters in regard to which the people wish to come into contact with the Government; seeing the people in their own homes; ascertaining their circumstances and especially their troubles and calamities; and seeking quietly, in personal contact with them, to improve their condition and to secure their easily won gratitude and affection. It will be a long time before the personal influence of the individual officer of Government ceases to be one of the most important features of life in the interior of India; and any failure on the part of Government Officers to treat the people with sympathy, kindness, and consideration, and at the same time with justice and temper, militates more against the interests of Government than perhaps any other active influence on inter-racial feeling.

Generally speaking, the officers of the Civil Service who are accustomed to travel among the people, especially in these Provinces where the temporary character of the Revenue Settlements leads necessarily to a desire to obtain a thorough insight into agricultural conditions, treat the people well, and in fact acquire a great affection for them; and in no part of the world, I believe, is kindly treatment and affection more fully returned than in the interior of India. But there are Europeans, sometimes of a class from whom, despite their youth, better things might be expected, but more generally of low breeding and defective education, who treat their Indian fellow-subjects in a way which leads to bitterness of feeling which it is most difficult to eradicate.

Ignorance of the manners and customs of the people, and or their real sensitiveness under an unmoved exterior, very often leads to this sort of thing. I have known even an officer high up in a Commission who appointed an hour at which to receive Indian visitors, and left them to sit on a bench outside his door with his menial servants, or to rest on the coping-stone of the well in his compound, until he was at leisure to receive them. He had a good reputation for office work; but it would have been a great blessing to the province to have been able to deport him and to keep him out of all influential work among the people of the country. I have seen an officer assault country carters, and actually beat them severely, because they allowed their carts to stray down the middle and on both sides of the road, so as to block his way while he was driving his carriage and pair. That officer, when I reprimanded him for his conduct, told me that he thought we were losing the country owing to such sentiments as mine; but there can be no doubt that a few cases of such violence and injustice do more harm than can be calculated.

I have known men who maintain that the old Indian proverb, "*pit par maro pet na maro*,"* shows that the people generally regard it as quite reasonable that at least a master should be allowed to beat his servant. This merely indicates an absolute failure to recognise that men are the same all the world over, and that right-minded men in the East are as much disgusted with physical violence as right-minded men in the West. The effect on Indian gentlemen of the sight of physical violence used by a European towards an Indian menial servant is just precisely what it would be amongst ourselves if we could conceive of it. They tolerate it amongst some of their own princes and big men, because they do not expect from these particular persons anything approaching to justice or to a recognition of the dignity of humanity; but they are shocked at any such exhibition on the part of the members of a race with the superior classes of which at least they have been accustomed to associate thoughts of better things. Such cases as I have indicated are within the experience of some of us; but they are distinctly exceptional. Exceptional as they are, however, they do incalculable damage; and they should be regarded with strong condemnation, and, wherever possible, repressed with rigour. There is no doubt that a great deal of good might be done by pointing out to young men who are destined for work in India that they must act there on the first principles of Christian gentlemanliness.

To return to the people of the interior—what a delight it is to see them in their ordinary life, to take part with them in little functions or ceremonies where that can be done without prejudice to the principles of religion. Formerly the officers of Government were not averse from taking part even in the religious ceremonies of the people. I do not think that this could be done without sacrifice of Christian principle and with-

* That is, "Strike me on the back, not on the stomach": does it mean, "Beat me rather than fine me"?

out producing a false impression among the people; and I entirely sympathise with the condemnation of the practice and with its authoritative repression; but I regret that in many places this change has led to a standing aloof from the people which is undoubtedly to be regretted.

Often when I have gone to a village, especially in my earlier days when I could go about amongst the country people without the pomp and circumstance of the head of a province, I have slipped into the home of an agriculturist during a marriage ceremony or on some other festal occasion. I have never sought to do this where there would be any risk of raising any caste question; but if you ask of a host whether there is any objection, he will point out the time when you can come without raising any such difficulty; and he will welcome the presence of an officer of Government as being most auspicious. That officer, on his part, will see something of the customs of the people and of their kindly life, which may well be useful to him in framing his conception of the character of those among whom he is called to work. The enthusiasm of such a reception is sometimes very great. The interest that the people show in our affairs, in our customs and life, when we show our interest in theirs, is surprising; and the bond of loyalty between the people and the Government is greatly strengthened by such mutual interest.

A man who only knows the towns and great cities knows nothing really of the life of India. To know the real India well one has to move about among the people in their village homes. What a delightful life it is! There is no part of his life in India that the Executive officer enjoys so much as his life in camp among the people; and there is no part of his life that is more important and useful both to him and to them. That he should know them in their own fields and homes, and in their own everyday life, is absolutely essential to efficient administration.

An officer on tour has two sets of tents. He pitches one set at one place; and, while he is occupied there, the other set moves on to his next camp, perhaps about ten miles off. During the day he is occupied with *mulakats** with those who are entitled to that courtesy, with informal talks at his tent doors or in the fields with the villagers generally, with the inspection of any local institutions and the conduct of any local inquiries, with the discharge of his office duties, and with efforts to make himself acquainted with all the circumstances and conditions of the village. It is a busy day; and by nightfall he finds himself ready for rest. At daybreak he is up again mounted on his horse, and on his way to his next camp. He does not go direct across country, but wanders round, taking in all the villages within reach, seeing groups of people, and perhaps inspecting schools, police stations, and other institutions on the way. Arriving at the next camp, he sets himself to do very much the same line of work as occupied him the previous day; and so in the course of a tour he becomes intimately acquainted with a considerable portion of his charge.

I have sometimes been three or four months on tour, seldom meeting a single European or speaking a word of English, but living among the people and talking to them in their own vernacular. Often in the evening they would come round the camp fire and sit beside me and chat to me about their affairs, telling me stories of their daily life or old legends connected with the country, and acquiring that kindly familiarity with a British officer which camp life induces, and which is so valuable in the administration of India. Often, too, a man of sufficient standing would invite me to his house to some small family entertainment or social function. For my part I not infrequently went to the houses of people who would not themselves have laid claim to a visit, simply for the sake of getting to know something of their home life. It is a grievous error so to increase the drudgery of office work, or so to reduce the European staff, that the European officers are unable to give a large amount of time to this camp life.

The calamities which too often fall upon the peoples of India

* Formal interviews.

are themselves sometimes a means of drawing the races together. Nothing binds officers and people together more than sympathy between them, and co-operation with one another, in dealing with calamity. A visitation of plague or cholera, in which the European officer sets himself to explain the measures of prevention and relief which have been adopted after careful inquiry and wide experience, and in which he associates himself closely with the people in dealing with the calamity, does more to bind the races together than any mere talk, however kindly. It is wonderful how he will lead the people, if he is himself careful indeed in regard to disinfection, but fearless in his attitude towards the disease. Their spirits are cheered, and they realise that Government is doing at least all that human power can do to mitigate the horrors of the situation.

My experience of famine has been very extensive. As Commissioner of Nagpur, I had to deal with the famine of 1896, and as Chief Commissioner I had to deal with the even more terrible famine of 1899-1900. I do not propose to record the sad experiences of those famines; but I think it worth while to note that the work which we then had to do brought us more closely into touch with the feelings, customs, and resources of the people than perhaps anything else in my Indian experiences.

We did not deal with famine in the way adopted by Joseph in the great Egyptian calamity. In Bengal, at Patna, there is a strange structure called the "Gola," which was built as a storehouse for grain to provide against famine. It is now used for little else than echo experiments. Railways and easy communication with the markets of the world have obviated the necessity for such measures against famine. We rushed the grain into the affected area by the mere operation of the law of supply and demand. We provided work for able-bodied adults that they might earn the money to buy the grain; and only the sick and infirm and little children were gratuitously fed. The simplicity of the country people, their confidence in the officers whom they had learned to trust, their patient endurance of the severest trials, and their deep gratitude for all that was done for them, made an impression on our minds which will never be effaced. It was also delightful to find how cordially many of the best Indians, official and unofficial, threw themselves into the work of famine relief. One learned to appreciate not only the patience of the common people, but also the devotion and pluck of many of those in influential positions. I remember Mr. (now Sir Reginald) Craddock, then my famine secretary and now Chief Commissioner of the Central Provinces, telling me that he agreed with me that some of our most valued friendships with Indian gentlemen were formed during the famine.

There is one thing which we must not allow the recent deplorable ebullition of anarchy to prevent, namely, our intercourse with the people. When passing through a town in Bengal soon after an abortive attempt had been made on my life, I was struck by the emptiness of the streets. Cursory observation led me to see great crowds gathered at points some little distance down the side streets, so that they might just catch a glimpse of my carriage as it passed along the main road. I inquired the meaning of this, and found that the local police had cleared the streets and kept the people at a distance so as to secure my safety. I issued orders to the effect that this was never to be done again: the police might take what precautions they deemed necessary in the way of having officers in plain clothes scattered about among the crowds that lined the streets; but I felt that we could not tolerate any prevention of the people from becoming acquainted with their ruler and showing him respect.

When we are unable to meet the people freely and frequently, we shall be unable to exercise the most potent influence for loyalty; and the impression created on the minds of the people, when they seem to be suspected as a whole merely because of the existence of a few miserable criminals among them, is deplorable. One of the great reasons why it is absolutely essential to suppress sedition and anarchy by the most effective measures, however severe, is that it is the essence of sound administration in India that the officers of Government should mingle freely with the people. People at home, even the authorities at home, do not adequately understand the necessity for this. The Indian Government itself sometimes seems hardly to realise it; but I think that there is no local government—at all events, there are exceedingly few officers with long and valuable Indian experience—who have any doubt of the vital importance of having officers going about freely among the people and learning at first hand their sentiments, their needs, and their condition.

The loyalty of the people of the interior is a very strong sentiment indeed. It is distinctly personal in its character. The vague abstraction of Government is not much regarded by the people of the interior. Their loyalty is to the King on the throne, and to the officers serving under him, especially perhaps to those with whom they come most in contact. It was the necessity of the case that obliged His Majesty, when as Prince of Wales he visited India in 1904, to confine his tour mainly to the great cities of India, and his intercourse with the people mainly to the chiefs and nobles. But the common people eagerly took advantage of every possible opportunity of seeing their future king. The enthusiasm with which Their Royal Highnesses the Prince and Princess of Wales were received everywhere was unbounded; and amongst those who displayed most enthusiasm were many of the people of the interior. They had to make very considerable sacrifices and endure considerable hardships to gratify their loyal desire to see the royal visitors.

I remember a large party of several hundreds of people from the interior being found seated one evening on the Calcutta maidan,* well supplied with parched corn, and evidently determined to spend the night there. They were asked what their purpose was. They said that they had come hundreds of miles to see their Royal Highnesses, that they had heard that they were to pass in procession along Chowringhee the next day, and that they were taking up their place on the maidan so as to secure to themselves a sight of the Royal visitors. The kindly

* The great open meadow between Chowringhee Road and the river.

Commissioner of Police, Mr. (now Sir Frederick) Halliday, entered sympathetically into their wishes, and took care that they had the privilege which they desired. This was typical of the action of thousands and thousands of village people, who flocked to the towns for the sake of seeing the Prince and Princess of Wales.

The impression created among the people generally by this visit was of the greatest value. The affections of those who came into contact with the Prince and Princess were won by their unvaried kindliness and courtesy. Every utterance of the Prince was marked by sympathetic appreciation of the feelings of the people and a deep interest in their welfare. The common people were delighted with that readiness to receive and graciously to acknowledge their acclamations, which has characterised the Royal House of England for at least three generations. The political effect of the Royal visit will not soon pass away. The visit of Their Majesties seven years ago may have been of benefit in preparing them for the exalted position which they now occupy. It was certainly not less important in its effects on the peoples of India.

The resolve of His Imperial Majesty to visit India and hold there a coronation darbar seems to me a splendid inspiration. I can hardly imagine the feelings of delight with which the announcement must have been received. Indian friends wrote to me about it with unrestrained enthusiasm. The Royal visit has been an unbroken success. I never feared for the safety of Their Majesties, any more than I should have feared for them anywhere else. But I can understand the anxiety of those responsible for their safety; for the half-brained anarchist may be met with anywhere. But the visit was courageous with the courage of imperial instinct and sympathy. The nation has joined in thanking God for Their Majesties' safe return and for His blessing on their tour, the beneficent influence of which will not easily pass away.

CHAPTER VIII

INDIAN LADIES

The Zenana system exists to a very large extent in India. The farther north one goes the more he finds of that system. In the south there is less of it. The *Zenana* is simply the vernacular name for that part of the house which is occupied by the women; and the *Parda** is that which divides the women's quarters from the rest of the house. The lady who occupies the Zenana is a *parda nashin*, or one who sits behind the curtain. Where the Zenana system prevails men, other than the head of the house and his sons, are not allowed to see the ladies. The ladies do not come into public life; and the worst feature of the system is that their influence is confined to the family circle, and does not reach society. It reaches even the family circle only within the home; the ladies cannot directly influence the men outside the house. Where it is strictly enforced, it goes even further than this; ladies themselves are not allowed into the Zenana of other ladies, unless they are very intimate friends indeed. My wife has always made it a practice to visit the ladies of any house with the head of which I have been on friendly terms. In several instances her first visit was paid to the lady with the same formalities as mine might have been; she sat outside the parda and conversed with the lady inside. Sometimes two or three visits were conducted in this fashion; and it was only when she became more intimate that she was asked to go inside the

* A parda is a curtain or screen.

parda. There are several Indian ladies who had never received any European lady at all until they received my wife.

No doubt this tends to make intimate relations between Europeans and Indians more difficult. The influence of ladies on society is wanting, where the parda system prevails. But at the same time it must be borne in mind that the Zenana excludes Indian gentlemen and ladies just as much as it excludes Europeans; and yet social relations between Indians are perfectly frank and simple. It will not do therefore to say that while this system prevails, any intimacy between Europeans and Indians is impossible. Above all, it must be ever remembered that the Zenana system is not in any way indicative of a low opinion of women, or of their want of influence. The system is not a part of the ancient Hindu life at all. It has been prevalent among Muhammadans; and it came into India in troublous times.

It undoubtedly sprang from an unworthy conception of the relations that ought to exist between the sexes. It owes its rise in great part at least to lawlessness, to dangers arising at a time when might was right, and to a jealousy of women, who did not take an equal place in family and social life, nor were regarded as fit to do so. It must not, however, be thought that, where the system is now practised, these views of women necessarily exist. The troublous times in which the system took its rise and laid its powerful grasp on the society of certain communities and of certain parts of India, have left behind them this survival of the distrust and anxiety by which they were characterised; and it is not easy in India to get rid of any system which has once laid hold of the popular mind. It is not true, however, that Indians have a low opinion of women. There are men in all countries whose estimate of women is tainted by the stain of their own impure minds; and these may perhaps be more common in India than in a Christian country. But the men who are worth knowing in India have no such views. They despise some women; and they view some forms of behaviour in women with grave suspicion. But for good women, whether European or Indian, they have a chivalrous respect and admiration.

Let it not be forgotten that the women who are secluded under the Zenana system are, as a rule, at least as much in favour of that system as the men who are related to them. They have been trained for generations to think that it is a mark of respectability and dignity. They do not indeed misjudge the freedom of European ladies. As a rule these latter are regarded by the simple Indian ladies of the interior as strange indeed in their customs, and as possessing powers and privileges which, however consistent with their own surroundings, are altogether unintelligible to Indians. Yet they no more despise the European lady for her freedom from the Zenana system than they despise her for her want of Hindu caste; but amongst themselves they hold that it is a mark of their social superiority that they are thus carefully secluded.

It is a curious fact that some of the strongest supporters, male and female, of the parda system object not only to the visits of men from outside, but even to the visiting of ladies amongst themselves, and to the reception by the *parda nashin* of European lady visitors, or even Indian ladies who do not belong to their family. No doubt this arises from an instinctive feeling that the influence of the system may be destroyed by the enlargement of view which arises from contact with the outer world in any form. At the same time it must be borne in mind that the system receives as strong support from the ladies of India themselves as from the men. It is therefore wrong to endeavour to hasten the throwing aside of the parda and the opening of the doors of the Zenana. Nothing is good for a race which does violence to the modesty and self-respect of its women; and until the ladies of India themselves begin to see the evils of the system, and that it is not essential to endure these evils for the sake of propriety of conduct and reputation, it will be impossible, without injury, to abolish the system. The remedy lies in the preservation of the peace, the inculcation of respect for the rights and honour of women, and the education of the women themselves.

It is, indeed, a strange system. To illustrate it, let me recall a visit to an Indian friend with whom I was on most confidential relations. I drove up to his house. He came to receive me at the outer gate of his residence, with the delightful courtesy of a Hindu gentleman. Taking my hand in his, he led me into the public apartments of his house. I was seated with great respect in his audience chamber; he called the members of his family together that he might introduce them to me. His sons, some of whom had reached manhood, came one by one and were introduced. Of his daughters, only the very little girls, under, perhaps, nine or ten years of age, were allowed to come. The other ladies of the family were behind the parda. The little girls were bright and intelligent, and at least as susceptible to friendly overtures as the boys, as bright and cheery and happy as the boys, and more inclined to conversation, comparing with the boys just as girls generally do all over the world. Their intelligent interest in anything that one had to show them or say to them was very marked. It was sad to think that in a short time they would be within the Zenana. This was not because their father had any less regard for them than for his sons; for, whatever theory may exist in the Hindu mind of the comparative value of sons and daughters, human nature is the same everywhere; and the father has very often as proud and as tender an affection towards his girls as towards the boys. It was merely because custom demands their seclusion.

Lady Fraser has told me that the Zenana quarters are very frequently most comfortably furnished; and the ladies are provided with all that love and care can devise for them. But, as one can see by visiting the Zenana of an empty house, the windows looking out upon the world are high up, so that there may be no temptation to the ladies to make themselves acquainted with that which is outside. The doors and windows which are lower down open only on courtyards or gardens, into which no one is admitted who would not be permitted to enter the room itself; and every precaution is taken to keep the ladies from contact with the outer world. The seclusion is most strict; the life is practical imprisonment.

Early in my service I had a civil case before me in which a lady of considerable property was required to give evidence. As she was a *parda nashin*, it was possible, under the law, to appoint a commission to examine her at her house; but this would have involved considerable expense in sending counsel for both parties to attend while she was under examination. The party producing her as a witness was of common interest with her; and it was determined, with regard to that common interest, that she should be examined in the court. A day was fixed, and she was brought to court. She came in a *palki* or palanquin, which, despite its name, was nothing else than a very small and uncomfortable box carried on a bamboo pole. One could hardly understand how it was possible for her to be in it without great discomfort. It had been carried into a room of the Zenana and laid down. After all the men had gone away, she had come, attended by her women, and had stepped into it. The thick curtain that covered one side of the box (all the rest being of wood) was then dropped and securely fastened. Her nearest male relative stood by while the box was removed from her room; and he walked with it through the streets.

When it was brought into the court, it was laid down, but not opened. I asked the counsel on both sides whether they were satisfied that the lady inside the box was the witness whom it was desired to examine. After conversing with those who had accompanied her, and addressing a question or two to the lady, they replied that they were satisfied. I then put certain questions to her; and she answered them—clear, intelligent answers, in a sweet, low-toned voice. I never saw her; no one in the court saw her. She returned through the streets to her seclusion in the Zenana, having seen nothing all the time during which she was out of it. I have had male criminals brought before me from the jail to give evidence. They indicated their interest in the occasion by attending to what was going on around them to a degree which made it difficult to extract their evidence; and they went back to their penal confinement, no doubt, inclined to mark that day as a red-letter day in the period of their imprisonment. It was not so with this innocent *parda nashin* lady. She had experienced nothing but discomfort, and had seen nothing of interest.

These ladies who are thus secluded are often very far from unintelligent. One knows this, not only on the testimony of the European and other ladies who visit them, but also from the fact that they are able, from their seclusion, to administer affairs of very considerable importance. I have in several cases had to discuss important business with *parda-nashin* ladies. I had, for example, on one occasion to visit a lady who was administering one of the small Native States on behalf of her minor son. He received me; and intimation was sent to the Rani that I had come. When she announced that she was ready, I was led through several doors and corridors to a room in which a chair of state was placed for me. This chair was in front of a thick curtain which hung at one end of the room. On the other side of that curtain, I was informed, the Rani was sitting in another room awaiting the interview. Her son and anyone in attendance on him would not sit while she was thus in presence, though unseen. I exchanged friendly greetings with the Rani, and solemnly saluted in the direction of the curtain, believing that she was making a friendly salutation to me on the other side. I proceeded to discuss with her the affairs of the State. I found that she had a very intelligent grasp of them, and thoroughly understood what it was she wanted.

I made it a practice as far as possible, to take my wife with me to such interviews, so that she might sit on the other side of the parda with the Rani, as she was acquainted with her. This was at least a security that the right lady was conversing with me. To me there was always a feeling of dissatisfaction, in that neither of us, in the course of our conversation, was able to look the other in the face, and receive that light upon our interchange of views which the human countenance so often gives. I recall one case in which that feeling was evidently shared by the lady herself. She turned to Lady Fraser and asked her in a whisper, which I did not hear, whether there was any objection to her slightly putting the curtain aside with her finger, just so far as to permit her to get a view of my face, so as to see whether I was giving kindly attention to the expression of her views. My wife, of course, said that there was no objection; and, although I was unaware of it, the old lady saw my face, and then expressed herself as more confident that I would give careful and friendly consideration to her wishes.

It must not be considered that the ladies look upon their position as in any way deplorable, or as oppressive; but it is impossible for them to feel other than a sense of great deprivation, however necessary or honourable they may consider that deprivation to be. Ladies of India are brave and self-sacrificing. Nothing perhaps shows this more clearly than the old and awful system of *Sati*. This word, which perhaps may be translated "constant" or "faithful," was the name given to the Hindu widow who, in the depth of her sorrow, and in the determination not to live the lonely and, in some respects, accursed life of a widow, but to accompany her husband into the unseen, laid herself on his funeral pyre and died by the fire which consumed his remains. This awful system was abolished by the British Government, and anyone abetting a sati is now liable to conviction for abetment of suicide or murder. This stringent law has tended to abolish the practice of this dreadful rite. The law was enacted in opposition to the sense of large and influential sections of the community; and, owing to the prohibition of widow remarriage by Hindu law and custom and the estimation in which widows are held, these stricken women lead lives of sorrow and humiliation.

Sati is not even now entirely unknown. I remember that, in the end of 1903, in the village of Kaltaki in the District of Gaya, in Bengal, a Brahman named Damodhar died of fever. His widow, a woman of about forty-five years of age, was frantic with grief. Some time in the afternoon of the day of her husband's death, his kinsmen came to remove his dead body to the burning ground, which was about five hundred yards from her house. The widow became extremely violent; and, seizing the feet of the corpse, she solemnly cursed them for seeking to take it from her. She threatened to cut her throat if they did not leave her in possession of the body. They left it for a while in the room where the man had died, and the widow sat down beside the body.

The story is that there was no one else in the room except an old woman, a widowed sister-in-law of the deceased; and this woman gave evidence that suddenly she saw smoke coming out of the waist of the widow, her sari (or shawl) appearing to be on fire. The widow ran out of the room, and as she went she shook her sari so as to increase the flames. She threw herself down in front of the house on some wood lying near, which took fire. Seeing that she was dead, and that her body was being consumed, the relatives brought out her husband's corpse and set fire to it, heaping up wood and straw which lay at hand. Both bodies were thus consumed to ashes. When the police arrived the fire was still burning, and people were throwing ghi* on it. Not less than sixteen people were ultimately committed to the Court of Session charged with an offence under Section 306 of the Penal Code, which deals with the abetment of suicide. I cannot recall the precise results of the trial; but to me the important points established were the determination of the woman to give her life on her husband's funeral pyre, the failure of her relatives to see any reason why this desire of hers should be frustrated, and the general approval of the community as indicated in their adding oil or ghi to the flames.

Another case occurred in the Patna District a year later, where a Brahman having died, preparations were made to cremate his body in the usual way, close to a sacred and wide-spreading pipal† tree, and near the shrine of the village deity.

* Clarified butter.

† The pipal is the sacred fig-tree.

The widow, accompanied by about a hundred women and children, followed the litter, and went on to the river about a hundred yards from the funeral pyre. There she bathed and dressed herself in new clothing, the women putting sindur and tikulis on her head. She then walked back to the funeral pyre, climbed on to it, and sat facing the east with her husband's head in her lap. Then her own son applied fire to the mouth of the deceased; and he and other Brahmans set fire to the pile by placing sticks soaked in ghi and oil in the little fire-places underneath. It was alleged that the woman took fire by spontaneous combustion. She stood up with her clothes on fire, and then sank down again and died. There were said to have been from two to four thousand persons present, crying out, "Ram, Ram, Sita Ram."

The nearest police station was eight miles off; and information was not given there until, two days later, a report was made by a man who seemed to think that he was risking his life in informing. On the District Superintendent arriving at the spot, he found the pile still red-hot, and people coming in hundreds from long distances to worship at the place. A lamp was kept burning as at a shrine; flowers and sweetmeats were being offered; and temporary shops had been erected under the pipal tree. Among the articles in evidence in the case there was an invitation issued by the son to the sraddha,* in which it was stated that his father was dead and his mother had become a sati. Another document showed the line of defence to be taken in case of prosecution. The last sati that had occurred in this village was about eighty years before.

These melancholy stories are indications of the manner in which superstition still prevails in India despite the education of which we hear so much, but which, in reality, has affected directly only a very small fraction of the Indian peoples. They indicate also, how old customs, however cruel and contrary to human nature, may survive even after they have been made punishable by law, and have fallen into desuetude for

* The sraddha is a funeral ceremony.

years. We learn undoubtedly in India that human nature is in many respects the same all the world over; but we also learn that it is not very difficult to persuade men, under the name of religion, to practices which cannot be soberly regarded as any other than inhuman; and we must never allow ourselves to think that those practices, which have received the sanction of religion for ages, can be easily eradicated from the minds and lives of the people. On the other hand, these sad stories elicit an altogether different characteristic of Indian life which it is well that we should not forget, namely, the courage and devotion of the Indian women, their determination and capacity to endure anything and make any sacrifice that their religion and their family duty may require.

If anyone is under the impression that because the Indian ladies live in a Zenana, secluded behind the *parda*, they have no influence on the lives of their relatives and are looked down upon by them, he makes a great mistake. He does not understand human nature. I have heard much from my wife and others of the dignified bearing and attractive manners of Indian ladies; and I have heard my Indian friends speak with the deepest respect of their mothers and sisters, and with the deepest gratitude of the debt they owed to them for their influence on their lives. I may add that I have also known many a man who, when in society in the outside world, had strong things to say about his freedom from what he called the superstitions and bonds of his old religion: he talked lightly and flippantly, and even contemptuously, of the gods which his people worshipped; yet in his own house he prostrated himself before the images of these very gods and practised the rites and made the offerings required by that religion. The reason was that the ladies of his family wished it; and he had not the courage of his professed convictions. An old friend of mine once said to me that what India most wanted was "a new grandmother." He meant that, as every man who knows the peoples of India knows, the influence of the ladies in the house is great, and that the older the lady the greater her influence. The mother in the family has a place not unlike the mother elsewhere; but her mother-in-law, the grandmother in the house, has an altogether exceptionally honourable place in the Hindu family. She rules among the women; and the women rule in the house.

It is a very hopeful thing to think of this influence of women in India when one sees the growing desire on the part of both men and women to have the women educated, and to see women take their place alongside of their husbands in the work of life, and become a real influence, not only in the home, but in the social circle and in the life of the people. No doubt there are not yet very many who have broken free from the *parda*, determined to help their husbands in their social and public life; but there are not a few such ladies, and they are a growing company.

Many years ago, when I was Commissioner in Nagpur, I went on tour with my wife in the Balaghat District, and the Deputy Commissioner, my highly esteemed friend Mr. Shankar Madho Chitnavis, then a young officer, accompanied us on tour. As we were all three together riding along one morning, we passed a *tonga*, or little Indian cart, drawn by fast-trotting bullocks. There was manifestly a lady inside, because there were curtains carefully drawn as we passed. These were so constructed that she could put them aside to see the country, but could draw them at any time to exclude the gaze of outsiders. I asked my friend, Mr. Chitnavis, whether he knew who the lady was. He told me that it was his wife; that she was very anxious not to be dissociated from his life; and that, as he had to go so much into camp, she had made up her mind to endure all the trouble of marching with him rather than leave him without the comforts and society of home life during the months he had to spend in his tents away from head-quarters. This was, at that time, very unusual action on the part of an Indian lady. It excited the admiration of my wife, who very soon, in the course of that tour, became an intimate friend of the Deputy Commissioner's wife.

Some time after this, when I visited Balaghat head-quarters

on Sessions duty, Mr. Chitnavis asked me whether Lady Fraser and I would dine with his wife and him at their house. He told me that his wife was anxious to know some of her husband's friends, and that he thought it would be an excellent thing for her to see something of our social customs. He said apologetically that he would not ask anyone to meet us, as his wife was still shy about meeting strangers, and desired only to see a lady who had become her friend, and an officer who had been so long a friend of her husband. Of course, we agreed. I took the lady in to dinner, and talked with her at one side of the table in Marathi; for she knew no English. On the other side of the table, her husband was talking to my wife in English; for my wife did not know Marathi. Sometimes the conversation became general in Hindustani, which was known, more or less, to all four of us. It was one of the most interesting evenings that I have ever spent. It was a delight to see the intelligent interest that this Indian lady took in all the affairs which concerned her husband, in the administration of the District and in life generally; and to understand something of the earnest desire she had to play her proper part, as the wife of a man holding such a responsible office among his people, was a very instructive experience. Our pleasant interviews were repeated not infrequently. Then I left Nagpur, broken down with famine work, in which one of my most trusted fellow-workers had been Mr. Chitnavis himself; and when I returned from leave I was sent to the head-quarters of the Government of India as Secretary in the Home Department, so it was not till after some years that we met again.

We next met, all four of us together, when I was Chief Commissioner of the Central Provinces, and Mr. Chitnavis was Deputy Commissioner of Wardha. I visited the station with my wife, and the Deputy Commissioner asked us to a station dinner. He told us that all the officers in the station would be there with their wives; that his wife now knew all his colleagues and their families. We accepted the invitation. It is the Indian custom, that, when the head of the Local Government

The figures from left to right are the Maharani Adhirani Radha Bai, Lady Fraser, Maharaj Kumar Udai, the Hon. Maharajadhiraja Bahadur Sir Bijay Chand Mahtab, K.C.I.E., Sir Andrew Fraser, K.C.S.I., and Mr. Harry L. Fraser.

comes to dinner, all the company have already assembled, and are ready to proceed at once to the dining-room. We, therefore, had only time to shake hands, and then went straight to dinner. I sat down beside our hostess and began at once to speak to her in Marathi. She answered me in English, good ladylike English, pronounced with wonderful accuracy. I said to her, "Surely you did not make me talk to you in Marathi in the old days when you knew English so well?" She answered that when we used to meet in Balaghat she did not know English; but she had since set herself to learn it. She had regular lessons from the station-master's wife and lessons at least once a week from the wife of the missionary, and had given her mind to the matter, so that she had made what they regarded as very creditable progress. She said that her reason for this was that her husband had made up his mind to visit England, and that she felt that she must go with him; because, as she added, "It is not good for a husband to live a life, and to know people and places, of which the wife is altogether ignorant."

This plucky lady was still an orthodox Hindu, and partook at the table of nothing but fruit and such light food as her religion allowed her to eat in the presence of strangers; but she was determined that she would live alongside of her husband as far as possible in all his life, and be a help to him after the manner of some of the good European ladies whom she knew, and after the manner also of some of the famous ladies of early Indian story. She did go to England with her husband. She thoroughly enjoyed her visit to that country; and she set herself to write a little book in Marathi to explain to the women of her country the life of England as she had seen it.

Curiously enough this history was practically repeated in the life of another Indian lady who was a great friend of my wife in Bengal. The Maharani Adhirani of Bardwan, when she found that her young husband was determined to take his proper place in social and political life as the senior Hindu nobleman of Bengal, determined also for herself that she would take her place beside him and render him all the assistance in her power. She applied herself to the study of English manners and the English language; and in a wonderfully short time had stepped out, in all dignity and modesty, from her accustomed seclusion into the social life of Bengal. She has been the hostess at great entertainments, at which His Excellency the Viceroy and Lady Minto, the Lieutenant-Governor of Bengal, and other notable persons in Bengal life, along with their wives, and also the leaders of both European and Indian society, have been gathered together. She takes the deepest interest in all her husband's doings; and the relations in which they stand to one another, and the manner in which they treat one another and live their lives before the public, are an example to all the people. Let this movement but go on, and one cannot doubt that the progress of social enlightenment and moral elevation of the people will proceed with ever-increasing rapidity; for the principal defect in the social system of India in the past has been this, that the women's cause has not developed equally with the men's.

The education of women is still deplorably backward. The most recent figures show that education has reached only a fringe of the female population. The figures of the last census in Bengal show only ·57 per cent. of women, against 11·86 of men as "literates." This is fairly typical of the state of things throughout India. For the size of the community it need hardly be said that the Christian natives of India have a vast preponderance of educated women; but the general desire for the education of women is spreading, not only among themselves, but, what is far more important, among the men. The men have hitherto, to a very large extent, been either wholly indifferent, or even antagonistic, to the education of women. The best of them are beginning to change their minds on the subject, and to realise how important it is for their own work and for the development of the peoples of India that the women should be educated. The number of female students in institutions of all kinds is increasing more rapidly every year.

INDIAN LADIES

In the parts of India where the *parda* system prevails, it was naturally an almost insuperable barrier to the progress of education among the women. Only the intimate and sympathetic knowledge of the people possessed by the missionaries led them to adopt and advocate what is known as the Zenana System of education. The late Dr. Thomas Smith, then a missionary in Calcutta, was the first earnestly and determinedly to advocate that system. It was surrounded with difficulties; but he saw that they were not insuperable. It was clear to his mind that agents for the education of these women must be themselves women; and, through the kindly relations which the manifestation of the spirit of Christ by the missionaries established between them and the people of the country, it became possible for the lady teachers sent out or employed by the Christian Churches to find their way into the seclusion of the Zenanas. They undertook the great task of enlightening their Indian sisters, and interesting them in matters of vital moment with which they had hitherto been unacquainted. The progress of education within the Zenanas has been of the utmost importance; and it has been successful to a degree which could hardly have been anticipated by any ordinary thinker, and was certainly very far from being anticipated by many who were called on to judge the system and to give it their countenance.

Side by side with this system of Zenana instruction the girls' schools which had been started before that system was evolved have been continued and extended; but, beneficial as they were, they were quite inefficient without the Zenana System, inasmuch as the little girls who had acquired a certain amount of education in the schools were carried off at far too early an age to the seclusion and ignorance of the Zenana. There they found an atmosphere altogether hostile to the maintenance and development of their education. Too often the elder ladies, with whom they were brought into contact, were entirely ignorant and even despised the education of which they had none themselves, and the necessity for which they failed to understand. When these girls were pursued into the Zenanas by the Zenana teachers, and when the elder ladies themselves were subjected to the kindly enlightening influence of these teachers, things began greatly to improve; and the progress of education among the women is much greater than the statistics themselves can show; for there is great reluctance to make known the facts connected with Zenana life. Perhaps the highest tribute to the system which the missionaries introduced was paid when the Indian gentlemen of Bengal, during my time, urged the Government to press forward with female education, and emphatically declared that the system to be adopted was the system which the missionaries had proved to be so successful. It is earnestly to be hoped that the Government will, in the system of aided female education, give full and fair play to the great missionary agencies to which the people of India already owe so much.

There was one very melancholy feature of that part of the recent unrest in Bengal which was tinged with sedition, namely, that the influence of the ladies of the family was sometimes exercised against the peace. I do not know that this was by any means very extensive. I am inclined to think that it was not; but where it existed it was very strongly marked. We knew from our secret information that there were sometimes ladies' meetings held, in which sympathy was extended even to anarchists who had been guilty of murder, and in which ladies gathered together in the Zenanas were urged to do all that they could to advance the cause of the wicked and mischievous propaganda. I was once talking to a friend of mine who, though a member of what is called the National Congress, was not an extremist; for he was very clearly of opinion that in the interests of India it was necessary for an indefinite period to maintain British rule. I mentioned to him this information that we had; and he told me that there was some truth in it. asked him for an explanation. He said that it was due to three causes. First, there was the generally impressionable character of women, especially when they were uneducated and unacquainted with the life of the world. Secondly, there was the natural sympathy of women with a mother whose son had been laid hold of by the law for a crime into which he had been led by sentiments, however mistaken and perverse, of love of country, and by which his life had become forfeit to the law. Thirdly, it was due to forgetfulness of what they owe to the British Government.

On this last point his statement was very strong. He told me that, though now an elderly man, he remembered well how his mother and grandmother had impressed on him in his youth the sense of peace and security which the British Government had brought to the homes of the people, how they spoke with strong affection of that Government, and of the great lady who ruled over the British Empire from her home across the black water. He also expressed strongly his regret that these memories were passing away, and that misrepresentations of the character and results of British rule were being introduced into the homes of the people. No man who knows anything of human nature generally, or of Indian human nature in particular, will fail to realise how great is a mother's influence over her children under anything like normal conditions of family life, and how great is the importance of securing that influence in favour of that which is in the highest interests of the people. It is one of the saddest facts connected with the writings of a seditious press, that they are often all that the son of a proud Hindu mother has to read to her in her seclusion. The poison spreads farther and sinks deeper than we sometimes realise.

CHAPTER IX

GRAIN RIOTS IN THE NAGPUR DISTRICT

In the end of September, 1896, when I was Commissioner of the Nagpur District, we had grain riots in the city of Nagpur and in different parts of the District, which were in their origin and principal features of a somewhat interesting and instructive nature. There was famine in the north of the Province, that is, in the Jubbulpore Division, as well as in the adjoining parts of the North-west Provinces. There was no famine in the Nagpur Division, but the prices of grain were very high. The reason of this was partly the demand for the export of grain from that part of the Province to the famine-stricken parts, and partly the determination of the grain merchants to hold up their grain in hope of still higher prices when the famine elsewhere should have developed. There was some distress occasioned by these high prices. People with fixed incomes found it hard to purchase for themselves even the necessaries of life; and there was a great deal of ill-feeling in the community against the grain merchants.

It was ascertained in the inquiries which were made later that a number of the *badmashes* * of Nagpur had set themselves to foment this ill-feeling and to incite the people to rise against the grain sellers and take their stock by force. The object of these *badmashes* was to stir up a riot and incite an attack on the grain merchants' shops, in the hope that, while the rioters were possessing themselves of grain, they might take advantage of the disturbance of the peace to break into the treasuries and

* Badma'ash is a man of evil life, also a habitual criminal.

secure the bullion and valuables belonging to the merchants. The rumour was very carefully and secretly circulated among the people that the Government would be favourable to any measure, the object of which was to bring the grain merchants to their senses. It was stated that the paternal Government deeply sympathised with the people in the distress occasioned by high prices, and reprobated the selfish and unprincipled conduct of the grain merchants in seeking to make large profits out of the misery of their fellow-countrymen. The people were told that Government would not tolerate any prolonged disturbance, but was quite willing to have the grain dealers robbed of a certain amount of their grain, provided that the disturbance did not last more than two or three hours, by which time it would be possible to give them a sound lesson without too seriously injuring them. These extraordinary statements were received without doubt by a large number of ignorant persons; and riots in Nagpur city and in several towns in the District were the result.

On Saturday, 19th September, there was an unimportant fracas in the Sanichari Bazar. There were only two policemen present, and they fled. The rioters had a noisy quarrel with the grain sellers and seized some grain and then dispersed. The far more important Bazar, the Itwari * Bazar, was held on the following day and passed off without disturbance. No particular importance was therefore attached by the District officers to what had occurred on the Saturday; and it is probable that the incitements to general rioting were more systematically given after that date, and that Monday, 28th September, was fixed for simultaneous risings throughout the District. I was at the time on a visit to the Balaghat District of the Division, where there were some signs of approaching distress. The Deputy Commissioner of that District had invited me to come and consult with him as to the measures to be taken there.

* Sanīchar is Saturday, and Itwar is Sunday. The bazars are named from the day on which the weekly market is held, or used to be held when the bazar was named.

The Nagpur District was in the hands of a very junior officer. Mr. Needham, the permanent incumbent of the office of Deputy Commissioner, was away on "privilege leave."* As the vacancy was a very temporary one the senior assistant, Mr. Blenkinsop, a civilian of about three years standing, had been placed in charge of the District. He was then a young officer of great promise, which has since been manifestly fulfilled in several important posts under Government; and he showed by his tact and judgment throughout the trying experiences of the riots that he was even then not unfit for the charge of an important District at a critical time.

In consequence of the disturbance on Saturday the 19th, and of the reports which he received regarding the high prices of grain in the Bazar and the consequent irritation of the people, especially of the Koshtis (or weavers), Mr. Blenkinsop agreed to meet the merchants and some leading representatives of the other classes at the Town Hall on Wednesday, 23rd September, to discuss the state of affairs. When he reached the Town Hall he found all the leading Baniyas † and about six or seven hundred people assembled. There was also a very considerable crowd outside the Hall. The meeting was held in view of the Budhwari ‡ Bazar which was established in the open space in front of the Town Hall, and not in the Budhwari Mahalla § itself. Mr. Blenkinsop, who had previously written to me for advice on the subject, explained that he as the representative of Government could not interfere with trade; but he suggested that it might be well for both parties to appoint representatives and discuss the matter with a view to an amicable understanding. This was done; and certain rates were voluntarily fixed for that day. Everyone seemed satisfied with this voluntary arrangement, and the Bazar passed off without any sign of trouble.

* "Privilege leave" is short leave or holiday on full pay.
† Baniya is a shopkeeper, usually a grain dealer.
‡ Budhwār is Wednesday.
§ Mahalla is a ward, or part of a town.

The arrangement did not, however, work well for more than a day or two. Complaints were soon heard that the middle men were not adhering to the prices that had been fixed and were also adulterating their grain, and wetting it. These complaints were submitted to the Deputy Commissioner personally, and by post to myself. I had seen Mr. (now Sir Gangadhar) Chitnavis, President of the Municipality, and one or two other leading citizens; and we had consulted as to the best means of relieving such distress as existed, and allaying irritation. The Indian gentlemen generally advocated the compulsory reduction of rates by Government, and the prohibition of the export of grain. They were told that such measures, though certainly consistent with Oriental ideas, were entirely opposed to the policy of Government, and could not be adopted. We discussed the propriety of having relief works for those who could not earn enough to secure the necessaries of life at current prices; but the unanimous opinion of our Indian advisers was that there was no such distress as to require this measure, and that those who were most discontented would certainly not come to the relief works. It was ultimately decided by the Deputy Commissioner, in consultation with his Indian advisers, to hold a small meeting of the leading citizens and merchants on Monday, the 28th, to discuss the matter after further inquiry and consideration. I was informed of this decision and agreed to be present at the proposed meeting. I therefore returned to head-quarters on Saturday, 26th September.

On the morning of the following day the Tahsildar informed the Deputy Commissioner that irritation was very acute, and that disorder was apprehended at the Itwari Bazar. At breakfast the Deputy Commissioner received a letter from Sir Gangadhar Chitnavis, saying that the grain merchants had abstained from opening their shops in the Itwari Bazar, and that there was much discontent in consequence. No doubt the merchants were afraid of violence; but their action increased the irritation of the people by making it impossible for them to secure the necessary supplies of grain. A good number of people came to the Deputy Commissioner's house along with the letter. Sir Gangadhar suggested that the Municipal Committee might buy grain and sell it to the people. There had also been a proposal that some well-to-do merchants should bring in large consignments of grain and try to break up the alleged combination of grain sellers to raise prices and to keep them high. In his letter Sir Gangadhar said that he would await the Deputy Commissioner's reply at the Town Hall, which was about two miles from the Deputy Commissioner's house. Mr. Blenkinsop went down as soon as he could; but Sir Gangadhar had gone home to breakfast.

News was brought to Mr. Blenkinsop at the Town Hall that there was a threatening of grain looting at the Budhwari Mahalla, where there was no open Bazar that day, but where there were many important merchants' houses and shops. He rode off in that direction with the City Superintendent of Police. They learned, however, that the rioters had moved off towards the Itwari Bazar, the unopened shops in which were understood to be full of grain which had been brought in for that day's market. They therefore pushed on to that Bazar. When they got there, they were met by an angry crowd demanding that grain should be supplied. They had come to the Bazar to buy, and there was no grain on sale. Mr. Blenkinsop despatched a messenger to the District Superintendent of Police to bring up some of the Special Reserve Police to protect the Bazar; and, meanwhile, he promised the people that he would try to make arrangements to have grain in the market by 4 p.m. if they would have patience. This promise was undoubtedly required, for there was no grain available. It was also quite a reasonable promise; for the merchants professed themselves to be quite willing to bring grain if they were protected from violence. It was because they had heard very credible rumours of an intention to plunder the Bazar that they had not opened their shops.

It was very much to be regretted that, instead of adopting this course, which they must have known to be likely to cause intense public irritation, they did not inform the Deputy Commissioner of the rumour and of their intention. Owing to their failure to do so, he had no chance of taking the necessary precautions to prevent lawlessness. The police were too remiss or too sympathetic with the people to give any warning. It is a very striking thing how often in India serious trouble may be brewing without anyone going out of his way to inform the authorities. Experience of this kind was met with in the north of India during the cow-killing riots, in Behar during the tree-marking disturbances, and in Lower Bengal during the incidents of the boycott movement. European officers and their most trustworthy Indian subordinates of superior rank require themselves to live among the people and in close touch with them, if they are to be ready for any mischief that may arise.

Some time after Mr. Blenkinsop had reached the Itwari Bazar a large crowd, headed by three or four young men brandishing lathis,* marched into the Bazar, down the main road through the city. On finding the Deputy Commissioner there, these *lathiyals*† lowered their clubs and appeared to mix with the crowd. Mr. Blenkinsop remained patiently at the Itwari Police outpost, awaiting the arrival of the District Superintendent of Police. The latter officer, Mr. Stuart, arrived soon after 3 p.m. with about twenty of the Reserve Police. Before it was possible to begin sales, however, news was brought that plundering had begun in the Shukrwari‡ Bazar; and Mr. Blenkinsop sent Mr. Stuart there with some of the Reserve men, remaining himself to maintain order in the Itwari Bazar. At the same time, he sent me a note suggesting that troops might be called out to maintain order. I did not receive this note till hours later, when I was myself at work suppressing the disorder in the Shukrwari Bazar. Mr. Blenkinsop did not think then that the people in the Itwari Bazar would proceed to extreme measures; for they had listened to him quietly, and had apparently accepted

* Lāthī is a heavy club often mounted and weighted with metal.
† Lāthīyāl is a man armed with a club, generally a professional ruffian.
‡ Shukrwār is Friday.

his advice to exercise a little patience. Soon afterwards he received a resport to the effect that there was a rising in the Budhwari Mahalla, and that the City Superintendent had been killed. The latter statement was not true; but it was true that there was serious rioting at Budhwari. He therefore sent a messenger direct to the Fort urging the immediate despatch of a detachment of Madras Infantry to his assistance.

Meanwhile, at 3.30 p.m. a messenger had come to me from Sir G. Chitnavis with a hurried note saying that there were crowds of discontented and riotous persons led by *lathiyals* threatening to plunder the town, and that his own house was in danger. At the same time several grain merchants from the town drove at express speed into my compound with the information that the city people had risen against the merchants. At that moment I was talking to Mr. Coxon, Deputy Commissioner of Chanda, and Mr. Mitchell, Inspector of Schools, who were in Nagpur at a Conference, and were staying at my house. They offered to come with me to the city, which was about two miles distant. We started as soon as my wagonette could be got ready, for only two of my horses had returned from camp. On the way we met Chuni Lall (the Agent of Rai Bahadur Bansilal Abirchand, the great Kamptee banker) in a pony tonga, Seth Agyaram's messenger in a carriage, and several other terrified merchants, who told us that the shops in New Shukrwari Bazar were being broken into, that the police had fled, and that the whole of that part of the city was in the hands of a mob led by *lathiyals* and *badmashes*. This Bazar is the richest in Nagpur and contains the business residences of some of the most important money-lenders and grain dealers. It was evident that there was a rising of some importance in the city.

I turned into the Bank of Bengal, which we were just passing. It lies at the foot of the hill on which the Sitabaldi Fort stands, about half a mile from the Commissioner's old house, and between it and the city. There I wrote a note to Lieutenant Jeffcoat, in command of the detachment of Madras Infantry, to send down men to my assistance at once. We then drove on to the city as fast as we could, leaving the troops to follow. At the end of the new Shukrwari road, as we entered the city by the Juma Darwaza,* soon after 4 p.m. we found a small body of about twelve or sixteen unarmed Indian police huddled together in terror. The road was crowded with a vast concourse of people, among whom could be seen men armed with lathis. I inquired where the Deputy Commissioner was, and was informed that he was with the District Superintendent of Police in the Itwari Bazar dealing with a similar rising there. I left a note with one constable for Lieutenant Jeffcoat asking him to send half of his men on to the Deputy Commissioner, and half into the Shukrwari Bazar after me. I then shouted to the police, so that many of the people heard me, informing them that the military were on their way to the city, and ordering them to form up behind me and follow my carriage at the double.

I drove my carriage at full speed down the street to where the shops had been broken into and were being plundered. The crowd, in a somewhat friendly manner, opened out before us. Many of them recognised me and saluted quite respectfully, even some of those who were carrying away little bundles of grain. Meeting with no resistance, we were soon at the grain merchants' quarter. We found the shops broken open, the doors even smashed off their hinges, the rioters in undisputed possession, and some of the shops completely plundered. The work of spoliation was making rapid progress when we arrived. The rioters thought that we had a large force behind us; for the information I had given to the police spread like wild-fire. We leaped from the carriage and rushed into several shops which were entirely in the hands of the looters. Wherever we appeared panic seized them. We knocked down a number of the ring-leaders, tied them up in their own pagaris † and deposited them in the strong room of a shop, in custody of some of the police until assistance should arrive. The noise in the street prevented

* Jum'ā is the Muhammadan name for Friday. Darwāza means gate (or door).

† Pagarī is a long cloth wound round the head, a turban.

people in one shop knowing what was being done in another; and we had forty or fifty prisoners by the time assistance came. At least one half of these were ringleaders armed with lathis, and carrying not grain, but bullion and jewels as their booty. All of them were strong, well-nourished men. By this time we had emptied the shops of the looters and closed them, and were proceeding to clear the street.

Meanwhile, Mr. Stuart, who had been sent by the Deputy Commissioner to this Bazar, arrived. We made over charge of the prisoners to him, and as there had been no signs of organised resistance we determined to leave him there and push on to the help of the Deputy Commissioner. As soon, however, as we had turned to go, a determined attack was made by the street rioters on the District Superintendent. We fortunately heard the alarm and turned back. We fastened the prisoners to each other by their own head-dresses and by ropes, and then fastened the foremost of them to the carriage. We directed about half a dozen of the small force of Reserve Police to remain as a guard in Shukrwari, and the rest (about six men) to follow close behind the prisoners with fixed bayonets and loaded rifles; and in this order we drove off to the Kotwali.* The crowd opened up to make way for my wagonette and the strange procession of prisoners, whom the wagonette in front and the armed police behind kept at a smart trot all the way.

The Kotwali was not far from the Shukrwari Bazar, and we soon deposited our prisoners in the cells, from whence they were removed the next day to the Central Jail under charge of a military escort. By this time it was about 5 p.m., and the men of the Madras Infantry, who had started with great promptitude, under Captain Jeffcoat, joined us here. While we were putting our prisoners in the cells we received news that a mob led by *lathiyals* was marching on Sir G. Chitnavis's house. We left some of the Madras Infantry men to guard

* The Kotwal is the Chief Police Officer of the city; and the Kotwali is his office.

the Kotwali, and took as many as we could (about a dozen) in my wagonette. I requested Lieutenant Jeffcoat, meanwhile, to march directly to the relief of the Deputy Commissioner. We drove off straight to the Shukrwari Bazar as fast as my horses could gallop. The sight of the Sepoys with us was, however, quite enough; and we only saw the mob disperse and the *lathiyals* vanish.

We left a few of our men as a guard at Sir G. Chitnavis's house and went the shortest way to the Itwari Bazar. We found that organised looting had started there, about half an hour before our arrival. The Deputy Commissioner had not sufficient force to prevent it throughout the Bazar, though he had kept the peace at the part where he was. While he kept the peace in one place the plunderers were at work in another. The leaders were armed with lathis and house-breaking instruments, but only a few shops had been opened. We passed into the Bazar just ahead of Lieutenant Jeffcoat and his men. We formed up all together, rushed the Bazar and arrested some ringleaders. The police, seeing that they had European officers with them and that the troops were close behind, soon quelled the disturbance without any bloodshed.

There was, however, a grave risk that the rioters, whose defeat had been due to panic, might rally and give very serious trouble. No one who has seen the large bodies of men armed with lathis, who were the main agents in the disturbances, or the sympathetic attitude assumed for the most part by the crowd, could have doubted that the danger was decidedly serious. We therefore asked Lieutenant Jeffcoat to send as many men as he could spare of the Lancashire regiment, a small detachment of which was at the Fort, to assist in maintaining the peace of the city. He sent us twenty-five men. These were kept at the Kotwali as a reserve and to guard the prisoners, who now numbered ninety men. The men of the Madras Infantry detachment were picketed in the principal markets for the night. No further looting occurred.

On Monday morning disturbances broke out in various parts

of the city, and mobs armed with lathis were seen to be ready for mischief. Meanwhile, if the outbreak had been renewed, it would, in all probability, have been more serious than before. The mob would have come prepared to resist. Mr. Blenkinsop therefore asked Major Graves and Captain Biddulph to bring out such of the Bengal Nagpur Railway Rifles and Nagpur Volunteer Rifles respectively as they could. These were sent down most promptly to assist us. At the same time Mr. Blenkinsop, with my concurrence, telegraphed to Kamptee to the General Officer commanding the District to send some men of the Lancashire regiment and of the Madras Infantry to relieve the men from Sitabaldi, whom it was undesirable to keep away from the Fort. Patrols moved about the city all night; the mob was overawed, and all remained quiet. On Tuesday we sent back the European troops and Volunteers, and retained only a few of the Native Infantry as guards in the principal Bazars, with a reserve at the Kotwali. From this time there was no renewal of the disturbance. All was quiet in the city.

The main causes of the disturbance were undoubtedly: (1) the discontented state of the Koshti * population, whom the mills had deprived of a great part of the profits of their own peculiar calling, and who did not readily turn to any other; (2) the rise in prices owing to the want of rain and to the demand for food grains from the North-Western Provinces and parts of Bengal; (3) the export of grain which led the people to fear that there would soon be no grain at all in Nagpur; and (4) the efforts of the *badmashes* to fan the flame of resentment against the grain sellers and rich merchants, so as to create for themselves an opportunity for robbery. It was very curious to find on later inquiry that the principal prisoners arrested were all of bad character, some of them having several previous convictions against them, and that one of the principal promoters of the disturbance was an ill-conditioned distant relative of the old Bhonsla family of Nagpur, who was well known for encouraging crime and reaping profit from it.

* The Koshtī caste is the great weaving caste of the Nagpur territory.

On the whole, the rioters were to all appearance fairly well nourished. There was no exceptional distress in the town. Attention had been drawn very particularly to destitute people from distant famine-stricken parts of the country passing through the town; but there was no local distress of an exceptional character, and nothing that private charity was unable fully to meet. Almost all the arrests made in putting down the riots were of able-bodied and well-fed men, mainly Koshtis, low-class Mussulmans, and professional bad characters. There were many poor people and women following in the wake of these; but we drove them away without arresting them. The rioters were mainly ill-disposed persons bent on plunder. But for the prompt action of the military authorities, and the fact that the civil officers engaged in restoring peace were generally well known and popular among the people, there would undoubtedly have been determined resistance and probably considerable loss of life. As it was, there was really very little violence. Not a shot was fired or a bayonet used. The only death that occurred was that of an old and feeble grain merchant, who was seized by a fit owing to his terror and passed away. Our sudden arrival on the scene, speedily followed by the troops, created a panic and quelled the disturbance in the city in an incredibly short space of time.

Although it was promptly quelled in the city, however, the disturbance spread to surrounding villages. There seems little doubt, indeed, as subsequent inquiry showed, that plans were made for a simultaneous rising in several towns on a later day in the week, and that the rising in the city on the Sunday was fortunately premature. When I was in the Kotwali shortly after noon on Monday, news was brought of shops being plundered in Paldi, a beautiful old village of considerable wealth, about three or four miles along the Great Eastern Road. I started off at once with a small body of Bengal Nagpur Railway Rifles; but we were too late to prevent the plundering of the shops of one or two Marwari grain merchants; and unfortunately, as we had no mounted troops or police, we were unable to follow the rioters across country. This was the only serious plundering that occurred near Nagpur. There was also an attempt to plunder the Bazar in Kamptee, which was frustrated by the military authorities.

On Tuesday the 29th, a telegram from the Tahsildar of Ramtek, a subdivision about twenty-seven miles from Nagpur, was received about noon at the Kotwali, reporting a rising there with serious danger to the Government Treasury. Mr. (now Sir Charles) Cleveland, then Commissioner of Excise, was with the Deputy Commissioner and me at the time. He kindly consented to go off to Ramtek at once with any mounted men that the General Officer commanding at Kamptee could spare. A telegram was at once despatched to that officer, who placed twenty-five men from the Battery at our disposal. This he did, no doubt, with the more alacrity, because there were then one or two European officers and ladies taking a holiday at the beautiful Bungalow on the top of Ramtek Hill.

Kamptee lies on the way to Ramtek, and Sir C. Cleveland, who had driven out in my dogcart, found the men ready with an empty saddle for himself, and before night he was clearing the streets of Ramtek of the rioters. He found that the town had been entirely in the hands of a mob of some fifteen hundred persons. The attack on the shops had been deliberately planned. Their doors had been broken open and in some cases removed bodily. They had been plundered of grain, sugar, oil and money. The police had been unable to repress disorder, and the merchants had been panic-stricken and unable to defend their property. Nineteen ringleaders were quietly arrested, some of whom were prepared for further action next day. More arrests were made subsequently. Sir Charles summarily punished some of the less important rioters, and kept the rest for more severe punishment afterwards. Amongst the arrests made were two Tahsili Chaprasis.*

Similar risings occurred at practically the same time in Khapa, Umrer, Katol, and other towns of the district, and

* *Chaprās* is a badge. A *chaprāsī* is an orderly or messenger.

officers of different departments were despatched with police officers in tongas * to restore peace. Some well-to-do people were among the ringleaders. In Khapa two members of the Municipal Committee were amongst those arrested for having incited the mob and led them in their plundering. The officers sent out were instructed to arrest the ringleaders in the riots, and either to punish them summarily or to reserve them for punishment; to direct the police to take special precautions against plundering in the Bazars; to urge the malguzars (or village head men) and villagers to defend their property, and especially their seed grain; and to do all they could to restore order and confidence. No doubt the rioting in the interior of the district was partly planned beforehand, and partly due to exaggerated and coloured reports of what had occurred in Nagpur. The people were generally alarmed, and the ill-disposed were encouraged in lawlessness.

The subordinate police failed in their duty in not giving warning of what was about to occur, and were quite inadequate to suppress the disturbances. They were ignorant of what was about to occur, or perhaps somewhat sympathetic. They were wanting in courage, and not unfavourable to the rioters. It is very seldom that the police fail in this way; but the circumstances were such as fully to explain in the East the rapidity with which disorder spread, and the measure of difficulty that was found in restoring the peace. The sudden raid of Sir C. Cleveland on Ramtek with a body of mounted European troops removed the impression that these plunderers could commit crimes with impunity in the remoter parts of the District; and the visit of European officers to all parts of the District had an excellent effect. No plundering worth mentioning occurred after the 30th.

It was somewhat painful to see how thoroughly panic-stricken the most respectable people of Nagpur, and especially the merchants, were in presence of these disturbances. One does

* Tonga (or *tāngā*) is a light two-wheeled cart drawn by ponies or bullocks.

not blame them for some anxiety, for the aspect of the mob was undoubtedly at times very serious; but what surprises one is that there was hardly any real attempt made by anyone to defend his property where the riots occurred. This is due, partly, no doubt, to a certain want of courage and vigour on the part of these classes in India generally, and also, and even more, to their distinctly law-abiding character, the objection, if not fear, that they have to take the law into their own hands, and the natural inclination to look to the Government for protection. This is a feature of Indian life that we have to take into account at every turn. If we want the peace to be maintained we must maintain it ourselves.

Sometimes we do succeed in getting men to defend themselves against dacoits * and robbers; but as a rule they look to us in every respect for their defence. There are always some distinguished exceptions; and there were some on this occasion. I well remember several Indian gentlemen to whom public acknowledgment was made of their plucky and devoted assistance. Two of these especially recur to my mind, both of them Brahmans from the Bombay side, Rao Bahadur Bhargo Rao, an Extra Assistant Commissioner, and Rao Bahadur Bapurao Dada, a leading legal practitioner and Vice-President of the Municipality. These two men and others were present throughout the riotous scenes in the city, did their best to keep the people quiet and to restore order, and were indefatigable in the assistance they rendered to their European brother officers and friends. It is well worthy of record that neither of them suffered in the least, either in his profession or in his social popularity, by the vigour and loyalty which he displayed.

* Dacoit (or *dakait*) is a member of a band of robbers.

CHAPTER X

THE KHOND RISING IN KALAHANDI

When the territories of Nagpur came under our rule, owing to the failure of Rajah Raghoji Bhonsla to adopt an heir, it was determined by the Government of India to form a new Non-regulation Province consisting of these territories, with the addition of certain adjoining tracts. This Province was called "the Central Provinces," and was formed by the union of the old Nagpur Province and the Saugor and Nerbudda Territories. It included the Vindhyan table-land Districts, the Nerbudda Districts with their great wheat-field, the Nagpur plain with its cotton and rice, and the Chhattisgarh Division, a low plateau of red soil forming the Districts of Raipur and Bilaspur, to which was added the Uriya District of Sambalpur. Of this Division I was appointed Commissioner in 1888, in succession to my old friend Mr. J. W. Chisholm, who had formerly been Settlement Officer of the Bilaspur District, and, therefore, knew that District as intimately as it was possible for any man to know his charge. He had also, as is the manner of men trained in the Settlement school, a very intimate knowledge of the vernacular dialects of that part of the country, a great belief in moving about among the villages in camp, and a thorough and sympathetic acquaintance with the people.

The Chhattisgarh Division consisted of two great parts, the one being the British territory, consisting of the three Districts above named, and the other the Feudatory Territories of fourteen ruling Chiefs, each of whom was then nominally attached for purposes of supervision to one or other of these three Districts. The area of the British territory was 25,000 square miles, and that of the fourteen Feudatory States 26,000 square miles. There were no railways in those days over any part of the Division, the only railway communication being a narrow-gauge line, opened about five years earlier, between Raj-Nandgaon (the capital of the Feudatory State of Nandgaon, which is in the extreme west of the Chhattisgarh Division) and Nagpur, the capital of the Province. The whole of this vast territory of over 50,000 square miles was, therefore, under the sole charge of the Commissioner of Chhattisgarh, assisted by three District Magistrates, until events occurred which led to the appointment of a political officer to the charge of the Feudatory States. The Division was then remote and backward, sparsely populated for the most part, and little known. It was spoken of in 1866 by Sir Richard Temple, the first Chief Commissioner of the Central Provinces, as "the trackless wilderness of Chhattisgarh"; and he justly prided himself on having made the first road with any right to claim such a name running from West to East, that is, continuing the Nagpur-Raipur road down to Sambalpur, a hundred and sixty miles off.

It was impossible for any of the District Magistrates or "Deputy Commissioners" to become acquainted with the real condition of things in the Feudatory States attached to his District, if he was effectively to do his duty and discharge his responsibility as Magistrate of the British District committed to his charge; and it was equally impossible for the Commissioner to do more than pay a flying visit to a few out of the fourteen Native States in the course of each year. The result was that, although a good deal was known of these States in a general way, there was little intimate acquaintance with them. The Chiefs, indeed, not infrequently came up to the headquarters of the District to which they were attached, and of the Division itself, to meet the Commissioner or Deputy Commissioner and talk over things with him in a friendly way. But on the whole the administration of the Feudatory States was unsystematic and not very effective; and what the people had of comfort and fairly satisfactory administration was due rather to the remoteness of the jungle villages, the simplicity of their manners, and the smallness of their requirements, than to any other cause.

At the time when the Central Provinces came under our rule, the present clearly defined distinction between Feudatories and Zamindars did not exist. All the petty chieftains of Chhattisgarh constituted a great class of more or less independent rulers. Their powers and privileges were by no means equal. These depended largely on the degree of remoteness of the territory of the chief in each case from the centre of sovereign authority at Nagpur; but the States were all alike in this, that while the most important of them was not wholly outside of the authority of the permanent power, the least important was not in every respect subject to that authority. When the authority of the British Government was established in these tracts the chieftains were divided into Feudatory Chiefs and Zamindars, according to the degree of their powers, as far as these could be ascertained by the inquiries instituted under the orders of Sir Richard Temple, and also personally undertaken by him with his usual energy.

The Feudatory Chiefs were left to rule their States. The more remote among them, having been the most powerful, were given authority subject only to the condition that they should generally administer their States under the supervision, and subject to the advice, of the Chief Commissioner of the Central Provinces, and especially that they should not execute any sentence of death without his sanction. The western and smaller States had similar authority; but in the exercise of their criminal powers any sentence of over seven years' imprisonment required the confirmation of British authority. The authority of all the Chiefs was thus to a greater or less degree politically circumscribed and controlled; but from the point of view of the law their independence is practically absolute, and they are not British subjects.

The ordinary Zamindars, on the other hand, are British

subjects, though as a class they have special privileges. Owing to the exigencies of the administration they were long allowed a number of extraordinary privileges, some of which appear at first sight incompatible with the position of an ordinary British subject; but it is noteworthy that, whenever attention has been drawn (as in the matter of police and excise) to the fact that any such privilege is inconsistent with the due administration of the law, it has invariably been held that it must be either withdrawn or legalised. The whole question of the relation of these two classes of Chiefs to the Government was generally decided in Sir Richard Temple's time on the principle indicated above, namely, that one clear line of demarcation was drawn between those who on account of their high powers and privileges under native rule should be regarded as more or less independent rulers, under the general control of the Government as feudal superior, and those who, though possessing certain special privileges, were not rulers at all; but details were worked out, and have continued to be worked out, in accordance with any later light thrown on the matter and the developing requirements of the case.

As I have said, the authority and control of the British Government over the internal administration of the Native States was exercised through the Commissioner of the Division and the Deputy Commissioner of the District, until certain events which occurred in 1878 and 1879. On the 1st January, 1877, Lord Lytton's great Imperial Durbar was held at Delhi for the proclamation of Queen Victoria as Empress of India. The native chiefs, small and great, from all parts of India were invited to be present at this Durbar; and Chhattisgarh chiefs went up to Delhi with the rest. Various honours were distributed at Delhi amongst the chiefs, and the Chhattisgarh Chief selected for distinction was the Rajah of Kalahandi. His is a somewhat important Uriya State. He himself was a man of excellent manners, and of more capacity and education than the Chiefs of Chhattisgarh generally possessed. He was a man who, on the whole, meant well; and he had some idea of administration and a great desire to improve the status and develop the revenue of his State. He was believed to have administered it well, and he was recommended for the honour of a salute of nine guns; to which honour none of the Chiefs of Chhattisgarh had up to that time been entitled. The recommendation was accepted, and the honour bestowed.

It was not long after this that the Rajah died, and Mr. Frederick Berry, of the Indian Civil Service, was appointed to go down and inquire into the circumstances of the State and report what measures should be taken for its administration during the minority of the heir. Immediately on the death of the Rajah, whose personal influence seems to have been great, and just as Mr. Berry was taking over charge of the State, a deplorable insurrection occurred.

Subsequent inquiry showed that the measures in the Rajah's administration which led up to this rising had been of some standing. The cause of the rising was the despair and rage with which the simple Khonds, who had been the pioneer cultivators of the soil in certain parts of Kalahandi, found themselves over-reached and superseded by a far more efficient class of agriculturists, known as the Kultas. The Khonds are a hardy, war-like race of men, well accustomed to jungle life. Their pluck in the presence of wild beasts and their skill as hunters are well known; but their style of agriculture is primitive and desultory. They are quite content to live in the simplest manner and from hand to mouth, doing only as much as the necessities of the hour seem to demand.

The Kultas, on the other hand, are very successful agriculturists of somewhat timid character and of frugal habits. They were naturally in many respects much more desirable tenants than the Khonds. They were more easily squeezed in the matter of rents, so long as the squeezing was done somewhat judiciously; and they were able themselves to get a great deal more out of the land. The Rajah therefore encouraged them, and gradually the Khonds found themselves ousted from the possession of their old villages and fields by these interlopers of superior agricultural capacity. This led to a strong agrarian hatred and jealousy.

In the middle of May, 1878, a meeting was held at Balwaspur, which was attended by a large number of the leading Khonds. They determined unanimously to massacre the Kultas. From natural reverence for their Chief, whom they indeed worshipped as an embodiment of the Divinity, they had been prevented from entertaining or manifesting any personal animosity against him ; but they planned to attack the European Superintendent of the State, Mr. Berry, and either murder him or at least restrain him from interference with their designs to wreak their vengeance on the Kultas themselves. They swore to carry out these designs, and kissed the sacrificial *tangi* (or axe) in token of their resolve. The execution of this purpose was remitted to the various representatives, that each might carry it out in his own neighbourhood. The result was that over a hundred Kultas were murdered, and many more would have perished but for the prompt measures taken by the Government, and on the spot by Mr. Berry, who, acting under the supervision and with the support of Col. Ward, Commissioner of the Division, dispersed the armed bands of Khonds and rescued the captured Kultas.

In the village of Kalamgaon twenty Kultas were murdered. This is a typical case, and the circumstances may be related. Four days after the meeting above referred to, news was received in Kalamgaon of the murder of Ishwar Gaontiya of Asargarh, a leader of the Kultas ; and his fellow caste-men were filled with alarm and prepared to flee. They found, however, that they were surrounded by armed Khonds, chiefly belonging to their own and the neighbouring villages. They were captured and huddled together in a house in the village, which was guarded all night. Besides placing a strong guard on the house, the leading Khonds present promised that, though the Kultas might be deprived of their ill-gotten lands and wealth, their lives would be spared. Next morning the number of Khonds had largely increased. The number of Kulta prisoners, including women and children, was about forty.

Early on the morning of the 20th May the leading Khonds came in and demanded the surrender of all the property that the Kultas had. When this had been given up, the Khonds prepared to remove their prisoners from the house. The latter, who were now convinced that their lives would be taken, tried to hide themselves where they could; but one after another they were pulled from their hiding-places and hurried outside. Here they found hundreds of Khonds collected, armed with axes and bows and arrows. The wretched prisoners fell at the feet of the leading Khonds and begged them to spare their lives; but they were told that none of the men among them would be spared. In the confusion one or two men did succeed in effecting an escape to the hills; and their story was told before Col. Ward when he made a judicial inquiry into the circumstances. The women, however, and most of the children were spared. The harrowing details of what followed were furnished to Col. Ward by the bereaved women and by the Khond prisoners themselves; for the latter were far too simple to deny their guilt, and gave what were shown to be clear and accurate accounts of what had occurred.

Twenty Kultas were murdered in cold blood. There may have been more; but twenty murders were proved. One old Kulta who had got a little way out of the thickest of the confusion was discovered by some of the Khonds. He came towards the foremost among their leaders in an attitude of supplication, holding grass in his mouth as a token of abject submission. The fierce Khond struck off the old man's head with one stroke of his axe and filled a small vessel he carried with the blood. This he intended to pour upon some of the fields belonging to himself and some of his friends, as an offering to the earth to secure her bountiful response to their agricultural efforts. The other men were not murdered at once; but the leading Khonds from the various villages which they represented were allowed to select victims, who were led away in different directions to be slaughtered in these villages.

One woman, Musamat Sari, the widow of one of the murdered Kultas, thus described the capture of herself and family, and the events which followed: "My boy Madho was carrying a *Banghy* * on his shoulder; my husband was carrying our little girl; and my brother-in-law had a basket of our goods. I was also carrying a little girl. We were running away from our village of Kalamgaon, when we were surrounded by several Khonds, led by Ude Khond, all of whom were armed with axes. They seized all the things we had with us which they thought worth taking; and we were separated and taken in different directions, two or three men going with each of us. We begged for our lives; but the men said they were going to kill all the Kulta men, and that I would not see my son or my husband again. Afterwards I heard that they had taken my husband to Billaikoni and killed him there in the idol's shrine. When the men had been carried off the man Ude came to me and asked me what I had in my basket. In hopes that he would save my boy, I gave him two saris,† some silver jewels, a silver waistbelt, Rs.103 in cash, and some other things. I gave them to him, and implored him to save my boy; but he took them all and ran away; and my boy was killed. Not knowing what to do, I returned to the village; but the Khonds turned me out saying I was not to go crying about the place; so I went away to the nullah.‡ Towards night I returned, but they again turned me out, saying that the widows would not be allowed to remain in the village. I got shelter for the night in one of the tolas.§ I never saw my husband or my boy again. When my boy was taken away to be killed my two other little children were taken from me, but they were afterwards recovered by the Tahsildar of Bhawani Patna. Being very young girls they had not been killed."

This is a sad story told in simple language, with no attempt to enlarge on the miserable details. The widow simply tells

* A bamboo pole, with a bundle at each end, carried across the shoulder.
† A sari is a woman's dress or shawl.
‡ A nullah is the bed of a stream or the stream itself.
§ A tola is the hamlet attached to a village.

how she and her family were intercepted in their panic-stricken flight; how the little property they had hurriedly put together was offered in vain as the ransom of her son's life; how her husband and son were carried off from before her eyes and killed; and how she was not even allowed to weep for them. It would be hard indeed to find a record of greater barbarity, more contemptuous ill-faith, and more ruthless cruelty; but practically the same story was repeated in every case that came before the courts in reference to the murder of the Kultas in this rising. It will be observed also that the woman particularly mentioned that her husband was killed in the shrine of the idol of the village to which he was taken. This was characteristic of the rising, and was a detail established in almost all the cases.

The rising was not only agrarian; it was also partly animated by superstition and religious fanaticism. The old ceremonies connected with human sacrifice which had been common among the Khonds in former days, and had been put down with difficulty by officers of the British Government some years before, were revived in connection with this rising. The victims were murdered solemnly in cold blood, after having been duly anointed and prepared for sacrifice. The huge and terrible sacrificial axe was ordinarily used; and the murderers struggled to dip their axes in the blood, and to secure small fragments of the bodies to bury in their fields as an offering to the powers of the earth. These details are given to indicate the character of the rising. As has been already stated, about one hundred Kultas were proved to have been murdered in this way; and there were no doubt many more whose cases did not come before the Commissioner and Superintendent of the State (Mr. Berry) for inquiry.

The Khonds determined to attack the camp of the Superintendent, who was marching through the State accompanied only by a small body of police. A large number of Khonds set out to attack his camp and take it by surprise. They were fortunately met by Gopinath Guru, who had been appointed to the post of Tahsildar of Bhawani Patna, the head-quarters subdivision of the State. This gentleman was an Uriya Brahman of the highest caste, and of priestly sanctity. He had been an officer of the British District of Sambalpur, and was selected on account of his administrative capacity and high character for the important post to which he had been appointed under Mr. Berry. He was a man of distinguished courage and resource as well as of high probity.

When he met this armed band of Khonds he was a few miles distant from the camp of Mr. Berry. As soon as they came in sight, he suspected that they intended to attack that camp. He had with him an orderly mounted on a pony. He immediately despatched this man to Mr. Berry's camp to warn him, and meantime he went out with great courage to meet the Khonds and hold them in parley. During that parley he observed that several of them kept their bows with their poisoned arrows on the string, ready to loose the fatal shafts at him should he attempt to leave them. He asked them what their intentions were; and they told him that they were going to the camp of the Superintendent Sahib to take him in charge and prevent him from interfering with their vengeance on the Kultas.

He endeavoured to dissuade them from this purpose and from their murderous designs, the folly as well as the wickedness of which he tried to impress upon them. The only result was that their demeanour towards him became threatening; but when he reminded them of his sanctity and of the danger which, according to their own superstition, must be involved in taking the life of so high caste a Brahman as he, they desisted from their purpose to kill him. The result was that an hour or two were lost to them. The Superintendent had time to prepare for their attack, and they were defeated. He then sent word to head-quarters to obtain necessary assistance, and with such forces as he could collect, proceeded to put down the rising. Police, followed soon after by a small detachment of troops, were sent down to his assistance; and the rising was suppressed and the ringleaders punished.

The inquiries which followed indicated such serious discontent throughout the State as led the Government to continue the deputation of Mr. Berry to Kalahandi, and to set about making an Agricultural (or Land Revenue) Settlement in the State, and providing for its administration with due respect to the existing rights of all classes of the population, including the aborigines. Those who were actually convicted of murder were, of course, punished according to law, due regard being paid to all the circumstances in each case; but when the law had been vindicated and peace restored, it was found by no means a difficult task for an officer of Mr. Berry's tact and capacity to carry out the necessary reforms in the administration. The services which he rendered were recognised hy Her Majesty, and he was created a Companion of the Order of the Indian Empire, while his brave and capable subordinate, Gopinath Guru, received the title of Rai Bahadur.

Soon after this, the Maharajah of the neighbouring State of Patna having died and his heir being a child, that State also was taken under management by the British Government. An Indian gentleman, also an Uriya Brahman of high character and proved administrative capacity, was appointed to the direct charge of the State under the immediate supervision and control of Mr. Berry. When these two States had been settled, and their administration had been reformed and raised to as satisfactory and efficient a condition as was consistent with their resources and with the character of their peoples, it was found possible to employ Mr. Berry's services more widely among the States of Chhattisgarh. The great capacity which he had shown in dealing with the wild tribes and simple peoples in these two States marked him out as the very officer required to help the Government in setting right abuses which more careful attention and more accurate information discovered in almost all the States.

The settlement of these two States and the improvement of their administration took some years of patient and unwearying labour; but when this work had been accomplished it was found possible to leave the charge of them to the Indian officers who had assisted in that work; and nothing more was required from Mr. Berry but careful supervision and somewhat frequent visits to the States. Details were left entirely to the Indian officers; and the administration was carried on in such a manner and with such expenditure as might reasonably be maintained by the Rajahs when they received charge of their States. Efforts were meanwhile made to train the Rajahs for the responsible position which they were to be called upon to fill.

Mr. Berry's services being thus available, it was determined by the Chief Commissioner of the Central Provinces, with the sanction of the Government of India, to appoint him Political Agent for the Chhattisgarh Feudatory States. He was to have his head-quarters at Raipur, the head-quarters of the Division, and he was to exercise on behalf of Government the supervision which it was entitled to exercise over the Feudatory States of the whole Division. He was to spend all the open season in touring among the States, and so becoming acquainted with the Chiefs themselves, with the character of their administration, and with the condition of the people resident in the States. His instructions were not to interfere unduly and unnecessarily with the power and authority of the Rajahs, and not to encourage the people to disregard that power and authority. He was instructed to be a friend and adviser to the Chiefs, to invite them to meet him at his head-quarters, to visit their head-quarters, and to take them with him sometimes on tour, so that he might become intimate with them, discuss with them freely and fully the principles of administration, and advise them in regard to any measures which they were carrying out in their States.

Going about freely among the people, he could ascertain whether there was any feeling of discontent, or whether there was practical injustice being done. He was not to encourage complaints; but he was to keep his ears open; and he was to endeavour to soothe discontent, to explain to people smarting under a sense of injustice the steps which they should take to have the matter righted by the Rajah or his officers, and to bring these cases to the notice of the Rajah privately and in a friendly way, explaining to him that the parties had been referred to him for redress. He was only to take up himself gross cases of injustice in which the Rajah had refused to do right, and grave cases of general maladministration which necessitated interference.

The two principles on which he was instructed to carry on his work were these, that on the one hand the Rajah as the ruler must be supported in his authority; and on the other hand that, as the British Government prevented the people from asserting their rights or setting their Rajah aside by force, the Rajah must consent to administer his State in a way which justified that measure of coercion of the people by the Government. The Government could not use its power to maintain the Rajah in his rule over the people, without being responsible that that rule was reasonably efficient, just, and consistent with their interests. In all his work the Political Agent was under the control of the Commissioner of the Division ; and both of these officers were specially instructed to exercise their authority and supervision in a friendly and tactful manner. No officer could have been found more fitted than Mr. Berry to inaugurate and carry out this wise policy; and during the years that he held the office of Political Agent a system of administration was introduced over the Feudatory States which has rendered it an easy matter for the Government, through a succession of political officers, to maintain that policy, and to secure at once the friendship of the Chiefs and the general wellbeing of the people.

CHAPTER XI

THE FEUDATORY STATES OF CHHATTISGARH

It was a deplorable misfortune which prematurely deprived the administration of Mr. Berry's services. He was stricken down by one of those sudden and terrible strokes of which we have experience in India. He was riding out on a Wednesday morning in May, 1889, in the neighbourhood of Raipur and came to a village where he met several funeral processions following one another. In his kindly way he drew up beside one of them and asked the bearers about the cause of death. They told him that there was cholera in the village; and he made inquiry as to the virulence of the epidemic, and found that many were dying.

It was a dry day in the hot weather, and he was to leeward of the body. There seems little doubt that more or less desiccated matter laden with germs was carried to him by the strong hot wind. It suddenly occurred to him that this might be so. He rode home and bathed and changed before he allowed his wife and child to meet him. He wrote and told me (for I was in camp) about this outbreak of cholera, and related all the circumstances of his meeting the biers to a friend in Raipur. All went well until the Saturday morning, when he suddenly fell ill; and by evening he was dead. Seldom, indeed, has the death of so comparatively young an officer evoked such widespread grief among the people of a province. Many chiefs and tribes and people of diverse races mourned with his European friends and brother officers over his untimely death.

I had held, for more than a year, the Commissionership of

Chhattisgarh by the time that he died; and I had visited all the fourteen Native States. Those that were accessible to head-quarters of districts I had visited by forced marches from these head-quarters when I was there on sessions or inspection work. The others I had visited in the course of a long cold-weather tour. In that tour through the southern and eastern States, and in one or two of my flying visits to the other States, I had been accompanied by Mr. Berry. It was deeply interesting to visit these States, to see their administration, to make the acquaintance both of the Rajahs and of the people, and to find how fully Mr. Berry had won the confidence of both during his ten years' work among them. They were in those days even more interesting, perhaps, than they are now; though Chhattisgarh is still, I should think, one of the most interesting charges in India. They were more interesting then, perhaps, because the Chiefs had still about them more of the old-world spirit and barbaric pomp and circumstance, accompanied by a certain uncivilised simplicity, the combination of which made their durbars or courts of very great interest.

The people, too, were for the most part unsophisticated, wild, simple, impulsive jungle tribes, with some residents of more cultivated country, far removed from the great centres of civilisation. At the same time there was the deep interest arising from the coming of the railway, the construction of which had by that time begun, the railway that was to cross the whole of the Chhattisgarh Division, running straight from Bombay to Calcutta by way of Nagpur. Many strange experiences came to us as the old-world life of Chhattisgarh began to give way before advancing civilisation.

In the course of one of his tours, Mr. Berry travelled with horses and camels by a hilly tract direct from the head-quarters of the Sonpur State to those of the Rairahkol State. As he crossed the border he found that there was a long-standing boundary dispute. He found that the Rairahkol people were constantly crossing over what the Sonpur people regarded as the boundary, and removing timber and other forest produce; and so with the people of Sonpur. The value of the produce was not of much consequence; but there were constant fights between the people of the two States on each side of the border, and not infrequently lives were lost. It reminded us of the old stories of border warfare in countries nearer home; but it had a weird sound to those who were accustomed to the *pax Britannica* in India, and were surprised to find such a state of things unreported and unknown. We obtained (under the rules) the sanction of the Government for the settlement of the boundary dispute by the Political Agent, under the supervision of the Commissioner; and we determined to settle it in the course of that cold-weather tour.

We called on the two Chiefs to meet us on the boundary of the two States as near to the disputed tract as the hilly and jungly character of the country would permit. The Rajah of Sonpur wrote a very courteous private letter to Mr. Berry, pointing out that, if he met the Rajah of Rairahkol, it would be necessary for the latter to comply with certain formalities which had been observed at the last meeting of the rulers of the two States, when the then Rajah of Rairahkol had, nearly a century before, prostrated himself before the Rajah of Sonpur and received a Khil'at (robe of honour) from his hand. The Rajah of Rairahkol was asked about this; and he replied, also in a courteous private letter, that he had no record of the alleged meeting, and that in any case he could not possibly comply with that formality now.

Mr. Berry and I talked the matter over. We determined to adopt the following somewhat amusing expedient. We arranged to pitch our camp one day in the nearest village on the Sonpur side, where the river formed an undisputed part of the boundary. The Rajah of Sonpur was to have his camp in the neighbouring village of that State; and the Rajah of Rairahkol was to have his in the nearest village on the other side. The Rajah of Sonpur was to come and pay me a formal visit in my tent, Mr. Berry being also present; and, while the Rajah of Sonpur was there, the Rajah of Rairahkol was to arrive, also to

RAJA KANHAYA LALL

Late Feudatory Chief of Khairagarh in the Chhattisgarh Division of the Central Provinces: a type of the old days before the railway.

THE LATE FEUDATORY CHIEF OF CHHUIKHADAN IN CHHATTISGARH, CENTRAL PROVINCES

He was a Bairagi and very typical of the old days when Chhattisgarh was almost inaccessible.

pay me a visit. Finding themselves together in the presence of the Commissioner, as they had not infrequently done in durbars at Raipur, the two Chiefs were to be introduced solemnly to one another, and were to make the usual Eastern salaam and then shake hands "like English gentlemen."

The next day we were to pitch our camp on the other side of the river in the territory of Rairahkol; and the ceremony was to be repeated *mutatis mutandis.* The Rajah of Rairahkol was to visit me; the Rajah of Sonpur was to arrive while he was there; and again they were to shake hands "like English gentlemen." After this double introduction, they were to sit down along with their diwans (chief ministers) and discuss the boundary question with Mr. Berry and me. The details of this arrangement were communicated privately by Mr. Berry to both the Rajahs, and were accepted by both as a perfectly satisfactory settlement of the important question of etiquette.

Accordingly we had our meeting; and it was always mentioned afterwards among the officers of Raipur as the "field of the cloth of gold." Both Rajahs got together as many elephants as they could and hunted out, from all their treasuries and throughout their States, as many gold-brocaded cloths as they could find, and had them as trappings for the elephants and hangings for their tents, and even as carpets inside and outside of their tents, so that the scene was one of really considerable splendour. Our discussion ended in the appointing of two persons to represent (one for each) the two Rajahs. Naturally enough the men appointed were the diwans. These men, accompanied by any villagers or experts that they chose to bring as witnesses or assessors, were to go round the boundary with us so that it might be demarcated at once. A number of the inhabitants of both States were also got together, to be ready immediately to put up, on the spot, boundary pillars along the line as laid down by us. Mr. Berry and I, accompanied by the diwans, went out very early in the morning, riding as far as it was possible to ride, and accompanied by a very considerable number of hardy, jungle people, on foot. We dismounted at the beginning of the disputed line; and we walked over it for six or eight hours on end. The diwans and the people, seeing that we were in earnest to settle the matter, and that the boundary we favoured was clearly indicated by the banks of mountain streams and the ridges of the hills, set themselves also to help us; and the matter was settled in two days' hard walking from about six in the morning till after midday. The boundary pillars were put up as we went along; and the dispute was finally settled in a perfectly amicable way.

This may be taken as an illustration of the methods generally adopted in our work among the Chiefs. We got hold of them and of the people, and simply worked alongside of them. During the course of work like this, we could not fail to get into the most friendly and intimate relations with our fellow-workers; and everything that we had to do, in the way of settling disputes, investigating cases and arranging points of State administration, tended to cement our friendship and strengthen the bonds that united us in our relations with one another.

The Rajah of Sonpur at that time was a very fine old man; and as his State contains a very considerable amount of first-rate agricultural land, as well as a good deal of valuable jungle, and is situated on the banks of the river Mahanadi, it was a State that was capable of great development; and to this he and his worthy successors devoted themselves with very considerable success. The present Chief has done so well that the Viceroy has given him as a personal distinction the higher title of Maharajah. The old Chief of Rairahkol was a man who had succeeded to his State as a mere boy, and was by that time in the eighth decade of his life. He had, therefore, been longer a ruler than probably any other ruler in the world. During all that time, without any great intellectual capacity or education, he had proved himself a good strong man. He was vigorous in constitution, temperate in habits, upright in character, and generally desirous to do justice and right. It was quite a pleasant experience to make these two men our friends.

A GRAVEYARD OF THE ABORIGINES IN CHOTA NAGPUR

A BODYGUARD OF BOYS

A number of the sons of State policemen and other servants formed by the Feudatory Chief of Patna into a bodyguard for my son while we marched through his State; a fairly accurate reproduction of his own guard except as regards the age of its members.

Our work was not always so pleasant. We sometimes found a Chief abusing his power, and permitting the administration of his State to become anything but a blessing to his people. Sometimes this arose from pure selfishness, from a desire on the part of the Chief to wring from the toil-hardened hands of his people as much as he could, in order to spend it on his own personal pleasure and comfort. Sometimes it arose from ignorance and indolence, and from the fact that the Chief was entirely in the hands of bad advisers. I remember the case of a very genial but stupid highland Chief of pompous but courteous manner, and of great hospitality and kindliness. As the railway came into the neighbourhood of his State, that State became the refuge and stronghold of bad characters from all parts of the country. They had their head-quarters under his protection, and from this safe retreat they raided British territory and the neighbouring States, leaving the people of the State in which they resided generally unmolested.

It was difficult to move the Rajah to take a serious view of these facts. Neither he nor his people suffered much from these scoundrels; and it was in his opinion the duty of the Government and of the other States to take measures for their own protection. To put his own police into an efficient state so as to co-operate with them in restraining these criminals would necessitate the removal of men who had long been in hereditary office, and to incur expenditure the direct advantage of which he did not see. It was true also that on all hands he was being robbed, and his revenue was being embezzled by untrustworthy subordinates, some of whom unfortunately were dismissed Government officials, and that his people were largely subjected to petty forms of oppression and exaction; but of this he was kept largely in ignorance by the unworthy men by whom he was surrounded and in whom he had misplaced confidence.

The Political Agent (both Mr. Berry and his successors) and I made many attempts to convince the Rajah of the necessity of reform; but, though courteous to us during his interviews with us, he was obstinately immovable in regard to his policy.

On the occasion of my fourth or fifth interview with him on the subject, I warned him that, if he did not comply with the requirements of the Central Provinces Government, and carry out the necessary reforms, he would find that the Government would be compelled to remove him temporarily from the State, and undertake the management of it until the reforms were carried out. His reply, given courteously enough, but sententiously, was to the effect that he had seen Commissioners come and go, but he himself had gone on for ever. I pointed out to him that there had already been one or two cases of the temporary supersession of Rajahs who had grossly mismanaged their States; but these were tales of what to him were remote and unknown places; and he did not give much heed.

On the next occasion he received a great shock. All his misdemeanours had been from time to time duly reported to the Government, and the Chief Commissioner (the late Sir Alexander Mackenzie) had seen the necessity for serious action. I wrote to Sir Alexander privately, and told him I believed that, if he would give me a private autograph letter, stating that the Rajah must be set aside for a time, all might be satisfactorily arranged without his being formally dealt with. Sir Alexander gave me the necessary letter. I went down to visit my misguided friend. He came to see me in my tent; and I took care that no one was within hearing. I then reminded him of the warning I had given him, and I said to him, "What I told you has come true. Here is a letter authorizing me to set you aside." He was very much moved, and, adopting the Oriental forms of supplication, he besought me not to set him aside, because even were he ultimately restored, he would find his authority over his people lost.

Knowing the character of the people, I recognized fully the truth of his statement. I therefore said to him, "I do not wish to injure you in any way, but these reforms are absolutely necessary. They must be carried out; you yourself cannot do this; and the authority must be given to one friendly to you who will

Photo by *S. A. Quddoos*

A GROUP TAKEN ON TOUR AMONG THE CHIEFS OF ORISSA

The Maharaja of Patna and the Maharaja of Sonpur are on my left, and the Political Agent (Mr. Cobden Ramsay, I.C.S.) is behind me.

carry them out on your behalf. The best plan will be this. You have not yet taken your father's ashes to the Ganges; and it would be regarded as very reasonable for you to do so. If you will go now, I shall lend you the services of an experienced Indian officer of good family, whom I can fully trust and whom I can cordially recommend to you as a loyal and kindly friend. You can summon a Durbar of the principal residents of your State, and you can explain to them that it will be necessary for you to be absent for a certain number of months, and that you have obtained the services of an able and experienced officer who will administer your State for you in your absence, to whom they must give the same loyal obedience as they would render to yourself. You will then give him a Sanad,* signed by yourself, accompanied by a Khil'at † of office." The good old man gratefully accepted this proposal.

I left the State and sent up the officer appointed, in time for the date fixed by the Chief for his Durbar. The Chief went off to the Ganges as arranged; and through this officer's earnest work, under the supervision and advice of the Political Agent, the Augean stables were cleansed. The worst of the local officials were removed; trustworthy men were put in their place; and the necessary reforms were introduced. As soon as the work was finished, the Rajah was informed, and he returned. His pleasure at finding things so much improved, and his loyalty to Government, were both evidenced by the fact that, with my consent spontaneously solicited, he appointed this Indian officer to be his own diwan, and continued the administration of his State on the lines laid down. The Chief remained my friend long after I left Chhattisgarh; and many were the kindly letters which I received from him after my direct connection with him was severed. When I returned many years afterwards on a visit to Chhattisgarh, as Chief Commissioner of the Province, my old friend had passed away; but his son was continuing the administration of the State in accordance with the later policy of his worthy old father.

* Sanad is a deed or document. † Khil'at is a robe of honour.

We were not always quite so fortunate in the issue of our dealings with the Chiefs; but it is wonderful how cordial and kindly were the relations between them as a body and the officers of Government with whom they were connected. A very striking illustration of this occurred at the time of the modification of the boundaries of Bengal in 1904, when the Chiefs of the Uriya States of Chhattisgarh (Central Provinces) objected to their proposed transfer to Bengal, mainly because they would thus be deprived of the immense advantage of the friendship and guidance of the Political Agent. They put their views on record in a remarkable petition, to which I shall refer more fully when discussing what has been called "the partition of Bengal."

The Native Chiefs are loyal to the British Government: not only the less important and influential Chiefs of the smaller States, such as those of Chhattisgarh, but also those of the larger Native States. It is very important for us to retain the loyalty of these Chiefs, both great and small. There is not the slightest doubt that they realise on their part the untold advantages which they derive from British rule. They have no desire to go back to the tempestuous times which preceded that rule, nor to enter into a ceaseless and precarious struggle for existence. They understand the benefits of peace both for themselves and for their people; and there is nothing that can alienate them from us, so long as we respect their position and are manifestly strong enough to secure it for them. Weakness in the administration of our own Empire fills them with disquiet, while needless interference with their administration, disregard of their dignity, and unsympathetic or bullying treatment fill them with disgust. As a rule they have been particularly fortunate in the political officers whom Government has sent to them, gentlemen of high tone and courteous manners and of sound judgment. Only such men should ever be appointed to political office in any native State, however small.

An interesting fact came to my notice in the course of a tour in the Bilaspur District of the Central Provinces. On the border of that district there is a beautiful hill called Amar-

A Darbar

A darbar at Orissa: an address being presented to the Lieutenant-Governor. A darbar ought, according to Indian ideas, to be arranged in rows on the right and left looking inwards across the open space in front of the dais.

kantak, which was transferred to the neighbouring Rewah State as a reward for the loyalty of its Chief. This hill is 3,500 feet high and has a very pleasant climate. It is greatly beloved by the people, especially of that part of India, as containing the source of the sacred river Nerbudda. Many shrines have been erected there, and it is a place of pilgrimage. On this account it has been greatly valued by the Rewah Durbar.

I went to visit it on one occasion and was much struck with the beauty of the place. On my way back to head-quarters I passed through the Zamindari of Laffa. The Zamindar was an old Kanwar, a fine jungle lord of thoroughly sporting character. I went out with him to a general beat, which he organised for big game of all sorts; and on my way back I talked to him about the beauty of Amarkantak. He told me that he was going there in the course of a few days. He said that the Rewah Maharajah was to pay his annual visit in state to Amarkantak, and that as many of the Hindu Chiefs of Bilaspur as were able to attend would go there to receive him and do him honour.

This struck me as very remarkable. The Rewah Chief had no authority over the Zamindars or Nobles of Bilaspur; but their respect for his ancient position, and the fact that he was one of their own race or clan, led them in a loyal spirit to go and associate themselves with his formal worship at Amarkantak. Their loyalty to the native Chief was entirely consistent with their loyalty to the British Government. There never was a Noble more loyal to our rule, nor more cordial in his relations with British officers, than this good old Laffa Zamindar, for whose memory I have a great regard, and in whose friendship, while he lived, I had great delight. The loyalty of the Chiefs of the Indian States is in my opinion very important, on account not only of the great extent of the territory—one-third of the area of India—over which they bear rule, but also of the influence which they have beyond their own borders.

CHAPTER XII

CHRISTMAS WITH WILD ELEPHANTS

THERE is no part of my service on which I look back with greater pleasure than on my tenure of the office of Commissioner of Chhattisgarh, of which I took charge in 1888. It must be one of the most interesting divisions in the whole of India. The people were simple, for they had lived remote. Even the ordinary village life had, I think, more of attraction for me than that of most other parts of the Province. There were also the fourteen Native States, of which I have already said enough, and there were many Zamindaris. These were large estates, the owners of which were British subjects. At the same time the remoteness of their estates, and the peculiar history of this part of the country, had given these Zamindars rights and customs which placed them in a position midway between the ordinary British subject and the Feudatory Chief. The Zamindars exercised authority over their people to a far greater extent than is the case with proprietors, even more wealthy and more powerful, in other parts of the country; and they exercised certain powers and rights in the police, excise, forest, and other departments such as were not possessed by Zamindars in other parts of the Central Provinces. Some of the most interesting work of the Division was done amongst the Zamindaris. In this chapter, however, I shall speak of sport rather than of work.

The Matin Zamindari to the north of the Bilaspur District is a wild, hilly tract of about 600 square miles, with a sparse population. This estate had, owing to the minority of the young chief, come under the Court of Wards, and was directly managed by the Commissioner of Chhattisgarh and the Deputy Commissioner of Bilaspur. During the lifetime of the last Zamindar the estate had become overrun with wild elephants, and many of the people had been driven from their villages. In the course of a tour in the Bilaspur District, I visited this Zamindari, and I found whole villages depopulated. The elephants came down, kicking the houses and the granaries to pieces and consuming the grain. Sometimes lives were lost of those who inadvertently fell in the way of the elephants, or who might be attempting to defend their property against them. It was manifest that measures must be taken for the capture of these elephants.

I accordingly wrote to Mr. Sanderson, of the Government Kheddah Department, and asked him whether he could arrange to conduct operations. I told him that, from the best information I could get, there were about sixty elephants in the herd which had taken possession of the estate. He replied that for him to bring up all the men and tame elephants required for the capture of this herd, and to carry through the operations against them, would involve very considerable cost on the small and far from wealthy Zamindari. But he advised me to secure the services of the neighbouring Maharajah of Sirguja for this purpose. He said that the young Maharajah was a plucky and exceedingly capable man, whom he had himself trained in Kheddah work; that he might be trusted to carry through the business just as well as he could do it himself, and that far from the operations being costly to the estate, the Maharajah would gladly pay to the Zamindar one-fourth of the value of all the elephants he might capture, as provided by law.

The border of the Matin Zamindari is the old Central Provinces boundary, and on the other side from us was the territory (including the Feudatory State of Sirguja) then administered by the Lieutenant-Governor of Bengal. The Maharajah of Sirguja, although he was my immediate neighbour, had hitherto been quite unknown to me, as he belonged to a different Province.

I wrote to him, laid the whole case before him, and told him what Mr. Sanderson had said. I received a courteous and cordial reply, stating that he was quite willing to undertake the operations; that he would take care to do no avoidable injury to the jungle; that he would begin his operations at once; and that he would let me know when he was ready to operate against the elephants, so that I might, if I chose, join his camp and satisfy myself that the operations were being conducted with due regard to the interests of the Zamindari.

Some months later Mr. (now Sir Charles) Cleveland, then a young civilian of two or three years' standing, was in camp with me on special duty in the south-west of the Bilaspur District in the neighbourhood of the Kawardha Feudatory State. We had been compelled to refuse invitations to more than one Christmas Camp, and had been pressed with work right over Christmas Day, 1889. We arrived in the course of our tour at the town of Bilaspur two days after Christmas, and found the station absolutely empty. The Deputy Commissioner, Mr. Meiklejohn, was in camp in the direction of Matin, and everyone else had gone off to some Christmas party. We settled down to a quiet life, but a telegram from the Maharajah disturbed us. It was brief, but momentous. "Thirty-four elephants are surrounded. Can you come at once to Basan?" The telegram was from Pendra, over forty miles along the Umaria branch of the Bengal Nagpur Railway, which was then under construction. We got down the map, and found that Basan was àbout sixty-five miles off as the crow flies, and eighty miles by village tracks round the hills. Telegraphing that we should arrive in two days, we sent off two elephants, one carrying a very limited kit, about thirty miles towards Basan. Next morning we overtook our elephants, driving part of the way and riding the rest. After a hurried breakfast we pushed on between twenty or thirty miles more, slept the night at a little village rest-house, and next morning reached the elephant country.

At Jatga, the present capital of the Matin Zamindari, we first came on the trace of the great marauders. We found their marks close to the hamlet and at the very door of the manager's office. Under a tree in front of the office lay the huge bleached skull of a wild elephant that had died some time before. We heard melancholy tales of the ravages of these monsters. Again and again as, map in hand, we mentioned villages which were marked on our proposed route, the remark was, "Deserted : no one lives there. The jungle elephants have driven man out." The Gaontya (or head man) of Jatga pointed, with a strange mixture of awe and triumph, to a sheer precipice near the Setgarh Hill about eight miles off, over which four out of a herd of five wild elephants, rushing along in panic, had fallen and been dashed to pieces. Forsyth tells the story in his "Highlands of Central India."

We pushed on over the hills through magnificent sal jungle and the wild hill scenery to Kudri, where, weary enough with our long and trying elephant ride, we gladly saw Mr. Meiklejohn's tents and received his cheery welcome. Kudri is about three miles short of Basan, to which we had been summoned. Our telegram had been received after a whole day's delay, as is the manner of these parts; and Mr. Meiklejohn had then started off for Basan, taking all his belongings with him and driving his camels before him like an Old Testament patriarch, because the servants feared to march without him. Suddenly, in the middle of the jungle, in grass about six feet high, his camels halted. He demanded an explanation. "This is Basan," said the guide. Basan had been deserted : the elephants had taken possession and warned off the human claimants of the village. Kudri was the nearest habitation of man, so he had pitched the tents there.

Maharajah Raghonath Saran Singh Deo Bahadur of Sirguja was in tents nearer to the immediate scene of the proposed operations. He had come out with a host against the wild elephants. About one thousand men and thirty-three tame elephants, most of them trained "Kumkis," accompanied him. He had found two herds of wild elephants, in all about thirty-five, at the Bahmani Nadi (River) about fifteen or twenty miles off. He had set to work with all expedition to run up a light fence about six miles in circumference, enclosing a valley and part of two hills below Setgarh. Round this he had posted at intervals eight or nine hundred men, mostly armed with matchlocks and provided with blank cartridges. Into this enclosure he had quietly driven all these elephants through fifteen miles of glen; and there they were surrounded by silent watch fires and sentries constantly on duty. The wild elephants wandered about unmolested within this large enclosure, but were not allowed to pass the guards; and near one side of it he had constructed a strong stockade, only about two hundred feet square. Having completed these arrangements, the Maharajah had courteously informed us that all was ready, and that we might join his camp if we cared to do so.

Next morning we set off to visit the Maharajah, whose tents were not much more than a mile from ours. He told us that one very large male elephant had been decoyed into the stockade the day before, and was there tied up and ready to be taken out. We started at once to see the process. We seated ourselves on the top of the broad wall of the stockade and saw the huge tusker. He was a splendid animal. His fore quarters were much heavier than in the tame elephant, and his figure was so massive that we did not think him so tall as we afterwards found him to be. A day or two later we had him measured by a man on a tame elephant. He set a bamboo against his shoulder; and we found that he measured 9 feet 10 inches. He was not standing quite straight, and must have been full 10 feet high at the shoulder.

This huge warrior had lost half his tail in some hill fight, and had a great scar on his trunk. We found him tied to some trees in the stockade. By careful manœuvring they slipped five cables round his neck, fastening the other end of each cable round the body of a tame elephant; thus there were five tame elephants in front of him. Similarly they fastened each hind leg to two elephants. The hind legs were also tied together by a

MY CAMP AS DISTRICT OFFICER

The illustration shows the well-trained riding (sawari) camel, and also the burden-bearing camels.

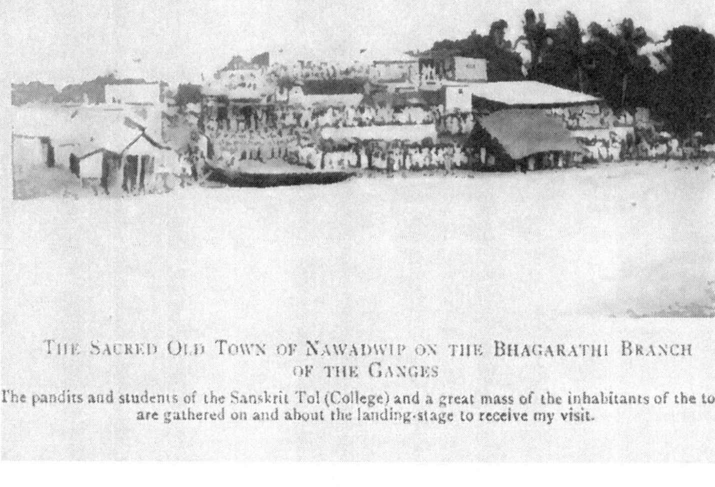

THE SACRED OLD TOWN OF NAWADWIP ON THE BHAGARATHI BRANCH OF THE GANGES

The pandits and students of the Sanskrit Tol (College) and a great mass of the inhabitants of the town are gathered on and about the landing-stage to receive my visit.

rope which, while leaving him free to walk, prevented anything like a long stride. Having thus securcely bound him to nine tame elephants, each of which carried a Mahout (driver), they undid the ropes which fastened him to the trees within the stockade and prepared to lead the forest freebooter away.

When he saw the gate of the stockade open he went out as fast as his captors would allow; but when he found outside that he was not to be permitted to choose his own path he began to show fight. He halted. The five elephants in front put forth all their strength, but could not move him. They roared and pulled, but he stood steady, leaning slightly backwards as in a tug-of-war. Then, suddenly, he swung his great body round, and dragged back the five for a little space, roaring as they came with rage and perhaps with fear. Then they recovered and the tug-of-war began again. A sharp discharge of blank cartridge behind him drove him on a little way. This scene was repeated several times. Occasionally the blank cartridge had to give way to a specially prepared cartridge with about a dozen snipe shot which tickled his fat flanks, and sent him gaily along for a time, his pace being kept moderate by the drag of the elephants behind. At last he was tied up to trees near the Maharajah's tents, about five hundred yards from the stockade. There, poor fellow, he raged awhile, kneeling down and pushing his formidable tusks into the ground, a grievous representation of Samson bound among his enemies.

Next day as there was nothing doing at the stockade we determined to have a look at the elephants in their own jungle haunts. Divus Augustus (as Sir C. Cleveland translated the "Deo Bahadur" of Sirguja's name), after some hesitation on the score of risk to ourselves, permitted us to go into the jungle on foot under the guidance of two of the most trustworthy of his trained men. They led us quietly through the forest by the paths cleared by the elephants. At last, with a gesture, they stopped us and pointed silently ahead. We peered through the trees and just caught sight of one large elephant. We heard others behind him and saw dark masses, the forms of which were undistinguishable, moving behind the trees. We indicated our desire for a nearer view; but the men had evidently been warned against this by the Maharajah, who was no doubt nervous lest any harm should come to us. As we did not wish to lead them to disregard his instructions, we returned to the camp, resolved, however, to have a good view of these elephants for ourselves. By the aid of a compass we carefully marked the direction we took. When we arrived at the stockade, we took leave of the Maharajah and went off in the direction of our tents.

As soon as we got out of sight, we turned sharply into the jungle. We went on along the elephants' tracks for a considerable distance. Suddenly we came to an open glade, and as we looked across it we saw the tusks of a great monarch of the herd gleaming through the trees. I had my elephant with me, and four of us, besides the Mahout, were seated on it, Mr. Meiklejohn, Sir C. Cleveland, my trusty servant Ramanah, and myself. It seemed to us that the elephants were going to cross the glade, so we pushed on to cut them off and get a clearer view. In the centre of the glade there stood a large solitary tree. As we reached it, the leader of the herd came out to look at us. We halted under the shadow of the tree. He came towards us, followed by fifteen elephants of all sizes. As he drew near, the situation seemed a little serious; and we prepared to do what we could to defend ourselves from attack. But after the elephants had stood for a moment looking at us and waving their trunks, as we remained motionless, the leader turned round and slowly crossed the glade to the other side, followed by the herd. Then, as they were about to disappear in the jungle he suddenly changed his mind, turned slowly on his tracks, and solemnly led them past again. The elephants thus marched twice across the open glade within twenty or thirty yards of us—a splendid spectacle. Moved by irresistible impulse, we followed them a little way; but when they got into the jungle again they quickened their pace and disappeared. We shall not readily forget that majestic procession, witnessed among the wild scenery of the sal-clad hills.

That night we spent some hours on the top of the stockade. We lay concealed among the branches of trees, which were placed on the top of the broad wall, that we might see something of the operations of the tame elephants which were employed to seduce the wild elephants into the stockade. The tame elephants had been well trained to their work. They came along through the jungle, grumbling to one another about the want of any really luscious food, till they reached the gate of the stockade. Then two of them turned in there and found sugar-cane laid down for their consumption. They attacked it with great gusto, and called to one another in triumphant tones about their great find. The wild elephants heard them; and one or two walked quietly into the stockade. There were men over the gateway who had orders to remain inactive as long as the elephants were going in, and to drop the portcullis as soon as any elephant made as though it would attempt to leave the stockade. Eight wild elephants walked in before any thought of going out. At the first indication of such an intention down came the portcullis.

The elephants then began to feel the walls of the stockade with their trunks to see whether it was possible to demolish it. Men were seated along the wall at intervals, armed with long bamboos with short, sharp needles at the end of each, with which an elephant could be pricked without being hurt. As soon as an elephant came to try the wall, the needle was applied to his head or trunk, and he started back, convinced, apparently, that he might undoubtedly injure himself if he attempted to run his head against the wall; and gradually they settled down in the middle of the stockade by the sugar-cane, with the two tame elephants on the most friendly terms. It must be admitted that these tame elephants showed the most extraordinary tact and intelligence in inducing the wild elephants to enter the stockade, and in their relations with them after they got inside; but one could not help feeling a certain sense of irritation at their treachery to their own kind.

After slipping off the wall of the stockade and having a few hours' rest, we returned to the scene of operations soon after dawn. The elephants were very much in the same position as when we left them. Through little portholes in the stockade, beside which the two trained elephants had taken up their position, two men, armed with the needle-pointed bamboos to which reference has been made, slipped in and, mounting each on his elephant, moved toward the gate of the stockade. From there with their spears they gently drove the wild elephants to the further end. The gate was then raised a little way and fifteen trained elephants, led by two huge tuskers, came in.

The process of tying up then began. About a dozen of the trained elephants surrounded the particular elephant to be operated on and hustled him into a corner. The two tuskers, meanwhile kept the others off. The trained elephants moved backwards on the selected elephant, and planted their hind quarters against him firmly on all sides so that he could hardly move. He and they formed one compact, oscillating mass, which reminded one strongly of a football scrimmage. A man slipping through one of the portholes of the stockade and between the legs of one of the tame elephants, got a rope round the hind leg of the wild elephant and dashed out again. This rope had been fastened to a tree outside the stockade. As soon as the elephant felt the rope he struggled with the tame elephants and shook them off, but he could not free himself from the rope. The operation was repeated until he was tied up by all four legs to trees in four different directions. It was very rarely that the first attempt to fasten the rope on any of the elephant's legs failed; and a very striking fact was this, that no wild elephant of them all attacked a tame elephant. Occasionally, one would lift his trunk inquiringly towards the head of the tame elephant where the Mahout (or driver) crouched with a black cloth round his waist, himself painted black and seeming part of the beast he rode; but a touch of the needle made the elephant lower his trunk and abandon his inquiry. The men who came in on foot to fasten the ropes, however, seemed sometimes to have a narrow escape for their lives.

On one occasion the elephant that was being tied up was a young one, about half-grown. Its mother seemed much agitated and alarmed about the treatment her son was receiving, and once or twice she charged past the two huge tuskers that were keeping the wild elephants off. Each time she scattered the elephants that were round her cub. At last the Maharajah gave the order to "knock her down." The larger of the two tuskers drew back until his hind quarters touched the wall of the stockade. The female elephant was occupied in anxiously watching her son and was sideways to the great male. Suddenly he charged straight at her, caught her on the side with the flat of his forehead with all the force he could, and knocked her down on her left side. She staggered tremblingly to her feet, and he stood over her, waving his trunk, as though to warn her that any action on her part in the way of interference in the work that was going forward would lead to a repetition of the punishment. She accepted the warning and stood perfectly still.

All the elephants were thus tied up. They were then taken out. The process was simply to fasten ropes from their neck to a certain number of tame elephants in front, and from the hind legs to a certain number of the tame elephants behind, the number being fixed according to the size of the wild elephant. The ropes that fastened them to the trees were then undone, and they were conducted in a most extraordinary procession to the camp of the Maharajah, where they were tied up. There they were approached gradually by men who gave them long pieces of sugar-cane from their own hands; and it was very striking to see how soon these elephants, receiving their food only from these men, became accustomed to their presence and reconciled to the altered circumstances. It was touching to see the anxiety of one of the female elephants about her two young ones. As she stood bound, the one about a year old would come running to her and she would quietly suckle him, he screwing his trunk out of the way in a most ludicrous manner. Meanwhile she would throw her trunk over his elder brother, some two or three years older, with a soothing and protecting air. When she was led out, the two young ones trotted before her; and she went without a murmur. The infant "Mouse," as we called him, would sometimes become excited, raise his little trunk and open his mouth and shriek louder than any of the herd. Once he caused great amusement by rushing at a rope drawn tight about two feet from the ground and taking it at a leap. The natives called the elder brother "Babu"; and many a time and oft he scattered groups of them as he charged about in wild excitement.

Next day we saw a beat which, though unsuccessful, was very exciting. We occupied a position on the top of the stockade with the Maharajah, among the leaf-covered branches. We sat there in silence for hours as the elephants were being quietly driven towards the wings of the stockade; then we heard the sound of the beating together of sticks, by which sound they were driven, and the elephants came crashing slowly through the jungle. Then matchlocks, loaded with blank cartridges, were fired; shouting began and ten or twelve wild elephants rushed into view, accompanied by as many trained ones. They came on at the pace of racing ponies. They dashed towards one wing, then across to the other, again and again. Two tame elephants near the gate then ran in; but apparently the wild elephants did not see them, or perhaps they did not see the gate. In any case they did not follow. The tame elephants came out again. The wild elephants apparently thought that the tame elephants were rushing in the direction from which they had come. They faced about and made a dashing charge through the beaters into the jungle. The whole scene did not occupy many seconds, but such excitement and commotion we had never witnessed.

Next day Mr. Cleveland and I took our departure for Bilaspur, leaving the Maharajah to his elephants and the Deputy Commissioner to continue his tour among the Wards' Estates. We had sent on our elephants twenty miles the day before, and came that distance on two kindly lent us by the Maharajah. We determined to push across country in a practically straight line, instead of going from village to village. We had one or two Gond guides, who knew the hills well. We passed through dense jungle for about forty miles, and descended on the plain over the Laffa Ghat by a path that only one European was known to have traversed before. We spent the night in a police outpost, and reached Bilaspur next forenoon. I had sent off a letter to announce my coming the day before I started. It arrived three days after us. It had been delightful, though almost uncanny, to be so far from post-bags and telegrams and official life. We had compressed into about half of the Christmas public holidays enough of excitement to last for months. We had passed over miles of wild mountains and forest, and had taken part in scenes such as we could hardly hope to witness again. We carried with us the most pleasant recollections of the Maharajah and the home of the elephants. Of these he managed, before the operations were concluded, to capture, if my memory serves me right, no fewer than forty-two. This brought some money into the coffers of the Matin Zamindar, and relieved his people from a terrible visitation.

The Maharajah of Sirguja, who is still alive, was then quite a young man. His State was one of the five Hindi Feudatory States handed over from Bengal to the Central Provinces in 1904. I have seen him several times of later years, and he continues to be quite happy in his relations with Government. He is most hospitable and friendly; and it is a pleasure to visit him, for he has a delightful family. His only defect is that he is too easily led or influenced by subordinates. He was a splendid sportsman in his youth, and continues still to take interest in sport and in his jungles. He is a humane and sensible man: he has a large number of captured elephants; and his system is to accustom them for a considerable period of the year to jungle life and for a few months only to his service. In the jungle they wander about quite freely, except that each wears a chain fastened to one hind leg, which serves to tie him up when necessary. They are in charge of men who periodically feed them with sugar-cane and other luxuries; and at certain periods they are led by these men to any part of the State where their services are required for burden-bearing or for assistance in forest work. The system works well, and the Maharajah and his elephants get on well together.

Before leaving the subject of elephants, I may mention an incident which occurred some time later than this in the Sonpur State to the south of the Sambalpur District in Orissa. I was on tour in the Feudatory States, and had several Rajahs and Zamindars assembled to meet me and discuss the affairs of that part of the country. Many of them had elephants with them, and one of these went mad. He had killed his own Mahout, who was, I fancy, not a great credit to his profession; and another man had barely escaped with his life from an attack made on him. The elephant was in the neighbourhood of our camp, and we slept all night with our rifles loaded in case he should attack our tents. We had arranged that in the morning we should go after a tiger in the neighbourhood, and our servants slipped into our tents before dawn and carried off our rifles to the spot where the beat for the tiger was to take place. All the weapons in the camp were thus carried off except my shot-gun.

In the morning I left the camp accompanied by a large retinue of Rajahs and one or two European gentlemen, of whom one was a very old man paying me a visit. About two miles from the camp, as we turned round the high embankment of a tank, we suddenly came face to face with the mad elephant. He charged straight at us, and we all fled; but there was no place of refuge near. It was manifest that we could not all escape with our lives. The use which the Maharajah of Sirguja had made of specially prepared snipe cartridges and their wonderful effect on the elephants occurred to my mind. I seized a Chaprasi (orderly) who was rushing past me and took out of the bag that he carried two of my No. 1 cartridges. I thrust them into my gun and turned round suddenly face to face with the elephant. I fired point-blank into the light-coloured spot at the top of his trunk. He roared with pain and swung round on his hind legs. I immediately gave him the second barrel behind, and he dashed off and disappeared in the jungle. He was afterwards captured and cured.

On this occasion I had one of many illustrations of the pluck and devotion often shown by the Indian gentleman. Among our number that day was Rai Gopinath Guru Bahadur, the Uriya Brahman Tahsildar, who received the title of Rai Bahadur for his splendid conduct during the Kalahandi insurrection. When the elephant first charged at us our impulse was, of course, to run away, which we all did. I did not notice that the Rai Bahadur kept close to me; but when I stopped to fire at the elephant, I heard him shout in Uriya, "Stand, all of you: the sahib is standing." When all was over, I turned to find him standing alone beside me, unarmed. He was my friend, and I was his Chief. He could do nothing to save me; but he could not leave me in danger: that was all. It was a wonderful escape; there is no doubt that some lives would have been lost but for my opportune recollection of my Christmas experiences among the elephants in the Matin Zamindari.

CHAPTER XIII

WITH TIGERS AND BIG GAME

Life in the jungles is exceedingly interesting and delightful. The jungle people charm us with their simplicity and friendliness; and our admiration is called forth by their resourcefulness and pluck. A number of illustrations might be given of the great skill they acquire in dealing with the wild beasts and birds, and in replenishing their larder. When I was on tour in the Sambalpur District very many years ago, I made arrangements for duck-shooting in one of the many excellent tanks in that district. On the day of my arrival, however, I had a slight attack of fever, and was unable to go out. In the afternoon a Gond Malguzar (or head man of the village) came to my tent with a present of one or two duck. With the kindly consideration of his class, he had refrained from shooting them, as that might have frightened the birds and interfered with my sport next day; but he had captured them. I asked him how he had done it. He explained the process, and agreed to show it to me.

I accordingly went with him on the following day at noon to one of the tanks in the neighbourhood. There I saw one or two inverted clay *garras** floating quietly with the wind in the direction of the duck, which were gathered in the middle of the pond. They floated amongst the duck, which looked at them with slight suspicion; but seeing that they were only clay *garras* took no further notice. After one or two had passed, however, there floated by another *garra* which had been constructed with so wide a mouth that it could be placed over the

* A *garra* or *garwa* is a round water-pot with a small opening at the top.

head and on the shoulders of one of the Gonds. It had two small holes in it through which it was possible for him to see. He swam quietly with the *garra* on his head into the midst of the duck, and as he passed he put up his hand and pulled one after another under the water, until he had three. Each duck, as it went down, made a slight flutter, but it was only momentary; and this *garra*, like the rest, passed through the midst of the birds and came gently toward the other side of the tank. Near the edge it went under water, and did not reappear. Instead, a man stepped out of the water under cover of the reeds, carrying the three duck in his hand. In this way the Gonds are able, without the necessity for a gun or a gun licence, and without expenditure on powder and shot, to replenish their food supply.

In the Balaghat District I was walking into camp with a Baiga* after a good ride from my last camp. As I came near my tents, I saw a pipal (fig) tree, with a number of green pigeons feeding on the fruit. I said to my companion that I must come in the evening and get one or two of these. In a very short time he turned up at my tent with half a dozen green pigeon in his hand. They were alive, but unable to fly. His plan was to take some bird-lime of his own private manufacture, and smear with it one or two of the branches of the pipal near the fruit. A bird would step on this lime, and then, feeling that there was something sticky and uncomfortable on his foot, clean it against the feathers of its breast. The result was that the wings of the bird adhered to the breast feathers. After this had been going on for a short time, the Baiga and his friends raised a sudden shout below the tree. The birds immediately raised their feet and attempted to fly away. Those whose feathers had been smeared found that their wings would not act, and fell like lifeless bodies to the ground where the Baiga made them prisoners. My companion had not been accustomed to meeting European officers, and did not

* The Baigas are a wild tribe with certain priestly functions among the aborigines.

know their preference for shooting their own game; so he brought these to me to save me trouble.

I had a more amusing illustration once of the kindly desire of the simple Indian, resident in the jungle, to meet what he believed to be the wishes of his European guest. I was passing through a small and remote Native State on a somewhat hurried journey towards head-quarters. I had to halt for a day to allow my camp followers to overtake me. The Chief told me that a panther had killed a goat very near my camp, and that he had arranged for a beat, so that I might get the panther. The beat was unsuccessful; and when it was over the Chief asked me if I could not stay until the next day, in which case, he said, he was perfectly certain that I would get the beast. I expressed regret that I must leave at a very early hour in the morning. Next morning he was present to say good-bye, and with him he had brought the panther in a cage-like trap mounted on wheels. It had been caught in the night; and he suggested that I should shoot the beast through the bars of the cage. He was somewhat disappointed when I declined to take that step; but his disappointment passed away when I told him that I should prefer to take the panther with me and present it to the small zoological garden at Nagpur.

The jungle tribes have a great variety of traps for wild animals. One of these is a little enclosure of thick bamboo fencing, within which a goat is tied near a spear firmly fixed in the ground at a particular angle. The goat bleats in the night, and so attracts the panther. The fence is just too high to allow the panther to see over, but is low enough to form an easy jump. The panther gathers himself for a spring, clears the fence, and is transfixed by the spear.

Another trap is to place a poisoned arrow in a fixed bow against a rock or a tree in such a position as to command the path by which a tiger is accustomed to come and go. To this bow are attached four strings, two on each side. The first on the right hand is a string high enough to be touched by the neck or body of a bullock, or of a man who may be passing

Awaiting the Tiger

The sportsman may be seen in his "machan" (literally, raised seat or platform) awaiting the approach of the beat. He may see a large number of wild beasts of many kinds pass below him, but he will not fire till the tiger comes.

through the jungle. If either of these touches this high string, the arrow is discharged harmlessly; for it is past before he reaches that spot in the path which it commands. The tiger, however, crouches low in walking, passes below that string, and comes to a second string, which, as he touches it with his foot, releases the arrow just at the right time to catch him behind the shoulder. The poison begins to work immediately, and he is found dead next day within a reasonable distance. The strings on the other side were precisely of the same character, so that any man or bullock coming from that side would be equally safe, and any tiger coming from that side would be equally likely to pay the penalty.

I once had a delightful tour through the Bastar State, a wild State with great possibilities of development, the name of which has been recently associated in the Press with a rising of some of the aborigines. I came to a certain village where they told me that they had been much harassed by a man-eating tiger, but that they had succeeded in catching it in a trap. They took me to see the trap, and, as one's nose bore witness, the tiger was lying dead within it. It was constructed in the following manner. A great tree had been cut down; its branches had been lopped off; and the trunk had been placed in a deep cutting into which it almost exactly fitted. The one end of the tree was on the ground in this cutting. The other end was raised by means of a prop which had been placed about half-way down the trunk within the cutting. To this prop a small goat had been securely tied. This goat bleated plaintively at night and attracted the notice of the cruel marauder. He turned in, seized the goat, and began dragging it out. The prop gave way, and the heavy tree fell upon his back, lying with dead weight upon him from head to tail; and so he was secured and left to die.

The villagers came together and lifted the tree in my presence. It was a strange sight to see the great tiger stretched out dead at the bottom of this cutting. The marks made by his claws on the ground showed the struggle that he had made; and one could not help feeling some pity for the awful sufferings which must have preceded his death. This feeling somewhat passed away when a *post mortem* examination exposed some of the contents of his stomach. Amongst these was the bangle of a young Maria woman, who had been among his victims. Her relatives pressed this sad memorial of the incident upon me, and were much pleased to receive more than its value in return.

The man-eating tiger is a terrible visitation in a countryside. The tiger does not ordinarily attack man. I have myself, when unarmed, met a tiger face to face in the jungle, and he has turned away growling at the disturbance, but altogether disinclined to enter the lists with me, not knowing his advantage. Ordinarily the tiger confines his attention to the lower animals, making a satisfactory meal or two on a good plump deer, or one of the cattle of a herd grazing in the jungle. The man-eater is generally one which finds himself unable, from some cause or other, to hunt with success. It may be that he has been wounded in a way that has maimed him without taking his life. It is generally due to the act of some Indian Shikari (hunter) provided with a very inferior weapon. From the hind leg of one man-eater of this class I extracted a slug which had broken a bone and rendered it impossible for the tiger to make his usual spring at his prey. Ordinarily one finds that the man-eater is either an old, mangy, worn-out animal, or one that has been injured in this way. He takes to killing men and women when he finds that he cannot otherwise satisfy his hunger.

There is another class, however, I believe: those trained as cubs by a man-eating mother to feed on men. I remember going out after a man-eater in one of the little hill Zamindaris in the east of the Raipur District. The Zamindar came out with me, and kindly took me to the scene of operations on an elephant. I took up my position in a tree which he had prepared beforehand, and the beat was organized. The beat came on over the hill for a considerable distance, and then stopped. From the place where I was awaiting the advent of the tigress, I could hear the shouts of the men, the blowing of the horns, and the beating of their drums; but the beat did not come any nearer. At last a man came running to me and said that the tigress had taken refuge in a cave. I sent to the Zamindar for the elephant, which he assured me was very staunch and would face any tiger. I took a large quantity of dry hay, and some grass a little damper, and pushed the elephant up towards the mouth of the cave. I threw down the hay and grass, and flung into it a piece of lighted fuel (cow-dung cake). The wind was blowing into the mouth of the cave. I pushed the elephant back, and took my station a few yards off, with my rifle levelled at the mouth of the cave to shoot the brute as she came out. She put out her nose and looked; but seeing me, she withdrew into the recesses of the cave. As I waited, still pointing my rifle at the cave mouth, I heard a sound somewhat between a cough and a growl on my right rear. Turning round, I saw that the beast must have slipped out by some other exit from the cave.

The elephant, which was supposed to be staunch, had begun to tremble so that my rifle was moving like a ship on a choppy sea. Doing my best, however, to steady it, I fired at the retreating tigress. I hit her, but I hit her low. I inflicted a severe wound on her stomach, and she turned on me at once. The elephant fled, and I had a few unpleasant minutes with the elephant tearing along, as fast as he could, and the tigress bounding along neck and neck with him just a few yards up the hill. I could not reload the barrel which I had just discharged, for I felt that the tigress might leap on to the elephant at any moment, and I was bound to keep the second barrel for her. For the same reason, I dared not risk firing the second barrel; for my aim would have been very uncertain, and I should have been left unarmed.

Fortunately for me, the elephant tripped and nearly came down. Nothing terrifies an elephant more than the fear of a fall; so he steadied himself and paused in his panic-stricken flight. The tigress shot ahead, and, finding herself ahead, went straight on. The elephant turned round and fled in the opposite direction. It was some little time before the Mahout (driver) could stop him; but nothing that we could do would turn him in the direction of the tigress; so I got down. I fortunately knew the country well, and judged that she had gone over a little knoll, and was probably lying cooling her wound in a soft, marshy piece of ground on the other side. Giving orders to all the natives to get into or remain in trees, I pushed cautiously forward up the knoll to a bush which was at the top of it. I peered through this and saw the tigress lying below as I had anticipated. Fortunately she was to windward of me. I pushed my rifle gently through the outermost branches of the bush, and levelled it at her. Just as I got my fore sight on her, she raised her head and looked round suspiciously. This gave me a good target; and I fired and shot her in the neck, breaking the spine and killing the beast.

I do not think that I have ever seen greater enthusiasm than marked our return to camp. The victims had for the most part been women, who were seized by the tigress as they were gathering the *mohwa* flowers, which are used both for food and for the preparation of a spirituous liquor; and there were tales of about thirty-five deaths within a short period before. We took a *charpai* (village bed) for the tiger's bier, and it was carried shoulder high into the camp eight or ten miles away. All the beaters danced round it; and as we drew near the camp they were reinforced by the villagers on every side. When we reached the tents there were hundreds, if not thousands, dancing round it and shouting, "Jai! Sirkar ki jai!" (Glory or victory to the Government). We found that the cave had many human remains; and it was apparently satisfactorily established that the tigress had been in the habit of carrying her victims alive to the cave and teaching two little cubs to kill them there. We were fortunately able, next day, to secure the two cubs, which had slunk away while we were dealing with their mother, but whose cries of hunger led to their discovery.

One other man-eating story may be told as an illustration of courage and devotion not at all unusual among these brave simple jungle people. I have in my possession a tiger's skin which has no mark on it, except a cut on its hindquarters. I had placed a young Assistant Commissioner on special duty after several man-eaters in the State of Kawardha in the cold weather of 1889-90. These man-eaters were holding the *ghats* (passes) between the plains of Chhattisgarh and the hill country of Mandla, and absolutely stopped the traffic which was carried by pack bullocks. I was engaged in inspecting Settlement work in the State. I fell in with my young friend one day as he was preparing to beat for one of the man-eaters. We had just organized the beat and placed our "stops"* in certain trees, near which we had taken up our position.

As we were about to send orders to the distant beaters to begin operations, a woman came running to us, and cried out that her son, a lad of sixteen years, had been carried off by the tiger from the village hard by. We at once set off for the spot, taking with us the few men whom we had retained as "stops." We found that the tiger had just carried off the lad into a narrow strip of jungle, which formed a sort of spur to the main forest. As we got near this strip, we met the lad's father returning with his son's body. The poor lad had his skull smashed, and was quite dead; but the brave old Gond had attacked the tiger with his little axe, and had inflicted so severe a wound on his hindquarters that the brute had dropped his prey and turned on the man. The latter had stepped up fearlessly towards him, and the brute had turned away and slipped into the strip of jungle.

We sent our small body of men round the fields to the far end of this strip; and we told them that when they got there they were to stand and shout, and make as much noise as they could without entering the jungle. Meanwhile we each got astride the branch of a tree. These two trees were at a little distance from one another, and commanded practically the whole of the end of the narrow strip communicating with the main jungle. Hearing the noise behind him, the tiger naturally

* "Stops" are men placed in trees near the guns to tap on the branches and turn the tiger towards the guns, if it tries to pass out of the line.

made for the dense forest. He came out looking to right and left in an angry and defiant way, right under the tree occupied by my friend, who raised his heavy twelve-bore gun to his shoulder. The animal saw the movement and paused to look up. My friend took advantage of this opportunity and fired. He struck the brute full in the chest. It did not move from its position; but its legs simply gave way under it, and it sank to the ground. There was only one bullet mark in the skin, and that was in the middle of the chest. When the skin was removed the operating Chamar (worker in skin and leather) cut through this hole. There was therefore no mark left on the skin at all except a long wound in the hindquarters, where we found that the blow of the axe had penetrated to the bone. My friend, who was successful in killing all the man-eaters, kindly left this skin in my possession as a memorial of the prowess of the brave old father.

Many years ago, when I was Commissioner at Chhattisgarh, I had to go out to Khariar (about one hundred miles from Raipur) to settle some urgent matters connected with that Zamindari. I took with me Mr. Chapman, a young civilian who had just joined. We sent notice to the Zamindar, a Chauhan Chief, despatched our tents and kit, and followed them a few days later. With relays of horses we rode straight out to the Khariar border. There the Zamindar met us. He was an enthusiastic sportsman, and eagerly offered to show us tiger, buffalo and bison, in the intervals of our work. We marched with him in five short stages to his capital, discussing *en route* the business about which I had come down.

At Petiapali we had news of buffalo. My own Shikaris had been left at Suarmar to mark down the man-eating tigress above referred to, which I was determined to get on the way back; and the Zamindar, who, by the way, had the title of Rajah, preferred that we should have his own people as trackers. He thought that this would prevent friction with the country folk. Dugari Majhi was the head man of a little village near Petiapali and was a well-known Gond tracker. He led us through fine sal jungle with here and there a thick clump of bamboos, and here and there a green glade with a little rippling brook, not dry in these jungles even at the end of April. We went a mile or two on my elephant, and then dismounting followed our guide on foot. We had two other Gonds with us, one of whom carried a *chagal** of water, to most men indispensable in jungle work. After a while we came on the tracks of a herd. A little further forward we came on a solitary Gond who had been left to try and keep the herd in view. Not a word was uttered, but he pointed forward towards a low-lying part of the forest which was still fresh and green. We pushed on with eager but suppressed excitement. A small Gond soon after swarmed up a tree and peered cautiously round. Coming down, he stepped out rapidly but silently, and soon stopped and pointed forward. Then we got our first glimpse of the herd just across a nullah, about three hundred yards to windward of us.

Dugari, who knew the jungle well, led us quickly off to the right. He calculated that the herd, which was quietly grazing, would move down the bank of the nullah, and that we should be able to cut it off. He was right; we came on it suddenly, face to face. The monarch of the herd was about one hundred yards off and facing us. Suddenly the herd took fright, turned round and dashed off. I could not resist firing at the bull as he fled, for I knew that there was no hope of any more stalking of the herd that day. I hit him in the hind quarters, but did not wound him severely. He separated from the herd, however, and we followed his lonely track. On a hard piece of ground we lost it, and sat down for a while to demolish a sandwich or two, while Dugari and his friends scattered to pick up the track again. They soon found it; and we immediately set forth. It was marvellous to see Dugari step out, touching lightly with his stick, as he went, faint tracks that were sometimes almost invisible to us even when pointed out.

We had walked about half a mile, Dugari in front, followed

* A large skin bottle carried by a strap over the shoulder.

by me, Mr. Chapman, and another Gond in that order, when suddenly the second Gond touched Mr. Chapman on the shoulder and pointed into a nursery of young trees. There was the bull standing not fifty yards off, rubbing his head against a young sal sapling. There were two thick bushes between us and him, but we saw him very distinctly. Mr. Chapman fired both barrels of his rifle, and I fired one of mine. We aimed at his neck, and thought that we must have finished him. He disabused our minds immediately. As we found out later, he had not been touched. All three bullets had been deflected. He turned and charged us with all his strength. Fortunately I was the nearest of the group with one bullet still in my rifle. I waited till he dashed out from among the bushes, having my rifle levelled at him as he came. His head was down, one horn almost sweeping the ground, and he presented a fine target. As soon as I got a clear view of it, I gave him my remaining bullet in the middle of the forehead just above the eyes, at about ten yards' distance, and leapt aside. I heard a tremendous crash and turned round to see him lying dead. The whole thing was over before we had time to think.

As we stood beside him, I said to Mr. Chapman that it was a very foolish thing to be standing with empty rifles beside so large an animal simply because we supposed him to be dead. I then opened the breech of my rifle, and to my surprise I found both barrels loaded. I must have loaded them instinctively as I leapt aside, and would, I hope, have been ready for the buffalo if he had charged again; but as the necessity had passed away I had forgotten the instinctive act. We were fairly excited, especially Mr. Chapman, who had up to this seen nothing of sport; but Dugari was calm and unmoved. I asked him whether he was not delighted. He replied, "It was not written that you were to be killed by this buffalo; and I think that the Rajah will give me a silver bangle because you are safe."

Next day we had a long weary hunt. We had done office work from dawn till noon, when we got news of a herd. We were led up close to it by the faithful Dugari. At last we saw a fine bull in the distance; but he also saw us and vanished like a ghost in the thick jungle, taking the herd with him. We followed their tracks a long way, and then lost them and began to make our way wearily towards the camp. When we were close to the tents we met the Zamindar with some villagers who gave us news of a great bull that had taken possession of the water supply of a village about four miles off. He was a crusty old solitary bull, and would allow no one near; so the villagers had to go a mile or two instead of two hundred yards for their daily supply of water.

It was by this time nearly five o'clock, so we rode off as fast as we could, taking no one with us, but trusting to get a guide at the little jungle village of Babupali, where the buffalo was. We found a man willing to guide us, who also told us that another man was posted in a tree close to the place where the buffalo was lying. We were told that he would point out where the beast was. We went on foot from the village. Within half a mile we came to the nullah with a strip of jungle like a spur from the neighbouring hill. We separated and moved stealthily towards the water supply from different directions. At last we heard the animal, slowly beating with his tail as he lay among the long grass and shrubs in the bed of the nullah. We tried to get sight of him, but could not. He heard us, however, and with a warning bellow came up to turn us off his preserve. He had to come out of the nullah sideways. We gave him two bullets in the neck and one in the triangle under the ribs as he came out. This troubled him terribly and the fight was soon over. His horns were the largest I had seen, and measured 10 feet 8 inches.

During our short stay with the Rajah we got three fine buffaloes, a tiger, a bear and a man-eating tigress—no mean bag. Tracking the buffalo is much more interesting than tiger shooting; but it is very rarely that it gives the same satisfaction to one's conscience. When the tiger is killed, there is a destroyer the less, either of man or of his possessions. It is rare to find a buffalo that is really offensive: the churlish old bull that we killed at the Babupali nullah deserved his fate for his selfish appropriation of the only water supply within reasonable distance of the village; but it is not often that the people suffer in this way from the presence of buffaloes. The damage they do is mainly damage to crops; and they are so like the tame buffalo, from which we get so much milk for our domestic use, that there is little satisfaction in compassing their death. Indeed, they are much finer animals, and I always felt compunction in shooting them.

We got no bison at Khariar. We did not attempt to go to the place among the hills where the Rajah told us they were to be found; but later on, in the Chanda District, when I was Commissioner of Nagpur, some friendly Gonds showed me bison in the jungle. It was in the rains; and I ran out from Chanda to a forest bungalow, some fifteen or twenty miles away, and slept the night there. My Gond friends, who had often been with me on other expeditions, woke me at three in the morning, and took me to a place quite close by where there was a salt-lick. We arrived there just after the herd had left, so we had a long stern chase. The fallen leaves were sodden with the rain, and it was easy to walk through the jungle without making a noise; and we walked at a great pace following clear tracks. As we were pushing on after having walked about ten miles, we heard a roaring such as one hears in the Zoo when the animals are to be fed. I inquired in a whisper from the Gond, who was beside me, what it meant. He said, "It is bison." The word he used was "Gaur"; for there are few sibilant sounds in the jungle language of the Gonds. They use sounds that do not travel. The noise was directly on our right, so I put two Muhammadan Chaprasis* who were with me into trees to mark the tracks we were about to leave, and, taking the two Gonds with me, we pushed directly towards the noise.

After walking a very short distance, we came to a glade in which I saw a sight which I shall never forget. Two great bison bulls had their horns interlocked and were wrestling with one

* Menial servants or orderlies.

Phot by Col. Bloomfield

A GROUP OF BAIGAS IN BALAGHAT

Photo by Sir D. Hamilton

FISHING-BOATS IN THE SUNDERBANS AT THE MOUTH OF THE GANGES

another. The cows of the herd were dancing round in frantic excitement with their tails in the air, and bellowing for all they were worth. The conflict had lasted for some little time; suddenly without any reason apparent to me, one of the bulls turned tail and fled, leaving his antagonist in possession of the herd. In the middle of the glade there was a large tree; nearer the other side from where I was, there stood a smaller one: the victorious bull went up to this and stood rubbing his horns against it. He was facing me, and the tree was more or less between us. I felt that I could not get a shot at him from where I was. I therefore made a sign to the Gond that I was going to creep through the long grass to the big tree in the middle of the glade and take aim from there. He shook his head, as indicating that the movement could not be carried out. I went down as flat as I could, however, and on hands and knees, holding my rifle close to me, I slipped through the grass till I got to the tree. Then I raised myself behind it, and cautiously putting my rifle round the corner of it, I fired at the bull. He presented a fine target, probably not more than fifty yards off. I felt that I had hit him, but he dashed off without a sound, the whole herd galloping away with him.

The Gond was so excited that, contrary to custom, he shouted, "Nahin lagla (You have not hit)." I held up my hand to silence him, and pushed on after the herd. As I turned a corner of a bamboo clump, not much more than a hundred yards off, I almost tripped on the dead body of the bull. We carried him to the tents, where the Gonds had a great feast. I sent the head and neck in a cart into Chanda, taking care that the carter was not a Hindu. My wife sent it straight on to the station at Warora in charge of a Muhammadan Chaprasi, and by eight o'clock in the morning it was with Johnson, the Kamptee taxidermist, who preserved it with perfect success, although it was the rainy season. Meanwhile, I suppose the defeated bull resumed the mastership of the herd.

The bison is much more attractive in appearance than the buffalo. He is even less offensive. The pleasure of pursuit in the long tracking through the jungle, with the feeling that at any moment you may come on the herd, is great; but the satisfaction of killing a bison is small except to our Gond companions, who like exceedingly to have a great feast of bison flesh.

The Gonds are wonderfully attractive people. They are absolutely without fear, and are intensely loyal to any one who associates with them in a friendly way. They expect to be regularly paid, and also to receive a full allowance of their ordinary food, while they are working with you. These conditions being granted, there is nothing that they will not do, so long as they do not suspect their European leader either of fear or serious incapacity. I sent two of my Chanda Gonds over to Burmah at the request of Captain Fryer, then private secretary to the Lieutenant-Governor. They did splendid work even in those, to them, unknown jungles; and Captain Fryer sent them home full of delight at his treatment of them, and with a handsome reward, which enabled them to buy a little land for themselves. It was touching to see the reluctance with which they crossed the water to Burmah. I was then Home Secretary to the Government of India in Calcutta. I received them there and put them on board ship. It was nothing but their perfect confidence in their old friend that induced them to go; and it was delightful indeed to see them return safe and sound, full of gratitude for the kindness shown them by Captain Fryer and his friends, and full of pride in his appreciation of their services. He had quite won their hearts. A man must be a little more than a good office man if he is to have real and permanent influence over the jungle peoples.

CHAPTER XIV

THE AGRICULTURAL COMMUNITY AND DEBT

To know something about the agricultural community is to know something about India, for the vast majority of the people are agricultural. In the Central Provinces we used to go about among them, and it was recognised as a duty to become acquainted with them. The Collector had to keep himself in touch with them, or he became, and was well known to be, an inefficient officer. He had to know the character of cultivation and the state of the crops in all parts of his District. The land revenue was paid to him at his own, or at one of the subordinate Treasuries. He was responsible for its prompt realisation, for understanding the reasons for any default, and for treating default leniently when the reasons for it were valid. The payments made by the Malguzar or Zamindar * are fixed not only on his home farm, but on the rents of the tenants. The condition of the tenants is therefore a matter of importance to the Collector, as well as the condition of the proprietor; and there is no part of a Collector's duty more important than going about among the people and, by frank talk with them and personal inspection of the village lands, ascertaining their actual condition.

This is also a duty which the people expect him to perform. They do not resent the fullest and frankest discussion of their affairs; but they very deeply feel any manifestation of in-

* The Zamindar is literally the holder of the land; and the Malguzar is literally the man through whom the revenue is paid to Government. Both of these terms are used for the proprietor of a village or group of villages.

difference. The Government is expected to understand them, and to be ready to help them when necessary. There are not a few who prefer the ryotwari system, under which the Government settlement of land revenue is made directly with the cultivator himself. There is no middle man to consume some of the revenue which ought to come to Government. But I myself prefer the old Central Provinces system, in which the settlement is made with the Malguzar, or village proprietor, in full cognisance of the rents he realises. To have a local man of some standing, to help the people over periods of temporary difficulty and to take a lead in village life, is often a great advantage. But it does not relieve the Revenue officer of the duty of knowing the condition of the cultivators. He must get beyond the Malguzar, and know the ryots as well.

The ryots like to be allowed to tell all their story. Any trouble they have, or anything that interests them, and still more any matter in regard to which they think that the Revenue officer can help them, will be poured into his ears, if he will listen. And he will be a very foolish person if, in the vast majority of cases, he does not let them say all they have to say. It sometimes may seem waste of time, but it is better and more valuable work than much for which the time might otherwise have been saved. To an earnest and sympathetic officer it is always a pleasure to hear what the people have to say; and to them it is such a privilege to speak freely, that they will take any order in good part provided that it is passed after they have had a kindly hearing and full consideration has been given to what they have said. Kindly and patient conduct towards the people enables an officer to carry them with him in a truly marvellous way. A missionary once said to me, "We may be of great use to you: the Government officer does his work righteously and conscientiously; but he has not time to explain things to the people. We go about among them and can explain." Missionaries do help in this way; but the Government officer who fails to try to find time to "explain things" makes a great mistake.

I recollect a case in which it became necessary to substitute Government servants for the hereditary Village Accountants who had become practically useless to the people. The measure was undoubtedly a sound one, and the Government determined to carry it out. Some of the old hereditary men fought for the maintenance of the old system, though the orders gave as full consideration as possible to their personal claims. One fine old man fought hard for his family office and dignity. The Deputy Commissioner, who was a man well known for a somewhat hasty manner of doing business, had called the case in which this man had petitioned urging his claim. Finding that there was to be opposition he adjourned it; and then, taking it up one day when the petitioner was absent, he struck it off in default. The man was furious, and declared that he would fight the case to the end, appealing "London tak."* I had succeeded to the charge of the District, and sent for him and tried to show him that he would gain nothing by all this expensive litigation. He said that he would not submit to injustice, and that he had a good case. I promised to come to his village and hear it.

I went soon after, and kept nearly a whole day free for it. My friend came with a mass of books and papers. I made him sit down on the floor of my tent surrounded with them, and listened to him and took notes. After some hours with him, I summed up the case to him, expounding the whole policy, and explaining that policy as applying to his claim. He listened quietly and respectfully. At the end he simply said to me in Marathi, "Does Your Honour really think that I shall gain nothing by fighting?" I replied, "I am sure of it, my brother." He unhesitatingly answered, "Then I shall sign"; and there and then he signed the agreement accepting the Government Scheme. He remained my friend till he died; and his son was one of the Indian gentlemen who pluckily stood by me years afterwards when I was engaged in suppressing the Nagpur grain riots. This is not a very exceptional case.

* "Even to London"—*i.e.*, to the Privy Council or to the Secretary of State, as the case might be.

I cannot even now think without astonishment of a case which moved me not a little at the time. When I was Sessions Judge in Chhattisgarh, I had to sentence a poor man to death for a savage murder. He was taken outside the court; and I heard great weeping and wailing. I ascertained that his women-folk were giving expression to their grief. When I went out to walk home they rushed at me, threw themselves suddenly at my feet, and cried for mercy. The constables who were near—like so many of the low class of police when untrained and officious—attempted to drive them away by force. I forbade this. And I asked the poor women what they wanted. They told me. I explained to them that I was as powerless as they, that I believed it was proved that the man had committed the murder, and that the law required me to pass the sentence. I went on to explain that the law gave them an appeal, that there was a higher court than mine, the judge of which might alter my order if he did not agree with my finding. I got a kindly Indian barrister to draw up their appeal for them there and then. I heard afterwards that the appeal was dismissed and the sentence carried out.

Some months later my wife and I were riding through a village far from head-quarters. Several women came, some to me and some to my wife, and touched our feet and said, "Peace be to you." I said, "Who are you?" Their answer was, "We are the women to whom you were kind when the man of our house was sentenced to death for murder." They had no ill-feeling to me for having passed the sentence; but they remembered with gratitude that I had listened to the story of their grief, and had done what I could for them. It is not difficult to win the hearts of these kindly, simple people; and they have a wonderful way of winning ours. It is worth while to get among them and help to mitigate their sorrows or increase their happiness.

Indeed, it is wonderful how happy their lives are. India is not a country in which the climate is favourable to hard work. I heard a fairly energetic European once say, "There are times in India when I feel very much disinclined for physical exertion.

I like to sit and think; and sometimes I only sit." The village folk do not, as a rule, work harder than they are compelled to do. Their standard of comfort is not high; and so long as their urgent wants are satisfied they do not care to exert themselves. They work hard enough when work must be done. At seed time and harvest they give weary days to toil, ploughing and sowing and transplanting and reaping, often in circumstances of much discomfort from rain or irrigation; but they do no more than they must. Yet in all they are cheery, and one may often hear the song of them that labour, as well as of those who see the joy of harvest.

To me it was always a touching spectacle to see a band of pilgrims on their way to Jaganath's temple at Puri.* They used to pass through Raipur, before the railway to Puri made pilgrimage more easy. They were going to fulfil some vow, to give thanks for some special blessing. They would come sometimes, nearly a whole village together, for hundreds of miles with their bullocks and carts and their families, and go singing down the road the praises of their God. They had looked forward to this pious journey for years, and expected much blessing from it. Often they would return weary and wellnigh stripped of all they had by the rapacious priests and temple servants. Often some of them fell victims to cholera and other ills incident to pilgrim life in India. Sometimes they had not even obtained a satisfactory view of the strangely unlovely idol they had gone to see. But they were going back to their old life, loyal and patient as ever, not understanding why things had not been made brighter for them, but not complaining.

St. Paul said † to the Athenians, "Ye men of Athens, in all things I perceive that ye are somewhat superstitious (or religious)." This is emphatically a characteristic of the Indian peoples. At the time of the great eclipse of the sun, in the last decade of last century, I happened to be at home on leave.

* The temple of Jaganath ("the Lord of the World," a form of Krishna) at Puri is one of the principal places of pilgrimage in India.

† Acts xvii. 22 (Revised Version): the margin reads "religious" for "superstitious."

The late Professor Copeland, the Astronomer Royal in Scotland, asked me to help him in respect of an expedition he was organising to see it in India. I gave him letters of introduction to some of the Central Provinces officers, and amongst others to the Tahsildar of Katol, a town on the line of total eclipse. When he came back he was full of the kindness he had received, and especially of the unstinted help the country people had given him. When I met the Tahsildar (a Brahman from the Konkan of Bombay) I congratulated him on his having made Professor Copeland's visit a success. He said, with a smile, "The credit is not mine. The Professor has a most venerable appearance, and I translated his title of 'Astronomer Royal' into Marathi as 'Astrologer to the Queen'; so the people received him with reverence, and gave him all the help they could."

I was greatly moved by the following incident. I had assembled many landlords and bankers to receive my thanks for the help they had given to the people during the trials of the famine which I had to fight as Chief Commissioner of the Central Provinces. The famine seemed over, for the Meteorological Department had given us good hope of rain; and I fixed my meeting for the beginning of July, feeling confident that the monsoon would have burst by then. But the rain had not come; and the sky was clear when we went to the meeting. Our hearts were full of anxiety. In speaking of it at the end of a long meeting in which the work of all had been detailed and many had received special marks of approval, I said that perhaps we had another year of trial before us, but that we prayed to the Merciful Father to deliver us from so terrible a visitation. As I drove away from the meeting, the sky was overclouded, and I had barely got under cover before the rain came down. As my wife and I sat at lunch there was shouting outside. Thousands were gathered with relieved and thankful hearts. They shouted, "Victory to our Chief Commissioner! He prayed for rain; and it has come." I spoke to them a few words of good cheer, and bade them go home and give God the glory. The scene greatly impressed us. It was full of gladness and of solemnity. They have the faith of little children; and "of such is the kingdom of God."

One of the greatest evils connected with agricultural life in India is the indebtedness of the people, and the difficulty that they have in obtaining command of capital on reasonable terms for carrying on agricultural work and effecting improvements. This has long attracted the attention of the Government and of those who are in any way interested in the welfare of the people. It is not easy to understand why there should be so large a proportion of the agricultural community involved in debt; for there are so many careful and prudent persons among the agricultural classes that many who know them would be inclined to say that habits of prudence and thrift characterise the people generally. The Hindu is certainly not necessarily improvident and unthrifty; and yet it cannot be denied that indebtedness is, to an extraordinary degree, characteristic of the agricultural classes.

There is one reason for this which is manifest on the face of it to any one who has practical experience of the life of the people, namely, that it is almost impossible for any man or any family that has once fallen into debt to recover. Therefore, generation by generation there is a tendency for indebtedness to increase. It is not the policy of the money-lender to sell up the debtor except under special circumstances. He will sell him up if he desires for himself, or for any one in whom he is interested, the property which the debtor owns; or he will sell him up when the debtor has become so involved as to be unable to pay what he regards as adequate interest for the money he has lent; but he will not ordinarily sell him up so long as he can extract from him a good profit in the shape of interest. Then, again, there is something in the climate of India that is against any great or special effort. The routine of life is as much as most men desire: special effort is irksome. Thus it is that, from generation to generation, the debt descends, sometimes without increasing in volume to any very appreciable extent, but without diminishing. There is one thing the creditor does not like in a debtor who has property such as to form anything like reasonable security: that is repayment of the loan, and the conditions of the debt are generally such as make the repayment of the principal very difficult.

Certain exceptional demands of the debtor for more money tend also to increase or, at all events, to maintain the amount of the debt. A man may be repaying his debt steadily year by year; but suddenly a marriage is to take place, which must be on a scale of expenditure such as will reflect credit on the family, and be a subject of pride to the married couple in after years. This expenditure may swallow up all that has been repaid, or even more; and the debt is left at least as heavy a burden as before. Or there may be a temporary or local failure in crops, from the direct consequence of which the agriculturist only escapes by incurring fresh debt. With a people who find it exceedingly difficult to get rid of debt when once incurred, and who have many occasions in the course of their ordinary life on which a sudden demand is made for money which they have not at hand, it is only natural that indebtedness should tend to increase.

It is an extraordinary thing also how difficult many natives find it to keep money. They are very sensitive to the public opinion of their villages. And that public opinion is frequently unfavourable to the prudent use of money, especially if that money is of the nature of a "windfall." I had once a native coachman who talked French. I forget how I discovered this very unusual accomplishment, for he never boasted of it. I discovered it one day by accident; and then I ascertained on inquiry that he had emigrated to the West Indies, where he had spent some years. I asked him whether he had saved nothing there. He told me that he had been very comfortable. His employer had been kind to him, and had paid him well; but he had longed to get back to his home; and, having saved over five hundred rupees, he had returned. Such a sum would in those days have kept him and his family in comfort for five years; or invested it would have made him a comparatively rich man. I asked him how he had invested his savings. He replied that he had not possessed them over two or three weeks. There was a feast to be given to his caste-fellows on his return, so that his position in the caste might be assured after his journeyings beyond "the black water"; and there were presents and entertainments to be given to his friends: how could he, after a long absence, refuse such calls? So all the savings of his exile were gone; and he had settled down to a life of work for which he had acquired both the taste and the qualifications during his absence. He was an excellent coachman, hard-working and conscientious, and simply devoted to his horses.

Another case occurs to my mind. A good Gond cultivator of great vigour and of no little intelligence had placed me under considerable obligation by services rendered to me in the jungle. As I was leaving that part of the country, I made him the present of what seemed to him a very large sum of money. He at once asked me to buy a little bit of land with it, and present that instead. I advised him to look out for a piece of land and buy it himself. He said that he feared that was impossible: his friends would think it so selfish of him to keep all that money to himself. So I got him to look out quietly for such a plot as would suit him, and report privately to me. I then got a trustworthy Indian friend to buy it for me, and handed it over to the Gond, who was allowed to enjoy it in peace.

Such incidents as these are quite typical. They indicate what is well known to all who know the people well, namely, that it is hard for the ordinary native of India to amass money. He lives up to his income: he is expected to do that. He is thrifty in that he can live on little; but as a rule he cannot save, unless he does it secretly: there are too many effective demands on his purse from his relatives and friends. It is a defect in social economy; but it has this redeeming feature, that it saves the country from a poor law: the people support their own poor: liberality is characteristic of the people.

The Settlement Officer soon learns this, and it greatly affects the assessment made by wise and considerate officers. There is nothing more disastrous to a district than a harsh, inconsiderate, and heavy assessment. An assessment may be actually just, and yet harsh and unwise. I remember having a talk, when I was a Commissioner of Division, with a Malguzar of many villages, a man of position and influence in that part of the country. He complained of the great increase in his assessment. I went over all the papers with him very carefully. It was easy to show him that owing to the construction of the railway and the general rise of prices, the assessments were perfectly just. My friend, an upright and honest man, admitted frankly that this was true. But he pointed out that he had saved but little, and that it was very difficult for him to reduce his expenditure at once within the limits of his reduced income. I represented the matter to the Settlement Officer, and to the Government, and his assessment was slightly reduced, and (what was much more important) the increase was made progressive over a term of years. This is a wise and reasonable procedure sometimes adopted in such cases.

To return to the matter of indebtedness, what strikes one as particularly noteworthy is the high rate of interest which money-lenders all over the country are able to exact. Cases are constantly brought to notice which actually appal one; the interest seems so extortionate. One is apt, from the experience which he has of a large number of such cases to denounce the money-lender and to regard him as one of the enemies of his race. It would be unfair to take up this position, and to pass a sweeping condemnation of the whole class. It is necessary to consider the circumstances more carefully, and also to bear in mind that there are many kinds of men with many different characters engaged in this profession. At the same time, it is undoubtedly true that a Government officer engaged in Revenue work, or in the administration of civil justice meets with a large number of cruel and rapacious men following the occupation of money-lender.

In some villages I have known the good old hereditary money-lender, whose family had followed this calling for generations among people who looked up to him very much as to a father. I remember one kindly old money-lender, with no very great capital, but just enough to meet the wants of the village community. He had very few customers outside his own village; and the villagers never dreamed of going to any one else. Their relations with him were very kindly. I do not think that I ever heard of his being in court as a plaintiff. Any disputes were settled by the village "Panchayat,"* whose authority is frequently exercised with great advantage. He gave the people his money when they needed it; they paid interest for it; and he was nothing but their kindly friend. This, however, is a state of things that one does not find often nowadays, and then only in the remoter villages in the course of a tour in the interior. One finds somewhat more frequently a Malguzar who lives on such terms with his own ryots.† He lends them seed grain, and sometimes gives them also subsistence during the time of ploughing and sowing and waiting for the harvest; and then he is repaid for what he has advanced, receiving in addition to that the interest on his advance and his rent. In many cases, I have found the relations between such a Malguzar and his ryots to be of the most kindly character, though this also is a phase of Indian life which is passing away with advancing civilisation.

It is not only as an illustration of the more simple and kindly past that one takes pleasure in such cases as I have indicated. They also serve as an explanation of the state of things in regard to indebtedness which has grown up largely under our own civilisation. There was no doubt a considerable amount of debt and of usury before our time; and traditions come down to us which show that the character and practice of the usurer were often even worse then than we find them now. The high

* The Panchayat is the Council of Village Elders: the literal meaning of the word is "Council of Five." The influence of these Elders, based on their age, character, and local experience, was very great: it is in many places now waning.

† The ryot or *rayat* is the tenant.

rate of interest then charged and the severity of the usurer's attitude may in some cases have been due to the fact that the remedy against a recalcitrant or negligent debtor was neither so simple nor so prompt in those days as it is now, and that therefore the risk of loss was greater. It must also be remembered that in those days there was much less capital. A loan was not so easily obtained. When the usurer came in with his advance of money he found a man, perhaps not a very satisfactory client, whose need had become pressing; and the transaction was one in which his position of advantage enabled him to get almost any return for the risk that he was running, and what he demanded was often exorbitant.

The ordinary transactions between creditor and debtor were mainly connected also with the advance of grain for subsistence, and of seed to the agriculturist. These were repayable in kind at the harvest. A very common rate of interest was *siwai* (literally "one and a quarter"): that is to say, the grain was to be returned with 25 per cent. of interest. This seems at first sight very high interest, especially as the debt had to be repaid within about six months; but when it is remembered that the price of grain is high at the time of sowing and low at the time of harvest, the rate does not appear to be so exorbitant.

Now, in India, custom, rather than either competition or reason, regulates to a very large extent economic conditions; and the rate of interest has a very unfortunate connection with this customary law. When, on the one hand, improved communications made markets accessible, and, on the other hand, the natural tendency of advancing civilisation substituted payments in cash for payments in kind, there was introduced that modification of the relation between creditor and debtor which changed these old grain debts into money debts. But then customary law prevailed to enable the money-lenders to extract from their debtors the old rate of interest. We find, therefore, that, even when the debts are contracted in cash, the rate of interest at which the agriculturist is being financed varies throughout India, in the great majority of cases, from 25 to

50 per cent. A man borrows money for seed grain for the *rabi* or spring harvest, and for subsistence during the period of preparation for that harvest. He may borrow the money about June or July, and he repays it seven or eight months later. He promises to repay it with *siwai*, that is, with interest at 25 per cent. Twenty-five per cent. for eight months is equal to 37½ per cent. a year.

Even this is not the worst. Usury laws were introduced by well-meaning but misguided authorities, with a view to benefit debtors, but really to their injury. I need not discuss the many ways in which usury laws are avoided; but there is one habit which is largely due to usury laws, and which has greatly increased the burden of the agriculturist in regard to the interest he pays: that is the habit of over-stating the debt and paying interest in advance. When a debtor was hard pressed for money and came to his creditor, the creditor found that the rate of interest which the law allowed was just about one-half of what he wanted. All that he had to do, however, was to double the sum the debtor required, and compel the debtor to acknowledge the receipt of that larger sum, while he only really received the smaller. This secured for the creditor all that he wanted in the way of interest, and for the debtor all that he wanted in the way of cash.

The necessity for this has passed away with the usury laws; but a habit once learned is not easily forgotten in India. Though an over-statement of the amount of the debt is still sometimes made in the bond, it is not necessary now to resort to this practice for the sake of securing a higher rate of interest; but the habit has been acquired of making a deduction from the amount actually paid to the debtor. This deduction is now made on the plea of having the first instalment of interest paid in advance. If a man is borrowing Rs. 100 at 25 per cent. and pays the interest in advance, he is actually receiving Rs. 75 at 33⅓ per cent. If the debt is payable in six months it is not less than 66⅔ per cent.

Thus the high rate of interest prevailing so widely in agricultural communities throughout India is due in part to customary rates for cash which took their origin in old days when security was less sound than now, and when recovery was much more difficult. It is also due to the maintenance, in respect of cash, of rates of interest which were reasonable for grain in view of the lower prices at harvest than at seed-time, but which are exorbitant in respect of cash. It is also in part due to the payment of interest in advance, a practice which appears to have its origin in the unfortunate lessons taught by the usury laws. The result is that the agricultural communities are deeply involved in debt, and are unable to obtain capital for the carrying on of their business and for effecting improvements on anything like reasonable terms.

CHAPTER XV

THE FINANCING OF AGRICULTURISTS

THE Government and its officers have had many a battle with the usurer. But there is nothing more difficult than to defend an ignorant peasantry against the consequences of their own thoughtlessness. It is necessary that the law should, as far as possible, be certain in its operation; and it is impossible to leave the laying down of the law entirely to the courts, especially when the Judges live apart from the people, and do not understand their circumstances. In older days the Judges lived more among the people, and had much less judicial work. It was wonderful how much of substantial justice was done in these days by men who did not discriminate much between law and fact, but were inclined to regard law as nothing more than the correct interpretation and treatment of fact. All the same, the idiosyncrasies of individual officers intensified the proverbial uncertainty of the law; and experience tended to show that attempts to interfere with contracts as made often resulted in injury to the people generally, and that the astute usurer could generally, by some means or other, get round such provisions of the Acts of the legislature or of the case-law of the judges as were framed for the protection of their debtors.

Early in my service I was employed as a Subordinate Judge in succession to a man who was well known to be very perfunctory in his work. I found that this man had not noticed a change in the Law of Limitation regarding the date in proceedings in Execution of Decrees from which the period of limitation was to count. Formerly it had been the date of final order in the last Execution proceedings; now it was the date of institution of these proceedings. I found a case of Execution pending against a Kunbi* Malguzar. I read the proceedings carefully. It was plain that the court had given a decree with great reluctance owing to the exorbitant nature of the demand. The old debt, which had been contracted by the present Judgment Debtor's father, had been paid off over and over again by the excessive interest demanded, despite the good security of the land; yet the debt had increased in amount. And now the Malguzar's village was to be sold.

I discovered that the usurer (who was well known as a relentless Shylock) had instituted his Execution proceedings after the period prescribed by the new law had expired. I told him so, and intimated that I would strike off the case and set the debtor free. I knew that it was necessary to see for myself that the debtor understood this. So I directed the Tahsildar† to order him to appear before me on the day fixed for hearing the case. He came, and I explained to him that as the debt had not been contracted by him, and had been more than adequately repaid already, I had determined to take advantage of a mistake in law made by his creditor and dismiss the case: his village was now restored to him; and he had better keep out of debt in future. He could hardly believe that the burden of years had rolled away. I record with satisfaction that I knew him afterwards for a long time, and that he kept free of debt. As for the usurer, he had many similar cases; and his mistake in law really broke his heart. His son, though not altogether estimable, did not inherit his father's ruthless disposition. By some such means as these, or otherwise, one was able sometimes to save a worthy agriculturist; but such efforts were sporadic and only affected individuals.

A far more extensive and systematic effort directly to relieve indebted agriculturists was made possible in the Central Provinces by the famine of the last years of the nineteenth

* The Kunbis are a good cultivating caste.
† Indian Local Land Revenue officer.

century. The Government is the great landowner. The "proprietors" of land realise the profits of their home farms and also receive the rents from the tenants of the other village lands; and out of these profits and rents they pay to Government as revenue a sum fixed from time to time on well-understood principles, retaining the balance as their own. Many of the tenants again have certain rights of transfer, which give their lands a marketable value. It is clear that this system has two great advantages. It gives the landlord an interest in the prosperity of his tenants; for he cannot pay his revenue unless they can pay their rents. It also gives the Government a direct interest in the prosperity of both landlords and tenants, on which the realisation of the assessed revenue depends. When agricultural trouble comes, the tenants look to the landlord, and both look to the Government, for sympathy and necessary assistance. This is the natural working of the system. I have seen it in the Central Provinces; and I have seen the other system of a permanent settlement, in which the payments to Government have no real relation to present conditions; there can be no doubt that under the latter system there is no such bond of intimacy and sympathy between the Government and the people as under the former.

Now when the famine came in the Central Provinces, the severest famine in all our history, apart from the relief works and other measures for the feeding of the people, it was necessary to take steps to help the agricultural community through the unparalleled crisis. Among these measures were the grant of "takavi" loans and the remission of revenue. The loans were given to Malguzars and ryots who needed them to enable them to purchase seed and carry through their agricultural work. The remission of revenue meant that the Government not only suspended, but actually wrote off revenue which the failure of the crops rendered it impossible for the Malguzars to pay. It was at once seen that the interests of the people and of the Government alike demanded that this liberality on the part of Government should be accompanied by similar liberality on the part of other creditors. Government could not agree to give advances or remit dues from the public funds merely to make it easier for other creditors to realise their dues. The law rendered it possible for Government to avoid this blunder, while helping the people.

The revenue is the first charge on the land: every other debt gives place to this; and "takavi" is collected so far like land revenue that it has a certain precedence. If the Government chose to do so, it could realise its revenue by selling up a defaulting Malguzar, no matter what the circumstances were that led to the default. Of course, Government would never sell up a man whose default was due to scarcity or famine, if he could be saved. But it would not abstain from selling him up if by that act of clemency it could not save him, but merely leave the creditor to sell him up, and realise for himself the money which ought legally and rightfully to find its way into the public purse. Therefore, the Government went to the creditors and said, "We will not help your debtors unless you also show them clemency, and place them in a position, after paying you what they reasonably can, to live in a fairly suitable way and carry on their agricultural work." The sensible or sympathetic creditor would have no desire to see his debtor sold up for the Government revenue: that would be to kill the goose that laid for him the golden egg. He would therefore naturally be willing to help the Government to set the debtor, rendered bankrupt by the scarcity, on his feet again. This was the basis of the great scheme of "debt conciliation" in the Central Provinces.

It was wonderful how it succeeded. At first a good deal of persuasion was required. But as the operations spread and became well understood, "suspicion gave way to acquiescence, and acquiescence to an apprehension lest one should be left out of the scheme." Creditors petitioned for "conciliation" as well as debtors. It was fine to see a "Conciliation Officer" at work. We gave our best Indian officers to the scheme. Such an officer would be seen sitting down quietly among the people, with the creditors on one side and the debtors on the other. Beside him were sometimes seated influential landlords and others, who acted as assessors with him in his work. Around this group, or in its vicinity, were other creditors and debtors awaiting their turn. In quiet and confidential conference the "Conciliation Board" ascertained all the assets and liabilities of each debtor. Its aim was to bring the amount of each man's debts within his paying capacity. It did not press wasteful remissions. If a debtor were in a position to pay all, no remission was adjudged; but solvent persons rarely applied.

Where its action was required, the Board not only arranged for remission, but also settled the whole method of such payments as it found right to order. Sometimes the whole estate was left with the debtor, suitable instalments being fixed for payment of such a portion of the debt as was not remitted. Sometimes part of the estate was given, and sometimes merely nominal payments, in full satisfaction of all claims, enough being left to the debtor to live on. The effect on the community was wonderful. Enormous debts were wiped out. A million of rupees of debt were remitted in the Saugor District, and about six hundred thousand each in the Balaghat and Bhandara Districts. The work was carried on in some other parts at the same time. Creditors felt that they were better off than they would have been by the mere ruin of their debtors. Debtors were set free from an absolutely unbearable incubus which had taken all heart out of them. I know of hardly anything that made a greater impression on the people; and the effect on their condition and spirits was very noticeable. It is especially delightful, too, to think that the work was done mainly by Indian officers, who threw themselves heart and soul into it, and did it with sympathy, tact, and uprightness. Men like Anant Lal, Ram Bhau and Ganga Singh showed what devotion to duty animates some of our Indian officers. All of these received from Government the title of Rao (or Rai) Bahadur.

Even such a measure as this, however, is temporary, and only meets a special crisis. The evil of indebtedness among the agricultural community demands more permanent measures. These have occupied the attention of the Government from time to time. But the root of the matter was never touched until the idea of co-operative credit was taken up and worked out by the Agricultural Department. The history of this measure is interesting as illustrating the manner in which schemes are framed in India.

The Agricultural Department owes its origin to the famines and to the desire to make the people less dependent on the amount and distribution of the rainfall. This Department concerns itself with matters affecting the interests of the agricultural community. It aims at assisting them in the selection of seed, in finding the best markets, in ascertaining the most marketable products, and in adopting new machinery and methods suited to India, and in other ways improving their cultivation and their staples. It also concerns itself with carrying out, or assisting the people in carrying out, permanent land improvements, designed both to improve agriculture in ordinary years, and also to make the people more independent in years when the ordinary conditions do not prevail.

In 1882 I was appointed the first Director of Agriculture in the Central Provinces, and entrusted with the task of inaugurating the new Department there. I was sent to other Provinces to see what had been done. The greatest progress has been made in the North-west Provinces and Oudh (now known as the United Provinces); and I remember the sense of hopefulness with which I returned to the Central Provinces to take the work in hand under my old Chief, Sir John Morris. But I was withdrawn from the work by one of those accidents which so often interfere with our plans in India, the sudden illness of the Chief Secretary, to whose office Sir John Morris transferred me. On my advice, Sir John sent for Mr. (now Sir Bampfylde) Fuller, then Assistant Director in the North-western Provinces, who had shown me over the work that was being done there.

Sir Bampfylde came with that unbounded energy that has

always characterised him, and full of zeal for the new work with which his association with Sir Edward Buck had inspired him; and the Department, in which Settlement work and Agricultural work were then united, was soon in first-rate working order. It was reserved, however, for the famine to turn more earnest attention to the agricultural part of the work, especially in regard to schemes for irrigation. But I must not allow myself to be drawn into reminiscences of the tours over the Province which I took with my old friend Sir Reginald Craddock, now its Chief Commissioner, and Mr. Harriott of the Public Works Department, now one of his secretaries, and of the great schemes which we planned and which they have carried out.

One matter which has long attracted the attention of Revenue officers and is now the special care of the Agricultural Department is the question of financing agricultural improvements. The lesson learned by the Government of India is well and briefly expressed in the following sentence from the Report of the Famine Commission, presided over by Sir Anthony (now Lord) Macdonnell: "We attach the highest importance to the establishment of some organisation or method whereby cultivators may obtain, without paying usurious rates of interest, and without being given undue facilities for incurring debts the advances necessary for carrying on their business."

The Agriculturists' Loans Act had been passed years before, the object of which was to enable the Government to give cheap loans in times of need. But it was too restricted in scope and too rigid in method to be very successful. At the same time it was distinctly contrary to the interests of the money-lender; and he made himself so objectionable to the cultivator in regard to other debts, that he was able, very often, to induce him to refrain from availing himself of the help of the Government. It is to the Madras Government that we owe the initiation of a system which seems more likely to meet the difficulty than anything that has hitherto been attempted.

The very question stated in the extract from the Famine Commission Report just quoted had engaged the attention of many philanthropists in Europe half a century before. And when Sir Frederick Nicholson was, under the orders of the Madras Government, making a special inquiry into the possibility of establishing "Land Banks" and "Agricultural Banks" in that Presidency, the scheme which had succeeded in Europe attracted his attention. The Raiffeisen system is well suited for country districts, and is therefore primâ facie well suited for an agricultural country like India; while the Schulze system is adapted to town life. The Government of India passed in 1904 "The Co-operative Credit Societies Act," which recognises both these systems.

The Limited Liability Societies are confined to those established among traders in towns, where want of intimate acquaintance with one another renders the members unwilling to accept unlimited liability. On the other hand, in rural villages, where all the people are acquainted with one another, where each can watch and know the doings of his neighbours, unlimited liability is perfectly reasonable. Experience shows also that it is the only possible foundation for successful work; and it is entirely consistent with the history and traditions of village life in India. The Village Community has always been regarded as a homogeneous body, and it is entirely in accordance with Indian sentiment that the Legislature has in this Act laid down the principle of unlimited liability for work in rural tracts.

The Raiffeisen system is wonderfully adapted to the democratic character of the Indian Village System. Even now there is a clear recognition of the common interest; and it is an essential feature of the old system that this common interest should be safeguarded by the Panchayat. Co-operation in the advancement of this common interest is still a recognised duty, although the recognition is not so strong as formerly. It is not wealth only that gives influence and position in the Indian village; it is rather sound common sense and wisdom, and a character for probity and uprightness. In their own villages the majority of the people have a character for honesty, which would much surprise those who know them only in the law courts. This character for honesty, this mutual confidence in a community, is the best basis of any sound system of co-operative credit.

There is not much capital among the villagers generally; but there is that which is more necessary than capital to the unlimited liability of the Raiffeisen system. It demands a restricted area of operation; a thorough acquaintance of the members with each other; a consequent readiness to incur unlimited liability in respect of the operations of the Society; no shares and no dividends, and consequently no private as opposed to common interest; readiness to render gratuitous service; strong public opinion in favour of rectitude in dealings with one another; repayment of loans from the profits or savings affected through the loan; and an indivisible reserve fund. These requirements are precisely what can be secured under the Indian Village System.

One of the ultimate tests of the success of the movement will be the ability of the banks to attract local capital. The capitalists are to a large extent the money-lenders, who did not at first look with friendly eyes on an institution which they suspected as having a tendency, if not being actually designed, to drive them from the field; but the capital even from this source is steadily increasing; and in many places local capitalists now readily deposit money in these banks. The money-lender is not necessarily the enemy of the public interest. The bad system which had grown up, as already described, had largely thrown him into an unfriendly position towards the community; but this is not consistent with the true spirit of Indian village life.

Joint Stock Banks are also being gradually brought into the movement as a financing agency. When I last examined the matter in Bengal, about 50 per cent of the capital of the Village Societies was already supplied by outside investors and Joint Stock Banks lending them money on business terms. The establishment of several central institutions has also greatly assisted individual societies in maintaining their own position. Such institutions are ordinarily formed by a combination of individual societies on the joint stock basis. They have more easy access to the money market, and are able to raise money on more favourable terms than individual societies. They have also another very important function, that of inspection and control. It is not to the advantage of the ço-operative system that the inspection and control of societies should be exclusively, or even mainly, in the hands of Government: self-reliance and self-help, which are surely among the main objects of the system, must be encouraged.

The system appeals strongly to any one who has studied with interest the traditions and practice of Indian life, and who not only sympathises with, but also admires, the general principles that underlie those traditions. It inspires such men with enthusiasm and hope. In its initial stages, at least, the history of its progress must largely depend on the personal character and influence of the officer in charge of the scheme, and of his subordinates. He must be a man of deep sympathy with the people, well acquainted with their manners and customs, able to go about among them in a kindly, frank, cordial way, and to talk with them in their own vernacular; and if, in addition to this, he has very considerable business capacity, he is an ideal man for the post.

In Bengal, I was able to secure the services of just such a man in Mr. William Gourlay, of the Civil Service, and he has inspired his subordinates with his own enthusiasm. His work has been very successful. The work has been going on in that province for only five years; yet when I last inquired there were over five hundred societies scattered throughout its Districts, including six central institutions, and the combined capital was about six hundred thousand rupees. The movement has hardly passed beyond the experimental stage; but the experiment has been most encouraging; and I trust that the zeal and energy with which it has been so far conducted will be maintained.

Serious and excellent work has been done in the districts

where societies have been formed. Their effect is noticeable already in the lowering of the rate of interest of the village money-lenders, and also in the moral and material improvement of the community. Co-operation has, however, merely touched the fringe of agricultural indebtedness; and it cannot claim to have made any appreciable impression on this vast Province as a whole. It has been necessary to proceed cautiously and to confine work to certain selected areas. The aim is to produce an organisation in which isolated societies, in compact areas in different parts of a District, will be grouped into local unions for the purpose of financial control, and then to link these unions to a Central Bank at District head-quarters. Ultimately it may be possible to establish a provincial bank to which the District banks will be affiliated. Some such system is necessary to enable the movement to stand alone, without Government support.

Such an ideal can only be achieved by an organisation of voluntary workers all over the Province. Mr. Gourlay has been most successful in securing the co-operation of such workers. There is perhaps no work in India that will conduce more to the elevation of the people generally and to the improvement of their economic condition. As Lieutenant-Governor of Bengal it was my privilege to acknowledge most devoted and effective service rendered in this matter by one or two of the most influential European merchants, by some of the most devoted and successful missionaries, and by many Indian gentlemen of position and capacity. There is no work that I can commend more cordially and more confidently to those who seek the good of the most important sections of the Indian peoples.

A good friend of mine, who has studied the subject as much as any man in India, estimates the indebtedness of the agricultural community in India at five hundred millions sterling. I understand that Mr. Gokhale accepts that figure; and I know European business men of much experience who do. Now I have already said enough to show that the people are probably paying twenty per cent. as interest more than they would pay if they were solvent. If so, they are overburdened every year to the extent of a hundred million sterling, or the cost of a South African war every two years. When we get to figures like that we are beyond our depth ; and of course it is only an estimate. But it is worth while trying to conceive what an intolerable burden usurious interest on such debt is on agricultural enterprise, and what the relief would be if the burden were reduced by the demand of reasonable interest. To realise at the same time that this relief would be accomplished through the development of self-help and co-operation fills one with enthusiasm. Men, whether European or Indian, who are interested in the future of the people, may well give themselves to this endeavour ; and if the assistance of a sufficient number of such men can be enlisted, success will unquestionably be attained.

CHAPTER XVI

LOCAL INQUIRIES

Going about among the people, one has so many controversies and quarrels to settle, so many cases to hear either formally or informally (the more informally the better) that he might be led to believe that the native of India is especially litigious. One very often hears this charge made against him ; but it is at least doubtful whether it is not due to a superficial view of the case. There is no doubt that there is a great deal of litigation, and that, in view of the numbers of the population and of the wealth and commerce of the country, there is more litigation than one would naturally expect. This may, however, be due, partly to the alteration in the habits of the people resulting from the system which we have ourselves introduced, and to the passing away of the local influences for peace and justice which used to prevail before our system; partly to the ignorance of our system on the part of the great mass of the community, and to the power which their knowledge of the system gives to the more powerful minority; partly to the centralisation of our law courts and the ignorance of native habits, opinions, and feelings, which far too frequently characterise the Judges; and partly to the improvidence of the people.

In the old days there was no elaborate system of Judicial administration. There was no attempt on the part of the Government to provide for the settlement of all disputes by highly-paid courts. The great majority of the disputes, which now arise among the people of the interior, either did not arise at all on account of the force of public opinion, or were settled locally by men of influence in the village. Our system has undoubtedly tended to deprive public opinion of a great deal of its authority, and has practically set aside entirely the authority of the elders of the village. The result is that disputes arise which would formerly have been impossible inasmuch as public opinion would have condemned the raising of such disputes; and at the same time the settlement of such disputes as arise is carried of necessity to the courts. The wrong-doer does not now go to the elders of the village to press his claim: he is not compelled, and he does not choose, to do so; for he knows that they would be able to take a just view of the case, and that he would in all probability fail to secure his claim, and would, at the same time, damage his reputation and influence among his own people. Or, if the wrong-doer is the man who is resisting a just claim, he declines to submit the case to the judgment of public opinion or to the elders of the village, and compels the claimant to go to court. I think it is largely on this account that the courts have so many cases brought before them which, under the ordinary circumstances of Indian life, would certainly have been settled locally and privately, and which it is most undesirable to have contested before the courts of law.

There is nothing more lamentable perhaps in the administration of India than the fact that the officers who preside in the law courts are animated for the most part by a desire to do right, and believe themselves to form the great refuge of the people against injustice, while at the same time the work they do is regarded by simple people in the interior as very much a matter either of chance, or of the success of somewhat questionable methods. It is a great help to those appointed to administer justice, to conduct investigations into questions of fact, as far as possible, on the spot, or to take advantage of local inquiries conducted by competent and responsible persons. This is exemplified in one of the most important branches of the administration, namely, in the Settlement inquiry as to the rights of the different sections of the agricultural community. There is no officer of Revenue experience who does not know the impossibility of anything approaching to moral certainty in regard to Revenue cases, unless he has the parties before him, and has them before him on the spot. When he is on the spot, sees the matter in dispute with his own eyes, and hears the evidence in regard to that matter in the presence of the villagers, themselves, he has some ground to hope that the evidence given before him is both truthful in itself, and also presented in a manner not calculated to mislead. Otherwise he may be misled by evidence which is deliberately false or which, though in its language apparently truthful, is yet distinctly misleading. This is, no doubt, true in any part of the world; but in our own country there is a strong force of public opinion which condemns, in the strongest and most emphatic manner, the giving of false evidence, and does not approve of the deliberate misleading of the court by the manner in which evidence is presented. In India public opinion is either indifferent or perhaps even inclines the other way. Litigation is a form of warfare; and all is held to be fair in war.

The very simplest illustrations may be given of this. A Civil Surgeon in a certain station in the Central Provinces told me that a pariah (mongrel) dog used to give great trouble to his servants by stealing their food, and often succeeded even in carrying off the meat supply of his own kitchen. He gave orders to his bearer * to let him know at any time when that dog came for purposes of theft; and he promised, for the sake of his servants and for his own sake, to shoot it. One day he heard the sound of a gunshot near his verandah. He was lying down resting after a very long morning in the jail and local hospital. Hearing the sound he sprang up and ran out. He saw the dog lying dead, and his bearer holding a gun which had just been discharged. The dog had lying beside him a small joint of good "club mutton." All the other servants had gone into the bazaar to buy their supply of food, and this servant

* The bearer is the valet: he is sometimes called "Sirdar." In the old days of the palanquin, the Sirdar (headman) and bearers did household work.

was alone in the compound. He told his master that, seeing the dog carrying off the mutton, he had rushed into his study; but not finding him there, he believed that he had not returned from his morning's work. He had accordingly himself seized the gun and run out with it and shot the dog.

A day or two afterwards, his servant told the Civil Surgeon that he was being prosecuted before the magistrate under one of the sections of the Penal Code. I forget whether the charge was one of mischief or of house trespass; but the allegation was that a valuable dog belonged to a resident of the town and that the Doctor's servant had come to the house of the owner, which was about three-quarters of a mile from his master's house, and had, out of pure malice, entered the premises of the owner of the dog and shot the animal. The Civil Surgeon sent his servant to an Indian Barrister, who was one of the leading practitioners in the small local court, and requested him to undertake the defence. At the same time he told his servant that he himself would be prepared to come and give evidence as to the exact facts of the case. He heard nothing more of the case for some time; and then he asked his servant when it was coming on for hearing. His servant replied that the case had been already decided in his favour. The Civil Surgeon inquired whether the owner of the dog had failed to bring forward any evidence; and he was told that, far from this, the owner had brought several witnesses to prove his story; but the servant added, "I brought four witnesses who told the truth."

The master inquired how it was possible that he could have got this evidence, inasmuch as there was no one in the compound at the time; and the servant said that he had ascertained that four men were willing to come and give clear statements as to the facts for eight annas, that is to say, two annas (or at the then rate of exchange, threepence) for each witness, and that the court had heard their statement and had acquitted him of the offence charged. The servant explained his conduct by saying that, when he found that he could get the matter settled in this way for eight annas, he thought it far better to do so than to trouble his master to go to court. Soon after, the Civil Surgeon met his friend the Indian barrister, and asked him about the case. He expressed his fear that, though the true view had been taken by the court, it was taken on the evidence of false witnesses. The barrister replied that that was none of his concern; that he had received a statement of the facts from the Civil Surgeon; and that, though he had some doubt in his own mind as to the truthfulness of the witnesses, he had no doubt as to the facts to which they gave testimony. He, therefore, allowed the court to follow its own judgment.

Here we have an illustration of the fact that false witnesses can be secured to give evidence at an absolutely nominal price: that no one seemed to be deeply interested in ascertaining the truthfulness of the witnesses on the one side or on the other; and that the court was content to deal with the statements of the witnesses by merely counting their heads and declaring that, as there was evidence as strong on the one side as on the other, the charge could not be held to be established. This may be perhaps an exceptionally clear case of the fabrication of false evidence; but it is indicative, if not of the general practice of the courts, at least of the danger to which the courts are exposed. When a man has made up his mind as to what are his rights, he often does not hesitate as to the means by which these rights are to be secured, and is quite prepared to secure them by foul means, if he cannot secure them by fair.

There is another feature of Indian life illustrated by this incident; namely, that false evidence is often used to establish a true story or a just claim. This is a very common thing. Many a good case has been destroyed by it. The statement of one witness is found to be false: it may be proved, for example, that he was not present to see what he says he saw. This discredits the whole case, and no doubt rightly so. But the case may be true all the same; and the other witnesses may be honourable men. The ignorant or prejudiced critic of police work is often among those who should be reminded of this.

LOCAL INQUIRIES

Formerly the Executive officers, in the earlier stages of our administration, were in the habit of deciding cases as civil judges between parties with whom in their Executive capacity they had become more or less acquainted, and of hearing evidence of which their local knowledge and experience enabled them fairly accurately to gauge the value. They may, no doubt, have made mistakes in law which had to be put right by higher tribunals, and they may sometimes have given way to personal bias in favour of persons of good reputation; but they were, at all events, less susceptible to the mistakes into which courts are led by false evidence at the present time. The old system was unsound in principle; and it was right to set it aside. But the new system has very serious disadvantages. The men who preside in the local courts now are too often men who have little or no knowledge of the people among whom they are dispensing justice; and they are led, by the accepted principles of the system which they are administering, to exclude from consideration any little knowledge they may have, and to decide cases entirely on the evidence presented before them, and on the pleadings of counsel on both sides.

Counsel also are in the same way far too often men who have been trained in the distant cities, and now reside at the head-quarters of the courts, without having any such knowledge of the people of the interior as would enable them to judge of their integrity as parties or as witnesses. The ordinary idea of an Indian practitioner is to win his case; he is, as a rule, by no means inclined to investigate the character of his own client or witnesses; and he has not, for the reasons above given, the capacity for treating effectively the case for the other side in cross-examination. The court is, therefore, in far too many cases, left to decide what is truth amidst conflicting evidence of which it is unable to determine the value.

A great remedy for this defect is local inquiry. Once, on my return from leave, I was posted to a certain District in the Central Provinces where there was a cantonment. There had been some friction between the regimental authorities and some influential and ill-conditioned persons in the town. A case had a short time before been brought against a certain officer of the regiment, and he had been convicted and fined. The opinion strongly held by all those who knew him, was that the conviction was erroneous; but the evidence was undoubtedly such as could not be got over.

Just as I arrived, a case was brought against two young officers for having gone to a village to shoot snipe, having assaulted certain villagers, and having been prevented from using their weapons only by having them taken from them. As I was the senior European magistrate, the case had been sent to my court. It was fixed for a date about a week later. On the day following my arrival, which happened to be a Hindu holiday, I went out to the village to shoot snipe myself. I had two or three people from that village and from the next to help me to beat. They did not know me, as I was new to the District. I talked away to them in a friendly way; and we had a very pleasant and successful morning together. At breakfast time I paid the men who were with me, and told them I should resume shooting after an interval of an hour or two, and that I should be very glad if they themselves, or any others whom they chose to send, would help me in the afternoon. They said that they would themselves remain. I had a talk with them in a free-and-easy way, and ascertained clearly the facts of the case which I was about to try.

The two young officers had come to the village to shoot. They had known nothing of the language, and had not been able to explain their wishes to the people. The agent of the non-resident Malguzar had happened to be in the village on business, and had told the people that these young men had no right to shoot there, that they would do mischief, that their guns should be taken from them, and that they should be sent about their business. The guns were handed over to certain men to carry. They retained them, and by signs explained to the young men that they must leave. There was no assault or violence. I took down the names of several of those who told me the story, not at the time they told it, but immediately afterwards, and on the plea that I was willing when I came back to have the same men again; and we parted on most friendly terms.

On the day fixed for the hearing of the case, I found that the witnesses for the prosecution, who were not of my beaters, were accompanied by the village servant, who was one of the men who had been talking with me. So when they came into the court and found that I was the magistrate, they did not tell the story that they had come to tell. The result was that the two young officers were honourably acquitted. The villagers remained my friends, and helped me in sport on more than one occasion afterwards. I did not make public my method of ascertaining the facts. It was quite sufficient for everybody concerned that the case had broken down, owing to the witnesses having an altogether different story to tell from that which was expected; and at my suggestion the Malguzar's agent gave a handsome donation to the local dispensary. A story like this, which is very far from exceptional, indicates the difficulties with which the courts have to contend, difficulties which, if known to the judicial authorities generally, are in my experience not fully realised by many of the Judges.

I shall discuss later on the work of the police, and shall refer to the criticisms often hurled at them by irresponsible persons, who are wholly ignorant of the constitution of the force and of its methods of working. Sometimes such criticism is made without due consideration by Judges who ought to know better than to condemn men unheard. I do not propose, therefore, to touch here on this subject at any length. But I should like to say that there is one point in which the police have a great advantage over the courts, viz., that they conduct their inquiries on the spot. The whole question turns on the character and capacity of the officer making the inquiry. This is never to be forgotten. If a low class, unintelligent, and possibly corrupt person is entrusted with an inquiry, it is not likely to be satisfactory; and the authority which would entrust an inquiry of any importance to such a person is much to blame: the Police Commission insisted on this most emphatically. But if an intelligent, upright, and well-trained officer is conducting the inquiry on the spot, the chances are that the inquiry is satisfactory, and the conclusions are probably correct. There may be mistakes made; but the chances are in favour of correct conclusions.

It is well that any police officer, however upright and capable, should have to establish to the satisfaction of independent Judicial authority any charge which he holds to be proved. But, on the other hand, if the Judicial authority is not satisfied, he should at least abstain from ill-considered denunciation of the police officer, and recognise any good work he has done, though not accepting his conclusions. I believe that one reason why Judicial officers often fail to do this is, that they are ignorant alike of the whole conditions of village life, and of the constitution and practice of the police force. If they knew how much easier it is to arrive at the truth on the spot, and how earnest are the efforts now made to make police investigations satisfactory, they would not indeed convict prisoners of whose guilt they were not themselves convinced—they could not do that; but they would hesitate to denounce the police on one-sided statements made in court.

There is another branch of inquiry in respect of which the ignorance of local circumstances and of general administration very materially detracts from the efficiency of the courts in administering justice. There is nothing more pitiable than to see an officer with no Revenue experience deciding a case of tenant right or of fixation of rent in a court at head-quarters. He has never looked carefully at a field or examined a crop; and yet he is called on to decide as to the tenant's status and the rent he should pay, on the evidence of contradictory witnesses of whose evidence he cannot hope accurately to estimate the value. The results are often most injurious to the district. This can be best illustrated perhaps by reference to experience of a definite kind. In the Chota Nagpur Division of Bengal, when I first visited it, I found that the action of the civil courts was operating to dispossess of their rights in the land that section of the agricultural community which was the most deeply interested in it, and at the same time the weakest and most ignorant. It is for the defence of the rights of the weak as against the strong that our courts exist; and yet the action of the courts in that Division was favouring the strong as against the weak, and depriving the true cultivators of the soil of their rights and interests in it, in favour of those who were many of them aliens, and all of them powerful.

The cause of this was simply that these powerful persons were able to secure good legal advice; they understood the procedure of the courts; and they knew both how to present their claims in a plausible way, and what kind of evidence was required to support these claims. Their unfortunate opponents were ignorant of the procedure of the courts, lax in their attendance at court, and unable to secure proper legal advice. There was one member of the Bar, who with great self-denial devoted himself, out of a desire to see justice done, to protecting the rights of these ignorant cultivators. He encouraged them to come to him, and took their cases either for nothing or at nominal fees, although he was a man quite able to command a lucrative practice. But, generally speaking, the members of the Bar were naturally inclined to take up only the cases of those who were able to pay high fees and to explain their cases intelligently.

Meanwhile, the courts were passing decisions upon the evidence submitted to them, without any regard to the real facts of the case, although in many instances the facts might have been easily ascertained. At the very time that such injustice was being done in the courts as tended to excite discontent and unrest among the agricultural community, a Record of Rights was being prepared by the Executive officers of the Government at enormous expense. Experienced Revenue officers were engaged in local inquiries, conducted on the spot, in the presence of the people, with all parties represented. These inquiries were designed to ascertain and record the rights of the different sections of the agricultural community. Although the Judges of the courts were meeting these Revenue officers in society every day, and were perfectly well aware of the inquiries that were being carried on, they closed their eyes to these inquiries and decided their cases entirely on the evidence produced before them in court—evidence which they ought to have known to be a most unsatisfactory basis for their decisions.

The action I took was simply to appoint a careful officer, who was admittedly one of the ablest lawyers of the Judicial Department, but who cared at least as much for the substance of justice as for its forms, to be Judicial Commissioner of that Division. After he had taken over charge, he met the Revenue Commissioner, and the principal Settlement Officer at a conference at which I presided ; and the whole matter of the rights of these agriculturists and of the current Settlement operations was thoroughly discussed. Mr. Carnduff, the Judicial Commissioner to whom I refer (now a Judge of the Calcutta High Court), had had a distinguished career as a Judicial officer in Bengal, and as Under Secretary and Secretary of the Legislative Department of the Government of India, and had the confidence of the Judicial as well as of the Executive officers of Government, owing to his soundness of judgment and his high legal attainments. He made an arrangement whereby all the Judges dispensing justice in the civil courts of that Division were invited to attend a series of lectures by the Settlement Officer on the principles and practice of Settlement work, so that they might understand what was the nature of the inquiries that were being made, and of the Record of Rights based on these inquiries. The result was a vital change for the better in the practice of the courts.

The same principle was, with the consent of the High Court, applied to a considerable extent throughout the whole Province. It was arranged that Judicial officers of original jurisdiction should be placed on special duty with Settlement officers to study settlement, when their services could be spared from their own special work. I have no doubt that this will tend greatly to the practical improvement of the administration of justice in cases between landlord and tenant, and other cases affecting the agricultural community. Surely the necessity for such action in this particular class of cases is only an indication of the importance of practical knowledge of the people, their customs and their interests, on the part of the officers engaged in the administration of justice. It is impossible without grave injury to the interests of the people to leave the administration of justice in the hands of men whose training consists only in the study of law books, and who are without that knowledge of men and of customs which intercourse with the people is necessary to supply.

There could be no more fatal error in Judicial administration in India than to suppose that the lawyer trained in English law is *ipso facto* able to dispense justice in the Indian courts. Yet it is an error that prevails far too widely, and is difficult to eradicate. It is of great interest in this connection briefly to recall the history of the formation of the High Court. Formerly there had been two Appellate Courts existing side by side, an arrangement which led to difficulties which are fully described in Ilbert's "Government of India," as well as in the Parliamentary Debates. In introducing in June, 1861, the Bill "for the purpose of forming one instead of two Superior Courts in India," Sir Charles Wood thus explained the position.* "There is the Supreme Court, consisting of lawyers and Queen's Judges sent out from this country, which has complete jurisdiction over the three Presidency Towns of Bengal [*i.e.*, Calcutta], Bombay, and Madras, and exclusive criminal jurisdiction in important matters over Europeans, in whatever part of India they may be. There is also the Sadar (or Chief) Court. That is a court of appeal for all the courts in the country, whether they are presided over by natives or by Europeans (*i.e.*, members of the Civil Service); and it also exercises over these courts a sort of superintendence, or what may be called the functions of

* Hansard's Parliamentary Debates, Vol. CLXIII, p. 647.

a Minister of Justice. In the evidence which was given before the Committee that sat on East Indian affairs in 1852-3, a strong opinion was expressed by those most competent to give an opinion, that it was desirable, with a view to the better administration of justice in India, that those two courts should be consolidated into one, which would unite the legal knowledge of the English lawyers with the intimate knowledge of the customs, habits and laws of the natives possessed by the Judges in the country."

This last clause is of immense importance. It was a wise and accurate statement of the circumstances and necessities of the case. It was reiterated in the following clear declaration of the intention of the proposed change: "The present Supreme Court consists entirely of Queen's Judges sent from this country, while the Sadar Court consists entirely of members of the Civil Service, who have risen through the successive stages of the Service, but who have not necessarily had the slightest legal training. With their great knowledge of local habits and customs will be united the legal training and knowledge of the English, Scottish and Irish Bars. Their knowledge of native habits and customs will be of the greatest assistance in guiding the opinions of the legal members of the court; and the union of these two classes of Judges will constitute a far better court than would be formed by either separately."

Fifteen was fixed as the maximum number of Judges under the Charter, and the Bill provided that one-third of the Judges should be barristers and one-third civil servants, leaving it to the Government to choose the remaining third from either of these two classes, or from natives or other qualified persons. Sir Charles Wood opposed an amendment by Mr. Vincent Scully to provide that one-half of the Judges (instead of one-third) should be barristers. He said, "To insist on one-half of the Judges being barristers would give the lawyers an undue proportion"; and the amendment was negatived.

These principles are as important now as they were then. A man trained in England is just as ignorant of local habits and customs now as then; and knowledge of these is as necessary as ever. If modern conditions demand more of legal training than formerly on the Bench, the necessity should be met not by reducing the number of civilian Judges, but by improving their legal training. Men with Indian and local knowledge are as necessary as ever.

The Bill was also clearly explained by Earl de Grey and Ripon ;* and there are two sentences in his speech which are relevant to the matter I am now discussing, and well worth quoting. "A very necessary and salutary provision was made for sending Commissioners to try cases in parts of the country distant from the ordinary courts; and also for the exercise by the High Court of a general supervision over the other courts in the country, which would place the Chief Justice somewhat in the position of a Minister of Justice. He believed that this measure would improve the administration of justice in India, strengthen the highest Court of Judicature in that country, and elevate the character of the other courts by placing them under its supervision."

In this connection, it is to be added that, in introducing the Bill, Sir Charles Wood had stated as one of its objects,† "that in important cases occurring in the various districts, justice as in this country should be administered on the spot by a trained Judge." He added, "At present, if an Englishman commits a crime which may subject him to serious punishment, he and all the witnesses must be brought to Calcutta, and the case must be tried there. In future an English Judge going into the country will be able to try these cases. At present when a crime is committed up-country by a European, the necessity of bringing him to Calcutta amounts in many cases to an absolute denial of justice. It may be impossible in a country like India to bring justice to every man's door; but at all events the system now proposed will bring it far nearer than at present, and where criminal offences are committed by a European—happily such offences are rare—the impartial

* Hansard's Parliamentary Debates, Vol. CLXIV, p. 1050.

† *Ibid.*, Vol. CLXIII, p. 653.

administration of justice on the spot will produce a most desirable influence on the minds of the natives."

All this is to my mind of vital importance. It has been, however, in regard to certain points almost, and in regard to others entirely, lost sight of. The personal supervision of the lower courts had, at least in Bengal, entirely fallen to desuetude; and it has only been revived of recent years with great difficulty. Even now any personal inspections are sporadic in character. Control and supervision exercised only by means of tabular statements and returns cannot but be imperfect and ineffective: the systematic personal visitation of competent Judges is absolutely necessary. Then, again, there is no such thing as going on circuit, or trying cases on the spot. This is to be deplored on the ground stated by Sir Charles Wood, that the impartial ad-administration of justice on the spot greatly impresses the native mind. It is also deplorable because it necessitates the transfer of some important cases to Calcutta, and leads to the transfer of many other cases on the flimsiest excuses; and such transfers are still too frequently nothing else than "a denial of justice." A Judge ignorant of local conditions tries such a case with a Jury equally ignorant; and the spectacle cannot fail to be, in not a few cases, far from edifying. Besides this, the present system involves another loss, referred to in paragraph 29 of the Despatch accompanying the first Letters Patent (1862), which points out that the trial of cases by competent Judges on the spot will be an object lesson to the local courts and "will materially tend to their greater efficiency."

The despatch left the responsibility for carrying out this important measure to the Governor-General in Council; but the Chief Justice was to be "habitually consulted in the matter." Few men who are acquainted with the administration of justice in the interior of Bengal will fail to regret that no action has been taken to carry out this policy. The majority of the Judges of the High Court are ignorant of the interior; and the people of the interior have no personal knowledge of the High Court. In India such a state of things has only to be understood to be condemned.

CHAPTER XVII

THE POLICE

In the last chapter I have made a brief reference to the police. I shall devote the whole of this chapter to that subject, of which I have had special experience. Perhaps the most interesting portion of my service in India was the year (1902-3) in which I travelled all over India, as President of the Indian Police Commission. This Commission was described by Lord Curzon's Government as a strong and representative Commission, and was appointed to inquire into the state of the police throughout India. At the time I was appointed President, I was Chief Commissioner of the Central Provinces. My colleagues on the Commission were—Sir Edward T. Candy, a distinguished judge of the Bombay High Court, the Maharajah Bahadur of Darbhanga, the wealthiest and one of the most powerful of the nobles of Bengal: Mr. S. Srinivasa Raghavaiyangar, a Madras Indian of great distinction ; Col. J. A. L. Montgomery, a Commissioner in the Punjab: Sir Walter M. Colvin, the leading criminal barrister in Allahabad ; and Mr. A. C. Hankin, Inspector-General of Police under the Nizam's Government, and formerly a successful police officer in the British service. The Judicial service was represented by Sir Edward Candy, and the Bar by Sir Walter Colvin ; the Executive service by Col. Montgomery, and the police by Mr. Hankin ; while the Indian views and experience of police work was well represented by two Indian gentlemen from Bengal and Madras. The Secretary to the Commission was Mr. (now Sir) Harold Stuart. We had a delightful time together. We had differences of opinion, of course; but we never had any discord. We were all anxious to find out the truth and to state it plainly.

The plan of our operations was as follows. Under orders from the Government of India, every Local Government had been called upon to appoint a local committee to investigate the state of the Police and submit a report. That Committee consisted in each Province of a District Magistrate and a District Superintendent of Police, with the addition of a Sessions Judge for all the larger Provinces. That committee submitted their report to the Government of India, through their own Local Government, which stated its views on the contents of the report and on police administration generally. These reports, with the letters of Local Governments, were forwarded to the Police Commission as soon as that body was constituted. As soon as these reports were read by the members, the Commission met and settled general lines of enquiry, and drew up a series of questions to be issued to witnesses. These questions were forwarded to witnesses who had been designated by Local Governments, and also to a few who were known to members of the Commission themselves. Witnesses were also invited to add anything they thought worthy of the attention of the Commission. At the same time a notice was published in the English and vernacular newspapers of every Province calling on any one who was desirous of giving evidence to apply for a copy of the questions and to submit answers to the Commission. Many availed themselves of this opportunity, especially in the Province of Bengal.

All the replies received from these different classes of witnesses were carefully examined by the Commission, who selected for oral examination those witnesses whom it was desirable to examine with a view either to the elucidation, or to the completion, of the evidence contained in their written replies. These witnesses were examined, during the Commission's tour, at convenient centres fixed in the different Provinces. Six hundred and eighty-three witnesses sent in written replies. Two hundred and forty-four of these, and thirty-five others, were examined orally. In the course of its tour, the Commission visited every Province in India except Beluchistan. It also visited all the four police training colleges in India and many police stations and offices.

As soon as the work in each Province was finished, there was a conference with the Local Government. Certain local officers, selected by the Government, were sometimes present at that conference; but ordinarily it was confined to the Head of the Government and his Executive Council, if any, on the one side, and the members of the Commission on the other. At that conference the evidence which had been received in the Province, and the impressions formed by the Commission on that evidence and on its inspections, were fully discussed. And, finally, there was a conference at Simla with all the Inspectors-General in India to discuss certain questions of procedure, discipline, and statistics.

The report was submitted on the 30th May, 1903, and published as a Parliamentary paper after the orders of the Government of India on it, contained in Home Department Resolution No. 248-259, dated 21st March, 1905, had been issued. The Commission had inquired into the adequacy of the organisation, training, strength, and pay of the police force in every Province; the arrangements for reporting crime, and the work of village officers and the rural police; the system of investigating offences; the suitability of the statistical returns; the general supervision of the magistracy over the police, and the control of superior police officers; the railway police and the inter-provincial police arrangements; and the attractiveness of the service to the proper class of natives. The report was unanimous, except that the Maharajah Bahadur of Darbhanga differed, to some extent, in regard to two questions, viz., the relations between the District magistracy and the police department, and the system of recruiting for the higher grades. As to the former, his recommendation was that there should be no connection whatever between the magistracy and the police. His view was based mainly on misreading of the Indian law on the subject, and a misconception of the state of things in England; and it was unanimously rejected after full consideration by his European and Indian colleagues. The other point on which he differed was that he proposed that the higher ranks of the service in India should be recruited by open competition, a view which did not commend itself either to his colleagues in the Commission or to any of the Governments concerned.

It was very striking to find in the course of our work in every Province of India how thoroughly alive all the best officers of Government were to the abuses which prevailed in the police, and how eager they were to see them remedied. No one among the non-official community who had suffered from police oppression or police blundering spoke more strongly about the necessity of reform than many of the police officers and magistrates who were examined. The Commission submitted a report which certainly showed that the state of the police was in many respects unsatisfactory, and proved the clear necessity for far-reaching reform. But this report was based, not on ill-judged or ill-informed statements made by prejudiced persons outside the force, but mainly on the statements of experienced Magistrates and police officers as to the difficulties against which they had to contend, and the evils against which they had constantly to be on their guard.

There still remained about the lower grades of the force, to some extent, the traditions of the old native system, where extortion and oppression had flourished unchecked. In these older days before our rule, village watchmen, and heads of villages, and even higher officials had connived at crime, and had harboured offenders in return for a share of the booty. Immunity from robbery and theft had been purchased either by a kind of tax paid to the criminal classes or by shelter afforded to them on the condition that they confined their operations to strangers. These things are not mythical stories of a forgotten past. In the course of my own service I have known places in which watchmen were employed who belonged to the criminal classes: so long as their employer paid them, he was safe from molestation. I have also known a case in which the ruler of a Native State gave shelter to dacoits on condition that they committed no robbery in his territory, but confined their operations to the neighbouring British Districts and gave him a share of the spoil. Under British rule great improvement had taken place; but it is not easy to get rid of such traditions.

A Commission in 1860 had done much to improve the police, and Local Governments and local officers had struggled more or less persistently to effect further reform. But reform is not easy to bring about in India; and the old traditions affected the work of the police in the most serious manner. The people are patient and not very ready to complain; and the low-paid official is sometimes a great scourge to a country-side. None but the officers well accustomed to go about amongst the people fully understood the state of things. There were certain special reasons also why the system introduced by the Act of 1861, based on the report of the Commission of 1860, had not succeeded. It was on the whole a wise and efficient system; but it had failed to accomplish what was expected. The reasons are set forth in the Report of the Police Commission of 1902-3.

The question had been too big a one to be dealt with by Local Governments. No Local Government could propose the far-reaching reforms and the great expenditure necessary to bring their police administration up to the standard of efficiency which modern conditions demand. It was a brave and statesmanlike act on the part of Lord Curzon's Government, in view of the strong representations made by Local Governments from time to time, and specially by Sir John Woodburn, my predecessor as Lieutenant-Governor of Bengal, to appoint a Commission, and determinedly set themselves to face and deal with the question.

There was no doubt left on the minds of the Commission as to the principal abuses which prevailed, nor was there much doubt or hesitancy as to the principal remedies which should be recommended. The abuses were frankly and clearly indicated, and the remedies were strongly insisted on. The subject was far too serious to be lightly treated. The recommendations of the Commission mainly affected the class of officers who should be allowed to investigate offences; the recruiting of such officers, their training, and the supervision to be exercised over them; the constitution and treatment of the village police, that is to say, of the village officers entrusted with certain police functions; the pay and position of the regular police; the investigation of offences, involving the establishment of a Central Criminal Investigation Department for each Province and for all India, to cope with the great developments of crime in modern times; and the pay and prospects, and general attractiveness of the higher grades of the service, so as to secure thoroughly competent Europeans and a much higher class of Indians than there had been before.

Throughout the whole of their investigations the Police Commission found that the lower grades of the police were looked upon with suspicion by the people generally, and that the officers of the lower grades, who had for the most part been promoted from the ranks, were, to a large extent, men of low position, inferior education, unworthy traditions, and inadequate training. The higher grades of the police were generally regarded with much more confidence. It was particularly pleasant to find that even the witnesses who spoke most frankly, not to say bitterly, were always bound to admit that the European superintendents* at least were, as a class, entirely beyond the influence of corruption, though they might sometimes be, according to these witnesses, not careful and efficient enough in their work, and too much in the hands of their subordinates.

The reforms which the Commission suggested involved a very large increase of expenditure on establishments, due to the necessity for giving much higher pay to the whole force,

* The superintendent corresponds to the chief constable of the county at home.

from the lowest to the highest grades. It also involved the recruiting of men of a much superior class for all appointments, from inspectors upwards. The effect of such improvement in the system of recruiting in other departments, notably in the Judicial Department, had been found most excellent; and their proposals were made by the Commission in the spirit of hope. They almost entirely commended themselves to the Government of India and to the Secretary of State. The financial burden, though enormous, was cheerfully accepted; and the results have been far more quickly realised than the most hopeful of the supporters of these reforms ever expected. The difficulties with which the police have had of late years to contend, both in respect of sedition and of the extraordinary development of crime adjusting itself to the development of civilisation, have been enormous and unprecedented. These difficulties would never have been successfully grappled with but for the wise statesmanship which led to the thorough inquiry of 1902-3, and to the acceptance of the necessary reforms notwithstanding the great financial burden involved.

When the conduct of the police force is considered, and when very unfavourable criticisms are made, it has to be borne in mind that the men of the lowest ranks of the force, who have been scattered all over the country, were of the poorest and most ignorant of the people and had not a full living wage. This was one of the evils to which the Police Commission drew particular attention. This state of things has been already improved to a considerable extent in every Province of India. It is not easy to estimate the evil done by these ill-paid and inconsiderate, if not often ill-conditioned, underlings in rural districts. The experienced officer knows what mischief such men, clothed with the authority of chaprasis* or constables, do in creating an unfavourable impression of Government among the people.

On one occasion I was on tour in the Balaghat District, when I was Chief Commissioner of the Central Provinces. I found in the remoter parts many complaints of the exactions and

* Orderlies, literally "men with a badge."

tyrannies of the constables and forest or Revenue chaprasis. One ryot (cultivator) told me that at the beginning of the rains he was ploughing his field by the road through the jungle. A policeman came by, who wanted to have a companion and guide on his way. He insisted on the ryot going with him, and would not even allow him to take his bullocks to the village. When the ryot returned he found that one bullock had been killed by a tiger, and the other had broken its rope and fled. Some time afterwards he found that it had been auctioned at a distant cattle pound, and that most of the proceeds of the sale had been utilised to pay pound fees and feeding charges. He had made no complaint until now, when a European officer came by. There were complaints all along the road of the exaction of gratuitous services of an irksome and oppressive kind by these officials. This is an illustration of what one finds too often in the interior. Such acts of oppression create a most unfavourable impression, and sometimes lead to the desertion of villages near the high road. Officers have to be constantly on guard against them, and to put them down with a strong hand.

It has, however, to be remarked that, despite these acts of oppression, which are not so rare as they might be, and despite many petty exactions and occasional instances of gross misconduct, it is not true that the people hate the police. It is a singular fact, of which the Police Commission had evidence in every Province, that when the transfer of a Thana* from one place to another is proposed in the interests of the general police administration of the District, the people of the neighbourhood almost invariably petition against its removal. It is recognised that, with all their defects, which must not be underestimated but vigorously remedied, the police are effective in preserving the peace and securing the safety of the community. With the material hitherto composing the force, it would have been impossible to secure this feeling towards the police but for the constant vigilance of the great majority of District Magistrates and superior officers of police. These men

* Police station.

often get little credit from official and unofficial critics for work of which they have much cause to be proud, and for which the people and the Government have much cause to be grateful.

In doing their duty there is a very serious difficulty with which police officers and magistrates have had to contend besides the readiness to give false evidence in regard to any story before the courts to which I have elsewhere drawn attention : that is, the ignorance of the common people of the interior, and the manner in which the subordinate police very often impose on that ignorance. This induces persons who are charged with offences to make confessions, even when they are quite innocent. The subordinate officer formerly entrusted with inquiries, would form his own theory, and then proceed to extract a confession. He did not set himself to prove an innocent man guilty, or to force him to make a false confession; but he thought he had got hold of the right man; and he tried to induce or compel him "to tell the truth."

Very early in my service, I was in quite temporary charge of a District, in which Sirdar Bahadur Rattan Singh was the District Superintendent of Police. Rattan Singh was practically as much a foreigner in the Central Provinces as I; for he was a native of the Punjab; but he had been, during almost all his service, employed in the Central Provinces Police. He was well acquainted with the customs and manners of the people, and had a great deal of natural intelligence; and, though not a highly educated man, he was a very efficient police officer, and had a general reputation for trustworthiness and conscientious discharge of duty. While I was in temporary charge of the District, a murder was reported from a jungle village about twenty-five miles off. The body of the murdered man had been found, and was identified as that of a man who had been going about giving advances to cultivators on behalf of a firm of grain merchants in a neighbouring district. He was known to have money with him for the purpose of these advances; and when his body was found it was manifest that he had been robbed. The body had been sent by the police to the

Civil Surgeon for *post mortem* examination. That officer found that, though it was greatly decomposed and almost devoured by jackals, he was able to certify that the skull had been smashed by some powerful weapon, and that one of the shoulder-blades had also been broken by some instrument, which, from the marks on the bone seemed to have had a sharp point.

No clue to the discovery of the murderers was found for some days. Day by day, as the law required, the reports of the local police were submitted to the District Superintendent and to me. In a day or two a report came, stating that two men had been arrested; that the evidence recorded against them was that they were suddenly found to be possessed of a considerable amount of money, and that they had confessed to the crime. The District Superintendent and I talked the matter over. We thought it was a case that, despite the existence of urgent business at head-quarters, necessitated a visit to the spot.

The Sirdar Bahadur and I accordingly started off very early the next morning and rode together to this jungle village. There we found the local police with the two men in custody. The police had added to their evidence the discovery in the jungle of a lathi (or club) stained with blood, which lathi was identified by some of the villagers as belonging to one of the two men. There was, however, one very remarkable fact about the club, namely, that the bloodstains were on the thin end, not on the thick end. This aroused our suspicions; for it did not seem natural that a man designing to beat another to death would use the thin end of his club. We asked the men about the circumstances; and they told us that they had met the man in the jungle, and that the lust of gain had led them to take his life with the club and remove his purse.

Rattan Singh asked my permission to do something which was not quite regular, namely, to examine the men on oath, proposing to administer such an oath as the men would undoubtedly respect. After some hesitation I agreed, subject to the condition that nothing that they said would be recorded or used against them. They were then called and asked what the circumstances were. No one was present with us at this inquiry except the eldest son of each of the accused: the local police had been sent to a distance. Rattan Singh asked the men to place their hands on the head of these little boys, and to swear by the boys' lives that they would tell the truth. They immediately proceeded to repeat the confession which they had already made; but they were observed to remove their hands from their sons' heads, and were told immediately to replace them.

They then said that they could not tell that story with their hands on their sons' heads. We informed them that it would be in their interest to tell the truth; and they proceeded with their statement. They said that they had come upon the dead body of the deceased; that it was covered with blood; and that they had observed a string purse so bound up in his loin-cloth that only part of it was visible. They had been averse to touching the bloody corpse; and they had pushed the thin end of the club belonging to one of them under the loin-cloth so as to raise it and secure the purse without touching the body. This, of course, explained fully the blood-stains at the thin end of the club. They did not know anything about the cause of death. They were told, however, by the subordinate police officers investigating the case, that the evidence against them was conclusive, and that they would be hanged on that evidence, but that, if they confessed, the Government would probably take a lenient view of the offence and would pass a sentence of a short period of imprisonment. They had accordingly confessed.

They took us to the place where they found the body. A careful examination of the ground, for some distance round the spot where the body had been found, led to the discovery of the clothes of the deceased lying near a pool in a neighbouring stream, and of the footprints of a tiger. The case was ultimately established as one of death by a tiger, which, after killing the man where he was about to bathe, had dragged the body for some little distance, and no doubt intended to make a meal of it later. The fact that these men had found the body and interfered with it had probably roused the suspicion of the tiger, which, with the natural shyness of its kind, abstained from further concern with it. The end of the case was the punishment of the police officers concerned for having induced a false confession. In a way, one was sorry for them. They were zealous officers, and there was little doubt in our minds that they really did believe in the guilt of these two unfortunate countrymen; but they had deliberately, by false statements as to the probable action of Government, led these men to make a confession whereby their lives were imperilled.

This was by no means an exceptional case. I have in mind the recollection of several cases which occurred later, in which the innocence of a person who had made a confession under similar inducements was clearly established. I remember the case of one poor woman, convicted, on her own confession, of killing her new-born child, being released by order of the Chief Commissioner on account of the fact that a child was born to her in the jail while she was still awaiting the confirmation, or (not improbably) the commutation, of the death sentence by the Judicial Commissioner. The personal experience which I had with Rattan Singh was very early in my service, and made a deep impression on my mind which has never passed away. It has often led me to insist on careful local inquiry by thoroughly trustworthy officers in such cases; and it was many such cases, which were brought to our notice on the Police Commission, which led us to insist on investigations being conducted by officers on whose judgment and integrity some reliance might be placed. This is the only effective remedy for such abuses.

There is undoubtedly a great tendency on the part of Indians to confess with a view of escaping the punishment which, through circumstances over which they do not see that they have any control, seems likely to fall upon them. The wife of a very distinguished officer of the Madras Civil Service told me, when I was on the Police Commission, a story which she thought was quite relevant to this part of our inquiry. It was to the following effect. Very soon after she had come from home, as a young lady, to reside with her parents in Madras, she reached their house from the tennis ground barely in time to dress for dinner. She went into the drawing-room and found that her mother had not yet come downstairs, but was in her own room preparing for dinner. She left the drawing-room in a hurry to run and change her clothes. As she was leaving the room she knocked down a little table with a valuable vase on it. The vase was broken to pieces. She lifted the table and then went upstairs, determining to tell her mother when she was dressed. When she came down she found her mother in the act of dealing with the servants about the broken vase; one of the servants had already acknowledged that he had accidentally thrown it down. Before she had heard what was going on, the young lady said to her mother: "I am very sorry about that vase. It was very careless of me. I knocked it down as I was hurrying off to dress for dinner." "But," her mother said, "Ramaswamy, the bearer, has just acknowledged that he broke it."

It turned out that the mother had told the servants that, if they would speak the truth, she would take into consideration any circumstances that might be favourable to the person who had broken it, but that otherwise she must insist on the price of the vase being paid by the servants as a body. The result was that, after some consultation amongst themselves, they had decided that Ramaswamy, who was a very good and favourite servant, should make the confession. He accordingly did so. It may be mentioned by the way that this plan of making a community responsible for the faults of a single individual, who cannot be discovered, is one which is not uncommon in India. It is one which is in accordance with Oriental ideas; but it is certainly one which ought to be adopted with great care. My friend told me the story with a view to showing how, from what might appear altogether inadequate considerations, an innocent person may be induced to confess to a fault.

THE POLICE

The police in the past have greatly erred in attaching undue importance to confessions. The result has been in two respects injurious to their work. On the one hand, a confession made to them, even if true, may be withdrawn before the court; or if it is made before a competent magistrate it may be withdrawn before a higher court. The accused may have regretted his over-frankness, or he may have learned, from persons whom he has met while in custody, that he was mistaken in thinking that a favourable impression would be created by confession. In either case, he withdraws his confession; and, the police having relied too much upon it, the case breaks down. On the other hand, it has sometimes been very injurious to police work to attach undue weight to confessions in that, satisfied with having obtained the confession and accepting it without careful inquiry, the inquiring officers have turned their attention entirely in the wrong direction. These lessons of experience have now been fully learned by the police; and in every part of India clear instructions have been issued forbidding the police to rely upon confessions except so far as they afford a clue to the obtaining of indisputably sound evidence. In this respect, as in many others, the police procedure is immeasurably improved, and their work has become immeasurably more effective.

All this indicates the difficulties with which those who are responsible for the administration of justice in India have to deal. These difficulties affect the police and the courts alike. There are many confessions made by prisoners in the hope of escaping from the meshes of the net in which they find themselves entangled, which are not prompted by the police, but by ignorant and mistaken views in regard to consequences. There is also much false evidence which is due to the desire of an ignorant person to strengthen for himself a sound case or to fill up the details of a true story. The police officer, however capable and however upright, may be misled by such confessions or such evidence, unless he exercises very special care. If he does not exercise the necessary care, he may greatly injure the cause of justice; if he does, he has very special opportunity of benefiting that cause, as his inquiry is conducted on the spot.

The Police Commission were supported by the sentiment of all responsible officers throughout India in thinking that the inquiry entrusted to them was one of vital importance; that their work must be done thoroughly and the truth told unreservedly; and that the opportunity for establishing the necessity for the required reforms must be fully utilised. It was reserved for critics at home to say that the Report was injudiciously outspoken. These men at home did not realise the evils that had to be obviated; nor could they understand how far mistaken economy might perpetuate these evils. We had to show clearly what the people concerned—whether officers or private citizens—found the police to be, and how far it was possible to make the police what they should be. Due allowance was made for exaggeration and over-colouring in the picture presented by some witnesses; but there was no mincing of matters, or under-statement of the facts, in regard to any abuse that was brought to light. Corruption and oppression were freely charged against the lowest ranks of the police; they were less freely attributed to the inspectors and sub-inspectors; while they were practically never alleged in connection with the higher grades. The force, as a whole, was prized or feared mainly as the officers of the higher grades maintained effective supervision and control.

To put the force on a thoroughly satisfactory footing and to remove the principal causes of abuse (which were, under-paying the lowest ranks, an unsound system of recruiting for the upper grades, and employment of men on duty for which they were not trained nor qualified) required an expenditure which had to be very clearly justified. The necessity for that expenditure was established; it has been incurred; and the results even already are excellent. The Commission were encouraged to urge this expenditure not only from Indian experience in other departments, but also from English experience in the police. Both in India in other departments of the Government service, and in

England in the police, courage in facing necessary expenditure had led to the very best results.

English experience is well worth a few words. We obtained and read the "Report of the English Constabulary Force Commissioners," presented to Parliament in 1839. It will repay perusal by those who set no limits to their abuse of the Indian Police. It will supply them with some choice phrases. Men would not in those days prosecute a thief or even report a theft; for that involved "throwing away good money after bad." They would not incur "the trouble and expense which are sustained in pursuing and apprehending felons." "The expense, trouble, and loss of time, in case of misdemeanours, are frequently more mischievous than some felonies." These are mentioned as "the motives to withhold information or abstain from prosecution," and as the causes of the failure to secure "the general support of the community in Police work."

We thought that if the police reform initiated by Sir Robert Peel had in England converted the state of things, described in that report as existing sixty or seventy years ago, into the state of things now existing, earnest efforts to reform the Police of India might in due time produce incalculable benefit. We have not been disappointed. Already reform has begun to tell, although some of the reforms are still in their infancy. The practical necessity for corruption in the lowest ranks has been removed by giving them a reasonable wage. An improved system of recruiting is securing better men for the higher grades. Men are not allowed to make inquiries and do other work for which they are not qualified. They are being better trained in all grades of the force; and the supervision and control are more effective.

It is true that the police are still sometimes harsh and even oppressive towards the people. So they always will be unless they are kept under control. The low-class Oriental official is a miserable tyrant: there are other places besides the East where this is the case. The Report which led to Peel's reforms is somewhat appalling reading; and there are places in Europe still where the police are worse than they are in many parts of India. Wherever authority in the hands of low-class uneducated men is unrestrained, it is abused. The only safety lies in supervision and control. But it is only those acquainted with the working of the police in the interior who understand what efforts are made to prevent abuse, how severely harshness and oppression are generally dealt with, and how immensely the police have improved of late years. Torture is a thing so rare as to be almost unknown, and is dealt with in the severest manner when it is discovered; and in regard to their treatment of the people generally the Indian Police are being trained on the lines laid down for the police force at home. The training schools and the constant instruction of their superior officers have effected a great change in the character of Indian constables.

Most of the denunciation of the work of the police that one now hears is based on the traditions of the days of their most defective work, on the too ready acceptance of tales invented by the criminal classes to cast discredit on police witnesses, and on complete ignorance of the present conditions of the force and of the rules under which inquiries are now conducted and supervised by officers of high character and sound training. The force is not immaculate: it is Indian and therefore human; but there are no well-wishers of India and its peoples who are more anxious to correct error and prevent abuse than the Magistrates of Districts and the responsible police officers of the higher grades. It is as unfair to talk of the Indian Police as some men talk of that force even in the House of Commons as it would be to apply phrases from the Report of 1839 to the London Police of to-day. The Government of India would not have been able to deal with the troubles of the last two or three years but for the splendid work done by the reformed police. Supervision and control will always be necessary. But with these, the Indian Police are capable of most valuable work.

It seems to me very deplorable to see how often the officers who preside in our courts are altogether unacquainted with, and make far too little allowance for, the difficulties against which the superior police have to contend. It is far too common for a Judicial officer, when a case breaks down, to give utterance to adverse criticism and even ungenerous abuse of the police, without reflecting on the possibility of mistakes being made innocently by men contending with the difficulties which the circumstances of inquiries in India too often present, and without any knowledge of, or consideration for, the efforts which senior police officers have made to secure efficiency and thoroughness in their investigations.

This is unjust to the police, who are not on their trial before the courts, and who are thus, often even when innocent, exposed to public obloquy and to such injury in their profession as constitutes not infrequently a serious punishment. It also tends to friction between the Executive and Judicial departments, which is inconsistent with the sound and efficient administration of the country. These two departments have one object, the maintenance of peace and justice in India; and they ought to pull together.

I should certainly be very far from discouraging Judicial officers from criticising the conduct of the police in their judgments, if these criticisms are made on good grounds, and with a due sense of responsibility on the part of the officer making them. Such criticisms are of great value, when their object is to bring mistakes and misconduct to the notice of the responsible officers with a view of improving the administration of the police; and they ought to receive most careful and courteous consideration. On the other hand, the hasty condemnation or denunciation of the police by Judicial officers is much to be deprecated. When unfavourable comments are made on a one-sided representation of the facts, without the police officer concerned having any chance of defending himself, they are unjust; and their most likely effect is to rouse a feeling of resentment and to defeat the only object that a Judicial officer should have in his criticism.

THE POLICE

When in the course of a trial the conduct of a police officer seems open to suspicion or to call for explanation or inquiry, it is necessary that the circumstances should be definitely set forth by the Judicial officer in his judgment or in a separate note, to be referred to the Executive Government, or to the superiors of the officer concerned, for such inquiry and subsequent action as may be necessary. The appearance of unfairness and prejudice in the utterances of Judicial officers is greatly to be deprecated. And the constant, and often unnecessary pillorying of the police by some of the courts is as mischievous in its effect on the administration as it is unjust in principle. The heads of the Executive and Judicial departments ought to be able to concert measures to prevent friction between the officers of these departments. It is an old Oriental proverb that, if you want good work and a straight furrow, you should "not plough with an ox and an ass together."* Men who are working for the same object ought to be able to co-operate and help one another; and friction in public duty ought not to be tolerated.

* Deuteronomy XXII. 10.

CHAPTER XVIII

EDUCATION

THE subject of education is one to which I have been led to give considerable attention during the whole of my service. The District Magistrate in the Central Provinces was in the old days directly responsible to the Inspector-General of Education for the primary schools of his district, and he was also expected to take a very active interest in the higher forms of education. He was assisted in this by any of his subordinates whom he chose to place specially in charge of that department of work, and also by an Indian officer called a District Inspector, who was in charge of the primary schools. The system worked well. No doubt in regard to higher education the department ought to be held primarily responsible, though here also the Executive officers of Government ought to render all assistance possible; but in regard to primary education nothing can compensate for a lack of interest or a want of sense of responsibility on the part of the District Officer. In the higher schools there are pupils, the majority of whose parents have begun to attach considerable importance to the education of their sons and will take an interest in pushing them forward; but if the primary schools are to be well attended the great majority of the pupils will be children whose parents require to be persuaded to send them. My opinion is that, in view of the circumstances of the Central Provinces and the condition of its peoples, education is far more efficient there than in perhaps any other Province in India; and I think that this is due to the effective assistance rendered to the Education Department by Revenue and Magisterial officers.

EDUCATION

I was placed in charge of education by one of my earliest Deputy Commissioners when I was a young assistant, and I have always taken a considerable interest in this branch of work. I do not intend, however, to write on the matter with any assumption of superior knowledge; because I consider that the question is an extremely difficult one, and that the conditions of the question have altered very considerably during recent years. Not only has attention been drawn particularly to the student class by certain very unfortunate events which have occurred, but the particular aspects of education which demand most attention now are not those which occupied us most in former years.

I must say that that which occupied us most in the Central Provinces was primary education. We felt a deep interest in the village school, because we regarded it as of importance to have at least some of the agricultural community as far as possible in every village throughout the country educated enough to be able to read their Village Papers and Accounts, and understand their transactions with their landlords and money-lenders. We regarded this as so desirable that we considered it expedient to use all our influence to make the schools efficient and attractive, and to get the people to take advantage of them for their children. There is one point to which too little attention is generally given, namely, the necessity for making the primary schools more popular by closing them when the parents need the help of their children during agricultural operations. This is done in the glens of Scotland: it is more necessary in the villages of India.

For a long time higher education was practically left entirely to the Education Department. Although District Officers visited the higher schools and colleges they did not, as a rule, consider it their duty to form any particular opinion as to their efficiency or suitability, but simply to encourage them. As, however, the demand for secondary education increased and a large number of boys and young men began to be gathered together in central places, the necessity for taking some steps to secure their physical and moral well-being was pressed upon the attention. It was not enough that the educational officers began to see this necessity. It was realised to be a matter deeply concerning the welfare of the people generally and the executive administration of the province.

It is sometimes said that education has been carried too far in India, that we are educating too many of our Indian fellow-subjects. In dealing with the limitations of unrest, I shall quote figures which show that there is no foundation for such a statement. We are not educating too many; we are still educating far too few. This is true in regard to higher education as well as in regard to primary education. There is no part of education that is being carried to excess. On the contrary, it seems to me that the demand for education, which has most naturally grown by leaps and bounds during recent years, has not been at all adequately met. The result has been that the education provided has become much less efficient than it used to be; the teachers have, as a rule, had to deal, each with far more pupils than he could give attention to; the inspectors and deputy-inspectors have had more schools under them than they were able properly to inspect and control; and boys and young men have been allowed to collect at educational centres without any adequate provision being made for their physical and moral welfare. In all respects the touch between teachers and pupils has become weakened, and the personal influence of the teacher has been less and less effectual for good. In many cases, too, owing to the underpaying and overworking of the Educational Staff, a spirit of discontent has been excited among them which is very serious in its consequences on their work and on their influence over the pupils.

Another great defect of our educational system in India of which parents of all classes are beginning now to complain bitterly, is the absolute want of religious instruction in the Government schools which the majority of the people at least still regard as the most suitable for their sons' education. It does not appear to me that this defect is essential to the educational system as laid down by the Government, but rather that it has arisen through a failure on the one hand to see the serious nature of the evils involved until they pressed urgently on the attention, and on the other hand to carry out consistently and determinedly the principles on which the educational system was based.

The Brahmans have always made a show of learning, and have, indeed, claimed a practical monoply of it. Of course, very many Brahmans are absolutely without education, many of them are mere menial servants; but it is the Brahmans as a class who have in India regarded themselves as the depositaries of learning. I have often thought that in this respect they were not unlike the ecclesiastics of the Middle Ages. The essential difference, of course, is that no one can be a Brahman except by birth. It is not difficult to make out a strong case against the Church of the Middle Ages in respect of the arrogance of the ecclesiastics and their contempt for the laity, as well as in respect of the vices of individuals or of groups among them; but, on the other hand, it is easy to see that in many respects they were a powerful influence for good, and that their education and training raised them in many respects far above the great bulk of the people. But in the Middle Ages the ecclesiastical monopoly of learning involved its neglect by the great body of the people, and meant also the absence of real progress. Even kings ruled who could not read nor write; distinguished soldiers travelled all over the world without learning; the great body of the people trusted to professional help in anything connected with reading or writing; and the general life of the world was wanting in intellectual vigour. That is something like the state of India now.

A writer on Indian affairs has told us that "the Brahmans of modern times are not in any degree more learned than their ancestors of the time of Lycurgus and Pythagoras." If this be true of the Brahmans themselves, it is more emphatically true of the peoples of India generally. While other once barbarous races have emerged from darkness, pressed forward into civilisation, and extended their researches into the arts and sciences in a manner of which the old world teachers and thinkers of the ancient civilisation of India could not have dreamed, her own peoples have stood still. They have made no moral or intellectual advancement: they have been asleep throughout these ages. As one travels about India one sees a strange mixture of civilisation and barbarism. There are the remains of the old civilisation, not only in wonderful buildings and works of art, but also in the elaborate philosophies and laws which have come down through many ages. But these remains are more like the empty walls or crumbling ruins of castles and palaces long deserted and falling into decay, while all around there is gross ignorance and darkness. A beautiful simple life is described as led by many of the people in the Indian Arcadia of olden times; and this is to be found in the villages of to-day. That life is, however, generally characterised by want of education; and the corrupt religion, which has long held sway, has been characterised by practices which our civilisation regards as inhuman and compels the Government to put down with a strong hand.

It is very interesting even now to go to some of the *tols* or seminaries of Sanskrit learning and find the teachers and the students living together precisely the kind of life that is described in the old Sanskrit classics. I once spent a delightful day with the teachers and pupils of the great School of Sanskrit learning at Navadwip. I was most kindly received in the good old way as "the illustrious model of all the Virtues," and they gave me their degree of "Ocean of Logic and Truth," and sent me on my way, after several hours of kindly fellowship, with words of encouragement regarding my work. It is interesting also to go to the indigenous village schools, where a Guru or religious preceptor gathers his pupils round him and teaches them sometimes a smattering of reading, writing, and arithmetic all in the old way of learning by rote, and committing to memory that which in the days when there were no books would otherwise have been lost to the learner.

But interesting as such experiences are, they leave the clear impression that there is little or nothing here of true education. The education as given to any other than Brahmans under the old system was exceedingly rudimentary, and while conveying to a few traders and petty landowners a little useful instruction, it really did practically nothing to educate and develop their intelligence.

It was very much the same with the Muhammadans. The Hindus form the great bulk of the population of India; and the Muhammadan system is in some respects foreign to that country. The Muhammadans, however, must be carefully considered in respect of education, partly because of their numerical importance, especially in the northern Provinces, and also because of the memories and traditions which are bound up with their history. Higher education among the Muhammadans, like higher education among the Hindus, was available for a very small section of the community. Men of learning devoted themselves to the instruction of youth mainly in the Arabic language and the sacred Koran; and as the Hindu dealt mainly with philosophy and law, so they dealt mainly with religion and jurisprudence. Here and there, connected with mosques and shrines, there were little religious schools in which the Muhammadan teachers gave altogether disproportionate attention to the training of the memory and failed really to educate their pupils.

It was with these systems among Hindus and Muhammadans that the Court of Directors of the old East India Company found themselves face to face, when they determined to deal with the matter of education. At first the Company which had become the rulers of India did not accept responsibility for providing popular education. In those days the Home Government did not even accept that responsibility in regard to the inhabitants of Great Britain, but left education to be managed or mismanaged by the people themselves. It was largely due to the great pioneer missionaries, and to a few distinguished statesmen, that education was at last taken up by the Company. In

India it is of the utmost importance that the Government should take the lead in such a matter. It is so still: it was even more so over half a century ago. The people of India had not then acquired—they have not yet fully acquired—the capacity for action on their own account. In great matters they look to the Government at least to lead them; their tendency is to expect the Government to do for them all that is to be done.

This is not always adequately realised; but though much has been done in educating the people in self-government, it will be a long time before the races of India can be left to manage their own affairs, even in regard to the matters which most concern them, and with which they are best acquainted. There are a great many Indians now, especially of the more intelligent and educated classes, who have a very clear idea of certain things that they want in regard to education. I am of opinion that their views ought to be fully considered, and as far as possible carried into effect. They expect this of the Government. They do not expect to have the whole work left to themselves. They want encouragement; they want a lead; the neglect to give it is interpreted as indifference.

In the latter part of the first half of last century the attention of the authorities both in India and at home was seriously directed to the moral and material condition of India; and there remains on record the Despatch of 1854 from the Court of Directors of the East India Company, which laid down in clear, though general, terms "the principles which should govern the educational policy of the Government of India." It set forth, in the words of Lord Dalhousie, "a scheme of education for all India, far wider and more comprehensive than the Supreme or any Local Government could ever have ventured to suggest." Before that there had been neither constancy of direction nor breadth of aim. The annual expenditure upon public instruction had been insignificant and uncertain, and its control had not been deemed worthy of the attention of any department of the State. The Despatch of 1854 was a new departure. This remarkable document starts with this noble declaration,

EDUCATION

"Among many subjects of importance none can have a stronger claim on our attention than that of education. It is one of our most sacred duties to be the means, as far as in us lies, of conferring upon the natives of India those vast moral and material blessings which flow from the general diffusion of useful knowledge, and which India may, under Providence, derive from her connection with England."

The object was not only to produce a higher degree of intellectual fitness, but to raise the moral character of those who should partake of education, to supply Government with servants to whose probity offices of trust might be committed with increased confidence, and to advance the well-being of the people generally. The material condition of the great Empire was to be advanced by the diffusion of the improved arts, science, philosophy, and literature of Europe. The vernaculars of the country were not to be neglected. They were to be utilised as the media of communication of European knowledge to the people generally, leaving the mastery of the English language, as a key to the literature of Europe, to those who aspired to a high order of education.

The responsibility for popular education was accepted both on the general ground of the duty of Government to secure the best interests of the people, and also on the particular ground that in India Government effort was especially required. At the same time, it was laid down that Government could not attempt to supply popular education by its own unaided efforts. The task was too great. It was indeed recognized that the people by themselves could not obtain an education worthy of the name. Government must, therefore, come to their assistance; but the work was not to depend entirely on its unaided efforts. History had shown that throughout all ages both Hindus and Muhammadans had given themselves to the work of teaching according to their lights, and that munificent bequests had not infrequently been made for the permanent endowment of educational institutions. It was hoped, therefore, that Government would be assisted by the people, and a Grant-in-Aid system was set forth.

The details of the administration of the Educational Department, and all the instructions of the Despatch regarding scholarships, textbooks, technical institutions, and female education need not be mentioned. Enough has been said to show how comprehensive a survey was taken of the necessities of the case, with what ability and forethought these were provided for, and the earnest and lofty purpose which animated the authors of this Despatch, the principles of which have again and again been accepted by the Government of India. The Despatch concludes by quoting with hearty concurrence the words used long before by Sir Thomas Munro of Madras, to the effect that any expenses which may be incurred in education "will be amply repaid by the improvement of the country; for the general diffusion of knowledge is invariably followed by more orderly habits, by increasing industry, by a taste for the comforts of life, by exertion to acquire them, and by the growing prosperity of the people."

This is a Despatch that fills me with admiration. It was written by great men at a great crisis in the history of India. I wish that it were better known to those who are making that history now. I cannot deal with it here at length. There are a few points to which I should like to draw attention; but I must pass unnoticed many that are important. Tempting as the subject undoubtedly is, I do not think it necessary to enter into any discussion concerning technical and scientific education. That is being taken up vigorously by the Government of India. There is only one thing which I feel it worth while to state in this connection: that is the strong impression that has grown up in my mind that technical and scientific education, such as will fit men for ordinary technical and scientific work, ought to be supplied in India itself. It will no doubt be necessary to send men from India to Europe for the acquisition of high expert knowledge in certain specialised departments, as it is necessary to send men away from England itself for that purpose. But it is not right that for ordinary education of a technical and scientific nature lads should have to leave their own country. This may be accepted as a general principle. It is especially applicable to the conditions of India. Effort should, therefore, be made to secure, as speedily as possible, a sound technical and scientific system of education in India itself. The people wish it; they would assist the Government in securing it; and it is emphatically in the interests of Government that it should be secured.

Although I cannot take up time with a full discussion of the Despatch, there are among its most important features, three that demand brief attention. These are the high place given to vernacular education, the Grant-in-Aid system and religious instruction.

Firstly, then, the importance attached to vernacular education. It has been humorously said that Englishmen have, to a large extent, modified the great commission of the Founder of Christianity, and have made it run thus: "Go ye into all the world and teach the English language to every creature." The English language is well worth knowing; but the framers of the Despatch were right in relegating it to higher education, and in insisting on the teaching of the vernaculars. They understood how absolutely necessary it was for sound government to maintain touch with the people through their vernaculars, and also how imperfect English education itself must be when the pupil, in all his home life and in all his surroundings, is separated from its spirit and true environment. Unfortunately there has been a tendency, based largely on the views enunciated by Lord Macaulay in 1835, but contrary to the later and sounder views of the Despatch, to starve vernacular education, especially in the higher schools and colleges. The result has been a want of touch between education and the life of the country, which is very much to be deplored. At present there is a revival, to a certain extent, of interest in vernacular education; and I earnestly trust that it may receive more attention in future. To sacrifice the vernaculars to English is to sacrifice the true interests of the vast majority of the people to the doubtful advantage of the few.

Secondly, there is the Grant-in-Aid system. This is of the very essence of sound educational policy in India; because it means that Government will aid local effort and develop self-help, while at the same time it secures the necessary pecuniary assistance of the people in work, the cost of which must be altogether beyond the unassisted efforts of Government in a country where the taxation must of necessity be kept as low as possible. It also enables the people to carry on education on their own lines, so far as these are worthy and efficient, their worth and efficiency being tested by a careful system of Government inspection. I do not for a moment mean to say that the manner in which Grants-in-Aid have been distributed by the Educational Department in the past has always been wise and effective; but the system itself is one which is capable of excellent administration, and is entirely suited to the circumstances of India.

The third point is the question of religion. The Despatch declared clearly in favour of neutrality in regard to religion; but this neutrality was accompanied by a sanguine confidence in the power of instruction in secular subjects alone to kindle a moral ideal, and to touch the springs of conduct. There is no doubt that there is some foundation for this belief, especially as stated by the authors of the Despatch. But their sanguine hopes have undoubtedly proved to be largely unwarranted. There is no one acquainted with the facts who does not admit that Government education in India has somewhat conspicuously failed to influence conduct and character. As has been well said, it has too much resulted in "the mere acquisition by the memory, or superficial understanding, of a body of information, much of it of a character alien to the real human life of the country." A good deal of this result, however, is due not to the principles contained in the Despatch, but to some neglect of them.

In speaking of Christian missions, I shall have to point out how erroneously the doctrine of neutrality has been interpreted by some officers of Government. Nothing could be more ridiculous than some of the action taken by such officers with regard to education. There was one Province in which at one time some of our best English classics were expurgated of all reference to the Divine Being and to Christianity. And, while that was an extreme and exceptional case, something of the same misconception has too often characterised the action of the department regarding religion. The Despatch, on the contrary, while distinctly laying down that no one is to be interfered with in respect of his religious belief, and that religious instruction is in no way to be taken into account in the inspection of educational institutions, also lays down, not only that grants may be given in respect of their educational work to efficient institutions which also teach religion, but that religious books may be placed in the libraries of Government institutions, and that private and voluntary inquiries regarding the Christian faith may be dealt with by the teachers in these institutions. I reserve for my chapter on Christian missions, some of the important sentences of the Despatch in this connection.

The really great provision in the Despatch for religious instruction was, however, the provision of an efficient system of Grants-in-Aid for secular education even to institutions teaching religion. This enabled good Hindu and Muhammadan institutions to receive support, and has led to the establishment of a large number of missionary institutions which receive Grants-in-Aid from Government. These are distinctly missionary in their character. Dr. Duff wrote in 1834: "I for one would not lend myself as an instrument in wasting the funds of the benevolent in Scotland, in teaching young men a mere smattering of knowledge to enable them to become more mischievous pests to society than they would have been in a state of absolute heathenism. On the other hand, if out of every ten who enter the school, even one were to advance to the higher branches of secular and Christian education, were to become in

"BELVEDERE"

The official residence of the Lieutenant-Governor of Bengal at Calcutta. It stands in beautiful grounds in the suburb of Alipur, on the other side of Tolly's Nullah from Calcutta. It is close to the spot where Warren Hastings fought his famous duel with Mr. Francis.

head and in heart a disciple of the Lord Jesus, and were a number with minds thus disciplined, enlarged and sanctified to go forth from the institution, what a leaven would be infused into the dense mass of the votaries of Hinduism."

These words by the great leader of missionary education who was also one of the most influential agents of educational activity in India, are a true declaration of missionary policy in regard to education. Missionary institutions have turned out, as Christian men, some of the finest Indian characters that I have known, men who were esteemed not only in the Christian Church, but by the entire community. And the influence of such institutions has been seen, not only directly in their converts, and in the influence that these converts have exercised, but also in those who, without formally accepting the religion of the Lord Jesus Christ, have been animated by its moral principles.

There are many now who attribute what is unsatisfactory in the results of our educational system largely, if not entirely, to the neglect of religious teaching. Dr. Duff and some of the early friends of education prophesied precisely such results three-quarters of a century ago; and the fore-knowledge of such results undoubtedly influenced the high-minded statesmen who framed the Despatch of 1854. But men in India did not then generally realise the possibility of such results, and they were somewhat careless on the matter. Now, however, among those who are thoughtfully considering the present condition of affairs, there adhere to these views hundreds and thousands among the best men of India: Hindus, Muhammadans, and Christians, Zamindars, and professional men, Government officials and business men. We have recently seen clear and vigorous exposition of the necessity for religious instruction in addresses presented to the Viceroy of India by the Indian chiefs of Native States, and in letters addressed to him by all the important princes whom he consulted in regard to the present state of affairs. It is pathetic to read how they describe "the absence of religious instruction in the schools as a potent cause of wrong ideas."

In British India, also, there is the same feeling. A very

striking deputation was received by the Viceroy in the end of 1908. It was a large and influential deputation of orthodox Hindu noblemen and gentlemen representing the Sri Bharat Dharma Mahamandal, the great Society of orthodox Hindus for all India. The sole object of their approach to the Viceroy was to secure his Excellency's sympathy with their views regarding religious education, so that "nothing will be wanting within your power to help us in our efforts to guide the awakening life of the Hindus throughout India by means of a spiritual religious education until they form a truly compact and noble religious nation, a loyal and peaceful and prosperous people." Similarly strong declarations have been made by Muhammadan associations as to the importance of religion in education. Distinguished individuals also have stepped forward, and strongly stated their views in favour of religious education, discipline, and moral training in schools. The Muhammadan representative of the old dynasty of Murshiabad, himself educated at Rugby and Oxford, the Maharajadhiraj Bahadur of Bardwan, the Maharaja Bahadur of Darbhanga, and others in Bengal have spoken strongly on the subject. The same feeling is shown in the remarkable movements for the establishment of a Hindu University at Benares and a Muhammadan one at Aligarh. To have religious education in a residential University is the main object of these movements. It is a sound aim; but I regret that the Universities should be sectarian.

During my first two or three years of touring in Bengal as Lieutenant-Governor, I was besieged by Indian parents occupying high positions of influence in the interior, such as landholders, lawyers, judges, district officers, and men of business, pointing out to me that they could not obtain a sound education for their sons at their own doors, and that they must, therefore, either train them at home under tutors, or send them to Calcutta or some other educational centre, to colleges where their moral and religious character ran the greatest risk of complete perversion. They implored me to devise some means whereby it might be possible to provide a less dangerous system of education for young men. They strongly approved of the principle of religious neutrality on the part of Government; but they urged that this was surely not inconsistent with devising a system whereby religious and moral training would not be altogether neglected.

This led me to propose the scheme known as "The Ranchi College Scheme." The object of this scheme was to have at Ranchi, which was the most healthy place for Indians of all parts of the Province of Bengal as then constituted, a college far away from the temptations inseparable from life in a great city; to provide in that college a thoroughly sound secular education in arts and sciences; and to surround that college by hostels, all of which would be built by private subscription, and supported by fees and scholarships founded by the benevolent. In these hostels the home life of the student would, as far as possible, be perpetuated under authorities, who would be subject to the supervision of the college authorities, bound to supply, not only physical comfort, but also moral education and discipline, and such religious instruction as the parents might desire. Hindus, Muhammadans, Brahmans, and Christians would each have their separate hostel or hostels. In this way Government would not be responsible for providing religious instruction, but would not interfere with it, except in so far as the maintenance of discipline within the college might require.

This scheme was cordially supported by private subscriptions raised with great enthusiasm. It was accepted by the Government of India and the Secretary of State; but it has not been carried out. The reason alleged for not carrying it out is the want of funds. If, however, more funds were necessary, it would have been easy to raise them; for the people felt very strongly the necessity for such an institution. There are men who feel so strongly on the necessity for higher education for their sons being accompanied by discipline and moral and religious training, that they do not hesitate to send them to this country not for any specialised course of study but in the hope of finding that training here.

EDUCATION

I had a talk in 1910 with a Muhammadan friend who was on a visit to this country. He was an old supporter of the Ranchi College Scheme, and had determined to send his children to the District school there, and then to the college. As the scheme had, to his great disappointment, been given up, he had brought his children, three sons and two nephews, to place them at school in England. He told me that the actual cost for schooling, apart from anything else, was £200 a year for each child. Besides that, he had clothes and other bills to pay; and he had also to make arrangements, at great expense, for the return of the children to India at least once every two or three years, so that they might not become utterly out of touch with their home. Something between £1,000 and £2,000 a year is being spent by this gentleman on the education of his children in England, while he would far rather have had them educated in a thoroughly sound Indian public school and college, such as were proposed for Ranchi. He told me that he would be willing to pay as much as that, if it could be done in accordance with anything like principles of justice in the adjustment of burdens, for the education of his children in Ranchi.

The most important Hindu perhaps at the present time in India was also to have sent his children to the District school at Ranchi, with the intention of letting them go forward in due time to the college. He looked about in vain for a place to which he could appropriately send them in India; and he also has now been compelled to incur the expense and the risk of sending them to England for their education, as well as the certain disadvantage of having them grow up out of touch with India, and with the people among whom their life work must be done.

There was another object which I had in view in proposing this Ranchi College Scheme, which included, as my remarks have already indicated, the idea of a good school at the same place. That object was to secure for the noblemen and great landowners of Bengal a place where they could have their sons educated, and also housed in a manner becoming their station, without sending them to a Chiefs' College, and thus separating them entirely from the traditions and influences by which they will be surrounded in after life, and from the people with whom they will have to do the business of life.

I know one particular case in which the son of one of the most distinguished families in Bengal was to have been sent to the Ranchi College. Instead of that it has been considered necessary now to send him to a Chiefs' College, which is intended for the Feudatory Princes of India. I do not propose to enter into the discussion of the kind of education that is necessary for the Feudatory Princes. The political department must be responsible for the decision in such a case. But I have no hesitation whatever in saying that to send a British Zamindar to be educated along with the future Feudatory Princes of India is an entire mistake. It puts him into a position where he cannot fail to have great difficulty in maintaining his self-respect. However great the position of a nobleman in British India may be, it is different from the position of the member of a ruling house in a Native State.

In respect of Bengal especially, I have not the slightest doubt that to take a young nobleman away from all connection with his own Province, and with those who are to do the work of the Province in future years, is a blunder. In his home life, which may be represented by the hostel in which he lives, he may be apart from others. But in the battle of life he has to meet with them on equal terms and hold his own with them; and he should be prepared for this by attending the same college. The noblemen of Bengal themselves desire nothing less than to have their sons educated in a manner which separates them entirely from other classes, and trains them in associations with which they will have no connection hereafter.

The Ranchi College Scheme was intended largely to provide for the separate home life of persons who, by their position, race, or religion, require a separate home life while attending school or college. It was also designed especially to meet the difficulty of religious education in institutions under the control of Government. Government cannot yet at least separate itself entirely from education ; and it is necessary, therefore, to devise means whereby the education which it provides shall not be divorced entirely from religion. But it must be borne in mind that another and even more important means of providing religious instruction is to do it through aided institutions. Both these methods demand attention and should be fostered. I am very strongly convinced that, unless we provide for religious training as well as for secular instruction, we expose the peoples of India to an unspeakable danger. We do more than this. We educate the youth of India in a manner that is strongly distasteful to their parents.

The people of India are naturally a religious people, and they have a strong belief in the influences of religion and of home life. If we fail to give religious instruction, we shall either find the people of India becoming by our influence, and against their will, agnostic and atheistic in their views, and wanting in religious and moral character; or we shall have them full of an altogether justifiable discontent with our system of education. It may be that they will take education into their own hands. It is not fair to compel them to do this; for, as I have said, the people need the assistance and the leading of Government in a matter of this kind. And, if they do, the strong feeling which at present urges them to appeal to Government for help to supply them with religious education will, when that demand is refused, lead them infallibly into a position of discontent and opposition. I regard the matter, therefore, as of the very highest importance in respect of the future of the people of India.

There has been great advance made in respect of higher education by the Universities Act passed by Lord Curzon's Government. This was one of the special services rendered to India by Lord Curzon. University Education was carefully inquired into by a strong Commission presided over by Sir Thomas Raleigh. On the Report of that Commission the Universities Bill was framed. It became law after the fullest discussion. It has not produced a perfect University system in India; no legislation can do anything of the kind. But it has made it possible to make any improvement for which the authorities have the pluck and the money. The new Regulations framed under the Act have already accomplished much: far more in the time than many of us thought possible. I was the first Rector of the University. I was consulted at every step by the Vice-Chancellor, the Hon. Sir Asutosh Mukerji, Judge of the Calcutta High Court. I saw all his work, and faced the difficulties with him. I have never seen more earnest, devoted, and effective work. No one who was not engaged in the work can understand the difficulty of getting the new Regulations through the Senate. Sir Asutosh was on special duty, and sacrificed his health to his zeal and his unremitting labour.

At that time there was sore trouble with the students. They were not wholly to blame; they had unprincipled and selfish advisers, who took advantage of their youth and inexperience to soil their best impulses by the most ignoble uses. It has been publicly said in the Press that the University neglected this matter. A prominent home writer deplored the fact that the interests of the University were at that time "in the hands of a Bengali Vice-Chancellor." This was an unjust judgment, pronounced in ignorance. Sir Asutosh tackled this matter with courage and wisdom. He and I worked together; and I approved all that he did. We put things right in scores of colleges without making any fuss or martyrising anybody; and we tolerated abuse in no college whatever which was subject to the University.

It is hopeless, however, to try to put things right merely by Regulation and Rule. We must have a proper system of Hostels, and a sound religious and moral training for Indian youth. It will cost money; but I believe that the money will be forthcoming. Men are now alive to the danger. They will help to provide the remedy. Government should be left mainly to deal with Primary Education, receiving there also assistance from the wealthy and benevolent. It is the latter who ought, with the assistance of Government, to provide higher education. The Despatch of 1854 says: "The higher classes will now be gradually called upon to depend more upon themselves." If the call had been made, it would have been answered. Government has greatly erred in not calling on the wealthy and public-spirited for their co-operation. It is traditional with the great families to help education; and much might have been done had they believed that Government would appreciate their help. I have never failed to secure a generous response to any appeal. All they want is to be treated as honoured and trusted fellow-workers.

CHAPTER XIX

CHRISTIAN MISSIONS

I WAS fortunate in falling in, at the very beginning of my service, with excellent missionaries, and in being thus led from the very first to take much interest in their work. In Nagpur there is a Scottish Presbyterian Mission which was founded under somewhat striking circumstances. In the Bhonsla days, in the earlier half of last century, there were troops stationed at Kamptee for the defence of the Resident, and among these there were several Christian officers who felt deeply concerned at the ignorance and superstition which prevailed around them, among a people for whom they had begun to conceive much affection. Some of these men set themselves to collect funds and to use their influence to establish a Christian mission at Nagpur. They applied to the Free Church of Scotland, which was then wrestling with the difficulties caused by its recent secession from the Church of Scotland as by law established. Their request was sympathetically considered, and the Church pluckily set itself to establish this new mission.

Mr. Hislop, who went out as the first missionary to Nagpur, was a man of much culture and capacity. Sir Richard Temple, when the task was committed to him of organising the administration of the newly formed Province (called "the Central Provinces"), found Mr. Hislop a valuable coadjutor. Mr. Hislop's intimate knowledge of local geology, and also of the peoples and tribes of the Nagpur country, as well as his intense interest in education and in whatever tended to the public good, was recognised by Sir Richard Temple, who treated him as a friend and helper in his work.

In many respects Sir Richard acknowledged the obligation under which he lay to Mr. Hislop. There is one interesting fact which may be recorded. Sir Richard was organising the educational department of the Provinces, on the lines laid down in the Halifax Despatch of 1854 and the orders of the Government of India thereon. In his scheme was included one high-class institution in each District, to serve as a model. In the Nagpur District Sir Richard placed this institution at Kamptee, ten miles away from the capital. His reason for this was that there was already an excellent missionary institution in Nagpur, and that Government ought not to enter into opposition with such an institution, but to use its limited resources only where they were really required. When, much later, a Government college was established for the Provinces, it was, in accordance with the same policy, located at Jubbulpore; and the Missionary College was left without a rival at Nagpur, until the increasing demand for higher education led to the establishment there of another aided college. The Missionary College bears the name of Mr. Hislop, who had died before a college department was founded.

When I went to Nagpur, the head of the Mission was the Rev. John G. Cooper. He and his wife had no family, and they lived entirely for their work and for the people of the town and surrounding country. I never knew kinder people, or people more generally beloved. Mr. Cooper's capacity for organisation and his sound common sense and perfect tact enabled him to bring the Mission, in all departments of its work, up to a high state of efficiency; and he and his colleagues were a great power for good in the Central Provinces. One of these, Mr. Whitton, was a great teacher, and under him the College achieved very exceptional success. As Professor and Principal he had great influence over the youth of the Province. It was my duty for many years of my service to keep myself informed of the state of education in the Province, and to watch the career of the students of its educational institutions. I do not think that any man was appointed to the Government service merely because of his having been a pupil either of the Government College at Jubbulpore, or of the Missionary College at Nagpur; but I have no hesitation in saying that some of the best servants of Government that we had, were men trained in the Missionary College. Even when they had not been led to embrace Christianity, they had undoubtedly imbibed principles of the greatest value to Government and to the people.

It was very remarkable to see the great affection that the pupils and students of the missionary institution and college had for their missionary teachers. On one occasion, when Commissioner of Nagpur, I had to go out to see some famine relief measures which were being carried out under the superintendence of the Rev. John Douglas. He had been set aside by the Missionary Council to village evangelistic work, and had his head-quarters at Dhapewara I arranged to start in the afternoon, as soon as my work in office was over, to drive Mr. Douglas in my carriage as far as I could along the high road, and then to go with him in his bullock tonga by the village roads to Dhapewara, where I had sent my tent. When we got into the tonga it was very late; for I had been detained in office. We became so engrossed in talk, that in the dark Mr. Douglas allowed his driver to miss the road, and we found ourselves in a village about five or six miles from Dhapewara.

A Commissioner is a somewhat important personage, and I was entitled, under the rules framed under the Land Revenue Act, to obtain a guide from one village to another in my route when travelling in the District. I went accordingly to the house of the Patel,* explained my position and the circumstances, and asked for a guide. The Patel at once called aloud for the Kotwar † to guide me to a village which lay half-way between his own and Dhapewara. Just then Mr. Douglas happened to speak to me. The Patel, hearing the voice, peered at him in the darkness and said (in Marathi, of course), "You are my old teacher." Mr. Douglas asked his name, and remem-

* Patel is the Nagpur name for the head man of the village.

† The Kotwar is the village servant.

bered him; and they had a friendly talk, to which I listened with great interest. As the Kotwar came up the Patel said, "I will go with you myself to Dhapewara;" and he walked with us the whole way in the dark, talking cheerily and familiarly with us both. He had been prepared to send the village servant half-way with the Commissioner of Division as the law required; but he walked himself the whole way with us from love of his old missionary teacher. I found also that my relations with the people were much improved through my acquaintance with their friend the missionary, and through his presence with me during my inspection.

It is not easy to overestimate the importance of the beneficent influence which missionaries have exercised in India. There are, of course, missionaries and missionaries. There are some men who mistake their vocation; they are by nature unloving and unlovable; and the mere fact that they are missionaries does not alter their nature. They are unsympathetic towards the natives; they are jealous, suspicious, and even hostile towards their fellow-countrymen. Narrow, ill-educated, and wanting in tact and judgment, they probably do more harm than good. Such missionaries are exceedingly exceptional. The pity is that one such man may prejudice an officer against missionaries and their work throughout his whole service; and, apart from the direct mischief that such a man does amongst the people, he is indirectly the cause of great evil by exciting such a prejudice.

There are certain missionaries who, although no doubt well-meaning, forget that not all the information that reaches them is accurate, and that not all the accurate information should be passed on. This leads to much misconception, to friction, and, I venture to think, to injury to the cause they have at heart. It is easy, of course, for an officer to show that he disapproves of such action on the part of the individual without losing his interest in, and much more without opposing, the cause; but it is unfortunately natural with some men to extend to a whole body the judgment passed on the individual. Sometimes, even when one is most firm in declining the intimacy of a mischief-maker, he does not escape the influence of that man's want of judgment. I recall an occasion on which I was attacked bitterly in the Calcutta press for having acted on information said to have been brought to me by a missionary. I suppose that he had given out that he was going to me. As a matter of fact I had refused to receive any information from him, or even to know the subject on which he was said to have come to see me. I did not contradict the newspapers: it is not our habit to defend ourselves from personal attacks. But the incident is illustrative of the mischief which a tactless and thoughtless man may easily do.

My experience, however, has been that the missionary who too readily listens to an ill-report of people round about him—whether European or Indian—or who could see no other view of any set of circumstances than that which is based on the information he receives, is comparatively rare, and that there is much advantage to be derived from friendly intercourse with the missionaries. To them, as a body, we owe the awakening of the conscience of the Government to some of the old abuses of Indian administration. We owe to them a representation before the people of the Christian religion and of the British character, which is higher and better than perhaps any other class whatever has been able to give. We owe also to them some of the best educational institutions in India, and some of the finest Indian characters. I should like to see all missionaries willing to enter fully and with kindly confidence into friendly relations with the officers of Government. They ought not readily to take up an unfavourable impression of the character and conduct of officers of Government, and least of all when these are their own fellow-countrymen. Officers of Government, whether European or Indian, are for the most part animated by a strong sense of duty. And, if the missionary is to exercise any worthy influence on them—whom he is as much bound by his duty to his Master to influence, as to influence any one else—he must acknowledge this.

On the other hand, that officer is altogether unwise who

ignores the missionary. An officer who disregards any source of information in respect to the customs and feelings of the people is unwise; and inasmuch as the missionary has special opportunities of contact with the people, there is special unwisdom in keeping him aloof. The missionary, however, when he is found to be a good and trustworthy man, ought to be far more than a source of information to the Government officer. He can be a most useful coadjutor. Not only his educational work, but also the beneficent aims which animate all his intercourse with the people, are such as to bring him thoroughly into line with a devoted servant of Government. To me it has always appeared intensely unsatisfactory to find a Government officer and a missionary standing aloof from one another and regarding one another with suspicion and dislike. Such a state of things has seemed to me to indicate that one or other of these two was in that respect at least unfitted for the position which he occupied. Of late years, when the country has been visited with plague and famine, the Government has been under special obligation to the missionaries for the efficient and devoted work which they have done ; and in not a few cases the value of that work has been publicly recognised by the Government of India and by the reigning sovereign.

In Nagpur, where I was stationed for many years, I joined the native Church and became an office-bearer in the congregation. I had regularly to visit a certain part of the congregation, along with another member of the Kirk Session, who was an Indian. This enabled me to know intimately the Christian families of the place and their concerns; and I acquired an admiration for the earnestness, simplicity, and high character of many of the native Christians. Our first pastor was the Rev. Mr. Timothy, who began life as a soldier in the 7th Madras Infantry, and looked forward to promotion in the army, as young native soldiers do. At the age of sixteen or seventeen, when a bright, intelligent lad, he was stationed at Raipur, about a hundred and sixty miles from Nagpur. There he met some native converts to Christianity. They told him about the Saviour, and roused his interest in "the new religion." They could not make things quite clear to him, so he decided to travel to Nagpur to see the missionaries. There was no railway; and he travelled by road. He had taken three months leave of absence; and by the end of that time he embraced Christianity and was baptised with the name of Timothy. He returned to his regiment, but became strongly possessed by the desire to do religious work among his fellow-countrymen. He took his discharge and returned to Nagpur, where he became a teacher. Meanwhile the mission established their own training classes for the ministry; and he was trained and duly "licensed," after the Presbyterian manner, to preach the Gospel. Then the Nagpur Christians, who had just been formed into a congregation, called him to be their minister; and he was ordained. He was, for many years, a beloved and faithful pastor of the native Christians. He lived a blameless and consistent life, and was much respected by the whole community.

The elders of the congregation were all natives except one missionary and myself. Some of them had very interesting life histories. These rise before my memory as I write; but I cannot give space to record more than one. It is illustrative not only of missionary work, but also of the most kindly relations that existed between Europeans and Indians about the time that I went to the Central Provinces. When I first knew him, Anant Singh was a contractor of good business capacity, and considerable means and position in Nagpur. His father, who was a Rajput, had been an officer in an Indian regiment. There was in the same regiment a European officer, Major Arrow, who was on the best of terms with the native officers, and was loved and trusted by them all. When Anant Singh's father was dying, he sent for Major Arrow, and committed his three children and their property to his charge; for their mother was dead, and he had no friends to whom he cared to send them. Major Arrow sent them to Mr. Hislop to be educated, making separate arrangements for their board as their caste required. Anant Singh met with an accident which imperilled his life. When in hospital and surrounded by Christian kindness and care, he thought out the great question of his relations with God, and decided to take his stand as a Christian. After he left hospital he applied for baptism and was received into the Church.

About this time I knew a young native who went to read the Scriptures every Sunday with a young Government officer. They talked over what they read; and the observations made and difficulties raised by the Indian, were often so frivolous and puerile as to lead his British friend to doubt his sincerity as an inquirer after truth. The young European officer fell ill and was sent home with the sentence of death passed on him by his medical advisers. He recovered, however, and went back to a very different part of the Province. Some years after he was present in the missionary church when his young Indian friend was publicly baptised. It appeared that the latter had continued privately to study the Scriptures in a remote district, to which he had been transferred, far away from any missionary influence. Absolutely discontented with Hinduism, he joined the Brahmo Somaj and became a Deist. This involved no separation from his people or his caste, for so long as a Hindu keeps himself from ceremonial impurity, he may believe what he likes. Here, however, he found that he could not rest. The Christ became more to him than merely one of many teachers, and he accepted Him as Saviour and Master.

Still, for about two years he saw no necessity for making any public confession of his faith, which would involve separation from his caste and all the beloved and sacred associations of his youth. But the conviction grew stronger within him that this course involved disloyalty; and with the quiet courage which has distinguished so many Indian Christians, he determined to sacrifice all that was dearest to him rather than be disloyal to what he believed to be the truth. He applied to the nearest missionary for baptism, and was received into the Church. For years after, he lived a trusted servant of Government, unobtrusive in his character and without reproach in his life. He served under me some years after his baptism, and I had many a conversation with him. It was interesting to hear him tell, in a very simple way, of his loss of faith in his old religion; of his struggle with the temptation to think that all forms of religion were equally mythical and perhaps equally useful, in raising one above the purely material and leading up to God, and that a man's belief mattered little if he just tried to do his duty as far as he could in the place given him in the world; of the great attraction which the character and teaching of the Christ had for him; and of the intellectual and other difficulties that he had with the Bible, and how he often would have turned from it altogether but for the Divine Son of God who spoke to him in its pages. He told me how the bitterness of separation from what he had loved and reverenced made him hesitate; how gladly he had found the apparent solution of his difficulties in the acceptance of Brahamoism, receiving the Lord Jesus as one of his many teachers; how even here he had not found rest; how more and more loyalty to the Christ filled his heart; and how after years of conflict he had reached that important point where he determined to enter the Church, a step which cost him less than he had anticipated, and which he never regretted. This case has special interest to me, because it is the story of a man who for years studied our Holy Scriptures for himself, and was led step by step into the Church of Christ.

I have known many Indian Christians very intimately; and I have seen the Indian Church grow from infancy, when it seemed impossible to let it take a step alone and without guidance, into a comparatively strong Church, more or less self-supporting, self-governing and self-propagating. It is a high estimate that I have formed of the character of many native Christians. I recognise the power of the Christian religion to elevate in the East as it has done in the West; and I see a future for the Indian Church the importance of which it seems to me impossible to exaggerate. There are undoubtedly some natives who are only nominally Christian, and who give an evil report to Christianity; but these are they who have been carelessly received, without instruction and without proof, into the Christian Church. The missionary bodies, as a rule, are careful in this matter; and we have no reason to be ashamed of our Indian brethren in Christ. For myself, I have Indian Christian friends for whom I have as high a regard as for my friends in the West, and whose characters I have recognised as becoming more and more Christlike as they submit themselves to His teaching and to the influence of His Spirit.

Apart from their converts, the influence of missionaries has been of the highest value. There are men who make no profession of Christianity, and who are animated all the same by the great principles of Christian morality; there are also some whose profession of Christianity is clear and decided, but not public. I remember a specially striking case. We had an applicant for baptism in Nagpur, who had received all his religious instruction while he was tutor in the family of an Indian gentleman whom we did not know to be a professing Christian. This gentleman had family worship in his house which this young man attended; and the latter was led to inquire into the truth of Christianity and joined the Church. His employer died some years afterwards still unbaptised; but several members of his family were received into the Church not long after his death. I have known intimately many such secret disciples.

To me the results of Christian missions are not small or discouraging: they are important and of the highest promise. The efforts that have been put forth by the Christian Churches for the evangelisation of non-Christian countries are indeed exceedingly inadequate. The command of the Christ in regard to this matter was lost sight of for centuries. Modern times have seen a revival of the missionary spirit, but by no means a worthy response to the Lord's commission. Such efforts as have been put forth by the Churches have, however, been crowned with wonderful success. No one who has taken any trouble to study the question, to see the work itself, to judge the character of those who have been really won to the Christian religion, can fail to recognise how wonderful the results have been, both in regard to the numbers of true converts, and also in regard to the elevation of their character.

Nor must it be forgotten that, in estimating the results of missionary work, account must also be taken of the spread of Christian principles, even where there has been no formal adoption of Christianity. This forms a very important element in missionary results. The sacrifices which the adoption of Christianity still involve, and other obstacles to the ready profession of that religion by the people, have prevented many who are intellectually persuaded of its excellence from embracing it as their creed. I believe that in this respect what we must look for is, that the Indian Church itself should awake fully to its responsibility for the religious condition of the peoples among whom it is set, and that there should arise great leaders among the Indian peoples themselves to secure a really widespread religious movement. In the elevating and civilising power of Christianity the hope of India seems to lie; but it must be Christianity not as a foreign but as an Indian faith.

I am not here writing a plea for missions or a defence of them; I do not understand any argument on behalf of Christian missions to Christian men stronger than the command and commission of the Christ Himself, requiring that His Evangel should be carried by the Church to every creature, even to the uttermost parts of the earth. The commission given by Him to the Church seems to me finally to settle the matter. Then again, to us who have received the Gospel of Christ in this land centuries ago, there is that other argument which rests on a fine principle of human nature: "Freely ye have received, freely give." Human nature when ungrateful and self-centred is degraded, and certainly is not the humanity of the Son of Man. It seems to me an almost impossible position to realise at all adequately what we ourselves have received in Christianity, and yet have no desire to impart that blessing. In the third place, there is in the case of India a special call to missionary effort, in the wonderful relations which have been established between that great country and ours. These surely involve great responsibilities, not only for its intellectual and economic progress, but also for its moral and religious condition. In the beautiful parable of the Good Samaritan, our Lord set forth the simple principle that the neighbour whom we are to love as ourselves is the man who is in need, and who is placed in such near relation to us that we can help him. India stands in this relation to Great Britain, and she ought to receive of our best. The obligation is all the stronger as respects the Church and the individual Christian, because the righteous principle of Government neutrality precludes the use of official influence on behalf of the Christian, or any other, faith.

These are among the arguments for missionary work in India that most appeal to me from the point of view of the Christian Church. There is a great lesson of Indian experience which also makes me feel strongly on the subject. That is, the universal need for the life that is in the knowledge of God, and the suitability of the religion of the Lord Jesus Christ to meet that need. I have found, in every page of the book of my experience, clearest evidence of the fact that human nature is the same in the East as in the West, that when we get below the surface we find that the desires and affections, the needs and capacities of men are practically the same. And my experience tells me that the power of the Spirit of life in Christ Jesus to cheer and purify the lives of men, and to elevate and transform their characters, is the same in India as in England. There may be flashes of light here and there in exceptional cases; but it is darkness that prevails among the non-Christian peoples whom I have known; and there is nothing more beautiful than to see the light of the Gospel breaking in on this darkness, not among the educated and more influential classes alone, but among the poor and depressed. I could tell of bright and worthy Christians in the humble homes of India, just as I could tell of them among the humble homes of the villages and glens of my own land.

I have referred to the righteous principle of Government

neutrality in regard to religion. It is a principle which has ruled my conduct, I most earnestly believe, throughout all my service in India. I have never consciously favoured Christian or Hindu or Muhammadan for his creed; and I have never used my official influence in any way to undermine or change the faith of any man. But I have never regarded the principle of neutrality as involving indifference or opposition to religion. Early in my service I had definitely to face this question. I was stationed in a District where there was one solitary European missionary. He had a service every Sunday morning in the Mission Church, which was attended by Europeans, Eurasians, and a few Indian Christians. Some non-Christian Indians also attended; because they liked to hear the missionary telling the story of Divine love. I attended the service regularly. The missionary had to go out on tour to preach in the villages. This necessitated his absence for a Sunday or two, and he asked me to conduct the service. I complied with his request. My superior, the Collector (or, as we called him in that Province, the Deputy Commissioner), an upright English gentleman, informed me that, as Indians attended the service, it was incompatible with my duty to Government to conduct it, especially as some of these were Hindus; and he requested me to cease from taking any part in the service. I told him that I could not accept his view of my duty, and that if he wished to press it, I should like the matter referred to the Local Government. He very courteously and kindly agreed to refer it "demi-officially." The reply was that, so long as I merely took part in a Christian service in a place to which no one was compelled to come, and did not force my views on the attention of the people, there could be no objection on the part of Government. I never had any trouble again in this connection.

There are some who seem to forget that the people of India are themselves distinctly religious, and they are far from having any aversion to a religious man unless he interferes with them in their own religion and its observances. It is also forgotten that the declaration of neutrality in regard to religion has been made by a Government distinctly professing to be a Christian Government. The simple and beautiful profession of her own faith made by Queen Victoria in the proclamation in which, when taking over the government of her Indian possessions, she declared the strict neutrality of her Government in regard to religion, made a profound impression on the Oriental mind and heart. There is also a very striking passage in the great Educational Despatch of 1854, one of the wisest and loftiest documents ever penned by British statesmen, which is well worth quoting. "Considerable misapprehension appears to exist as to our views with respect to religious instruction in the Government institutions. These institutions are founded for the benefit of the whole population of India; and in order to effect their object, it was and is indispensable that the education conveyed in them should be exclusively secular. The Bible is, we understand, placed in the libraries of the colleges and schools; and the pupils are able freely to consult it. This is as it should be; and, moreover, we have no desire to prevent or discourage any explanations which the pupils may, of their own free will, ask from the masters upon the subject of the Christian religion, provided that such information be given out of school hours. Such instruction being entirely voluntary on both sides, it is necessary, in order to prevent the slightest suspicion of an intention on our part to make use of the influence of Government for the purpose of proselytism, that no notice shall be taken of it by the inspectors in their periodical visits." It is in this way that I have always interpreted the principle of neutrality.

There is another argument in favour of missionary work in India by the Church which demands a moment's notice. Like other non-Christian lands there is at the present time in India an awakening from the slumber of centuries, the beginning of a new life. All parts of India, so far as education and association with the West have directly affected life, feel the unrest which comes from intellectual awakening and the revival of national spirit. There is an effective demand, which cannot be refused, for the education, the industrial methods and the civilisation of the West, to be applied in India on Indian lines. The peoples of non-Christian lands, and the peoples of India among them, are pressing forward to a place among the civilised nations of the world; and they will take that place. We have no right to complain of this. It is the result of our own policy. We have worked and striven for it. The best statesmanship of Britain has realised that India is not under our control to be exploited for our own advantage, but to be educated and advanced in the interests of its multitudinous peoples. There are elements in the present unrest which we deplore, elements of anarchy and crime. But these are not to be accepted as characteristic of the whole. The intellectual unrest, the newly awakened ambitions and aspirations, are what we ought to have anticipated and ought to welcome.

What, however, is the result? These non-Christian races are no more negligible. They were asleep and remote from our civilisation. Improved communications have made them our neighbours; and contact with our civilisation has awakened them from the sleep of centuries. They already have their influence on ourselves; that influence will grow. As they become more civilised and more conscious of their power, they will, with their teeming millions and incalculable resources, exercise an influence on the future of our race which it is impossible to estimate. To me it seems that to give them civilisation without Christianity is to withhold that to which our civilisation owes all that is best in it, and by which alone it can be kept pure and healthful. They cannot adhere to their own religions; they are breaking away from them; and yet many of the best of them realise the necessity of religion for worthy and beneficent life. To leave them without religion may make them a probable source of danger in the future history of the race.

One of the greatest educationists of his day, one to whose efforts India generally, but especially Bengal, owes more educationally than to any one else, made use three-quarters of a century ago of these striking words: "If in India you do give the people knowledge without religion, rest assured that it is the greatest blunder, politically speaking, that ever was committed. Having free, unrestricted access to the whole range of our English literature and science, they will despise and reject their own systems of learning. Once driven out of their systems, they will inevitably become infidels in religion; and, shaken out of the mechanical round of their religious observances, without moral principles to balance their thoughts or guide their movements, they will as certainly become discontented, restless agitators." These words, uttered nearly a quarter of a century before the transfer of the Government of India to the Crown, have been strangely fulfilled in our day.

It is felt, not by Christians only, but also by Hindus and Muhammadans throughout India, that religion is necessary to the healthy life of the people. This partly explains the Hindu revival which has recently attracted considerable attention. There are those who regard this revival as the answer of the non-Christian faith to Christianity. So far as it is genuine, it seems to me to be just as much the protest of naturally religious races against the secular education and materialism now prevailing in schools and colleges. It is to some extent the genuine expression of the reluctance with which the orthodox Hindus see the religious beliefs of their fathers dissipated by Western education and enlightenment, while nothing is supplied in their stead to meet the moral and religious wants of our common humanity.

Of course, it is also in some measure, especially perhaps in the West of India, due to the more selfish objection of the Brahmans to the subversion of their old influence and position. It is also very largely due to an attempt on the part of men who have no sympathy with any religion, and least of all with Hinduism, to divert the religious sentiments of the Hindus into a political channel. There are such men in all parts of India, but especially, perhaps, in Bengal. One effect of the influence of these sham supporters of the Hindu religion has been to induce thoughtless, fanatical, and half-trained youths to associate their religion with particular forms of violence and sedition, which are really altogether inconsistent with its true teaching.

I do not think that this Hindu revival constitutes any menace to the success of missionary work. I believe that the influence of Christianity is growing in a most remarkable manner. There is opportunity now such as never existed before. There is a toleration, nay rather a welcoming, of Christian teaching which is without precedent. For there is a desire for religion growing up amongst all classes which makes them ready to listen to any religious teacher whose life and character commend his teaching. With this unexampled opportunity there is the unprecedented urgency to which I have referred. I think that this opportunity exists as much among the higher and more educated as among the depressed and ignorant classes.

There has been some talk of dropping the educated and turning exclusively to the lower orders, because the former have refused the call.* I have no sympathy with this view. Some of the best Indian Christians whom I have known have been educated in our colleges, and have belonged to the learned professions; and, whether as laymen or as mission agents, they have exercised a far more powerful influence in supporting and spreading the Church of Christ among their fellow-countrymen than other Indian Christians have been able to do. Let us by all means have the gospel preached to the poor; but let us also aim at securing for the Church the learning and influence of the best class of Indians. In our enthusiasm for the salvation of blind beggars, let us not overlook the possibility of enlisting a St. Paul.

I believe that the outlook of Christianity in India was never so favourable as it is at present; and I feel that the evangelisation of its peoples is assured if the Church in the West and the Church in India are found alive to their responsibility and faithful to their duty.

* *Cf.* Acts xviii. 6.

CHAPTER XX

INDIAN UNREST: ITS CAUSES

A GREAT deal of attention has been of late directed to India in respect of the unrest which has forced itself so much on our notice during recent years. My own impression is that this unrest is not widespread, but confined to a very small section of the Indian community. The mass of the people are unaffected by it. The unrest itself is not by any means wholly evil. I do not for a moment desire to under-estimate the serious incidents which have recently occurred, or the state of unrest of which they are the outcome. I do desire, however, that they should be correctly interpreted, and that an exaggerated impression of the state of things in India should not be created or fostered. There is real unrest. Some of it is natural and inevitable; some of it is only wicked and deplorable. That which is evil has also, no doubt, been strengthened by that which is natural in the situation.

Among the natural causes of unrest may be taken the pressure on life arising from the high prices which prevail. Trouble more or less serious may at any time arise in India in scarcity or famine, just as similar causes may produce trouble in any other country. An illustration of this is contained in the account I have given of the grain riots in Nagpur, which were due to the holding up of grain supplies in anticipation of a rise in prices expected from the demand from districts and localities where scarcity prevailed. Under economic conditions which suddenly make even the necessities of life almost unobtainable by those who have fixed incomes, we may expect much distress and dissatisfaction which may give trouble to the Government in a country where it is believed to be able to do practically what it wills. The economic changes which have taken place in India of late years have most seriously affected what in Bengal are called the *bhadralog* or respectable classes, people of comparatively small means and fixed incomes. Among them are middlemen amongst the land-owning classes, who receive a fixed proportion of the revenue of the land, which they hold under the larger Zamindars, who have managed to keep for themselves any increased emoluments which result from the rise in rents. Among them are also to be found many of the official and professional classes, whose incomes have been fixed years ago when prices were much lower, and are not easily raised to meet the sudden rise in prices.

I know at least one district where, when I first went to India, one could get as much as one hundred and fifty seers (three hundred pounds) of grain for the rupee (then two shillings), where a man would now consider himself very lucky if he got fifteen. When it is realised how simple is the life of the Indian, and how large a proportion of his expenditure is on the necessaries of life, it will be seen how very serious may be the effect of such a rise of prices upon many classes of the community. The change has been produced by the enormous improvements in communication which have now brought Districts, at that time practically inaccessible, into close touch with the markets of the world. There can be no doubt of the great advantage of this change to India generally; and I am able to testify strongly, from my knowledge of the people, that the standard of comfort has been greatly raised throughout the country, and that the condition of the people generally has vastly improved. There are, however, classes which have been very severely hit; and they are classes of some consideration and influence.

A very intelligent Bengali friend of mine was talking to me about the discontent which prevailed among many classes, and which produced a distinct tendency to criticise the Government adversely. In the course of conversation he told me that families in his position had frequently found it necessary to cut down their domestic establishments; that the ladies of the family had to perform duties which formerly had been left to servants; and that many comforts of the home life to which the members of the family had been accustomed had ceased to be obtainable. He said, "This sends people out with loud complaints against the Government. Dissatisfaction with our circumstances produces political unrest. In fact," he added in his Oriental way, "it is with us even as it is with the dogs. When we are uncomfortable at home we come out into the streets to bark."

It is no easy matter to say what, if anything, can be done to assist the people under these circumstances. Economic changes, which in Europe were carried out in the course of generations, have been effected in India within a few years owing to its contact with the West. I have long been of opinion that the matter deserves the sympathetic consideration of the Government; and I am glad to see that the Government of India have their attention seriously directed to this matter, and are making the inquiry regarding it which many of the people demand. It must not be understood that I attribute the worst forms of unrest and political agitation to high prices and to the consequent pressure on certain classes. I merely mention this as one cause of dissatisfaction; and in a country like India, with so many incomes and salaries fixed by custom, it is by no means a negligible cause. It in some measure explains the toleration or even approval, with which the foolish and mischievous babblings of professional agitators were long received by many, by whom they would otherwise have been strongly condemned. It was hoped, perhaps, that these wild utterances would draw the attention of the Government to trouble and dissatisfaction which were real, and in respect of which the sufferers, in accordance with Oriental usage, looked to the Government for help.

Closely allied to this is the great depression among some of the industrial classes. This also is due mainly to economic causes. Manufactures have enormously developed in India of late years. Not only has there been a great increase in the import of manufactured articles; but there have also been innumerable mills and factories established throughout the country. Many of these are now worked with native capital; and the labour employed is, of course, mainly native. There is no doubt of the enormous advantage of all this to the Indian community in general; but the history of the introduction of machinery in our own country should enable us to understand how injuriously such changes must, for a time at least, affect some of the labouring and industrial classes, how discontent may easily spread among them, and how susceptible they may become to the mischievous influences of thoughtless or unprincipled agitators. This, to a very large extent, explains the success of what has been known as the "boycott movement" in Bengal. With the desire to foster native industry the Government and its officers have the greatest sympathy. But true "Swadeshi"* has been perverted by unscrupulous agitators to ignoble use, and has been degraded by selfishness, political disaffection, and race hatred.

The industrial depression is a matter to which the Imperial and Local Governments in India have now for some time been giving anxious attention. All that is now being done to develop local industries, and to introduce and stimulate technical education, indicates the interest that Government takes in this matter and the recognition of its great importance. In India such a matter must be dealt with by the Government. The people still look to the Government to help them in all kinds of difficulties, and the lesson of self-help has to be learned, not only by the common people, but even by those also who claim to be the educated and enlightened classes. It is not easy for the Government, especially where financial pressure exists, to meet its

* "Swadeshi" means "of the country," "indigenous." Some of the leaders profess that their object is merely to encourage indigenous industry. But the impression that they have given to their followers is sadly illustrated in the evidence of Ganesh Balvant Vaidya in the Nassik Conspiracy Case. He mentioned "Swadeshi," and being asked what be meant by it, he said, "I mean a movement for the collection of arms, the preparation of material for making bombs, etc."

responsibility in this matter; but it is necessary for the happiness of the people, and for the stability of Government, that it should find the means. It is in my opinion also of vital importance that the measures taken to this end should be taken in India itself. Not only must local industries be encouraged in India, but technical and industrial education must be available there. It is practically impossible, and also politically dangerous, to compel the natives of the country, to any large extent, to go abroad for instruction and education. The present compulsion is destroying many of the best of the rising generation. It may be necessary, no doubt, at least for a time, to send some young men abroad for education, if only for the purpose of obtaining duly qualified teachers; and it will probably always be necessary, in India as elsewhere, for specialists in any department of intellectual or industrial work to come into contact with the best workers abroad; but our aim should be, as soon as possible, to supply the necessary education in India, and to supply it in great measure by Indians themselves. Only thus can the work be done which the circumstances demand.

In connection with this subject of technical education I cannot help referring to a philanthropic scheme recently inaugurated in Bengal by one of the leading merchants of Calcutta. He proposes that, in the interests of the young, an experiment should be made with land reclaimed in the sundarbans, at the mouth of the Ganges, in the way of holding out inducements to young men of energy and of some education to devote themselves to agricultural pursuits. He offers generous support to the scheme, which seems to commend itself to many right-thinking people in Calcutta. It appeals to the Indian love of agriculture and to the earnest desire of many young men to find an honourable and worthy outlet for their energies. His object is to give them a useful career, and to save them from the injurious influences of selfish and unprincipled agitation. If the experiment succeeds it may have very important results. I do not see why it should not succeed, if the Government sees its way to encourage it. The rules for settling cultivators will have to be modified if this scheme is to go on. They are framed to keep out land-speculation. But they might be modified to meet the necessity of any well-considered scheme framed by men who can be trusted. I mention this now as showing how the situation impresses a large-hearted fellow-countryman engaged in commercial work in India. His view, he explains, is that such measures as this, as well as the enlightened measures of political reform recently carried out by the Government, are as essential as measures of repression in respect of the present unrest.

I pass now to a phase in the unrest which is, perhaps, more familiar to people at home than any other, the unrest of the educated classes, the unrest which is due to the education which we have ourselves given to the people of India. I shall have to refer immediately to the small proportion of the people of India who may justly be included among the educated classes. I have, however, no desire to minimise the importance of these classes or to refuse to pay earnest attention to their reasonable demands and aspirations. We have created these classes; and we have given them their hopes and aims. We are bound, on that account, as a matter of justice as well as of policy, not to ignore their reasonable claims.

We are bound by the generous promise of the late Queen Victoria, in Her Majesty's great proclamation transferring the government of India from the East India Company to the Crown, a promise which was solemnly renewed fifty years later by King Edward VII. We are bound by this promise, as well as by the principles of justice and sound policy, to see that, as far as may be possible, His Majesty's "subjects of whatever race or creed shall be freely and impartially admitted to offices in his service, the duties of which they may be qualified by their education, ability, and integrity duly to discharge." As I look back on my thirty-seven years' service in India, I see little cause to be ashamed of the manner in which this obligation has been met.

I do not propose to deal with the appointment of Indians to the purely Judicial Service of the Crown. They have long held some of the highest appointments in that Service. It was easy to find men in India intellectually qualified for purely legal work, and for judicial work, so far as that is purely legal, while the publicity of the work in the courts and a system of revision and appeal, sometimes perhaps too elaborate, made it, at a comparatively early period, a safe and wise measure to place judicial work largely in the hands of Indians. I propose rather to look at the part taken by Indians in the executive administration of the country, that is, at the number of executive appointments held by Indians. Here I do not intend to mention the lower classes of appointments, which are practically all in the hands of Indians: there is no question about these appointments; there is no desire on the part of the educated classes to hold them. What really demands consideration is the progress made in filling the higher executive appointments by Indian gentlemen. Although I have seen the great progress made in this respect in the Central Provinces, where most of my service was rendered, and also in other Provinces of India which I have visited during my service on two important Commissions which took me to every Province in India, I prefer to deal with the facts as they exist in Bengal. I do so for two reasons, both because there has been more agitation of recent years in Bengal than elsewhere, and also because I know the figures well, as they had especially to be dealt with by my Government in connection with agitation.

Before I came to India, in 1871, there were no members of the Indian Civil Service in Bengal at all. Three Indians joined the Service at the end of that year. All of them were drawing Rs.400 a month. At the end of 1908, when I gave over charge of the Province of Bengal, there were thirteen Indian civilians in the graded list, drawing monthly salaries of from Rs.776 to Rs.2250. Besides these there were ten Indians, not members of the Indian Civil Service, holding posts which had ordinarily been reserved for that Service. So that, as against three such appointments in 1871, there were twenty-three in 1908. Besides this, the Provincial Service in 1871 consisted of one hundred and seventy-seventy officers employed as Assistant Collectors and Assistant Magistrates, of whom forty-five, or just over one-fourth, were Europeans. At the end of 1908, there were three hundred and sixty-one members of that Service, and only forty-five, or one-eighth, of them were Europeans. The total addition to the Provincial Service, the officers of which do the same work as the junior officers of the Civil Service, by which addition the strength of the former Service had been more than doubled, was composed of Indians. These figures indicate the great progress that has been made in the employment of Indians in the Executive Service of the Crown in Bengal.

Perhaps, however, the earnestness of the Government in seeking to carry out the royal promise is more clearly seen when the importance of the offices now held by Indians is considered. In 1871 the highest position held by an Indian in the Executive Service was the comparatively subordinate one of Assistant Magistrate or Assistant Collector. There were no Indians as District or Sessions Judges, or as Magistrates, or Joint Magistrates. Recently we have had Indians employed not only in these capacities, but also in the higher office of Commissioner of Division; and during my term of office as Lieutenant-Governor, I had an Indian officer holding the Executive appointment of next highest rank in the Province to my own, as Senior Member of the Board of Revenue. The principle of appointing Indians to Executive offices, for which they possess the necessary qualifications, has thus been steadily kept in view. At the same time, they have been more and more appointed to high office in other departments of the Government Service, such as medicine, education, law, and engineering, and more recently in the police department.

His Majesty's recent proclamation to the chiefs and peoples of India will doubtless secure the constant prosecution of this policy in the future. It ought, however, to be distinctly laid down and kept in view that it is just as unsound to appoint a man to Executive office on account of his race or creed as to debar him from office on the same account. For District Boards or Legislative Assemblies, it is not only justifiable, but necessary, to appoint a man because he represents a certain interest. It is desired that he should speak and fight for that interest. For an Executive Council, or for any Executive office, the very opposite is the case. The man who comes to represent and fight for a particular interest is *ipso facto*, and to that extent, unfit. What is wanted is a man who can hold the scales justly between conflicting interests and favour none. Subject to this necessary condition, the policy above referred to should be consistently pursued.

While all this has been going on steadily in regard to offices under the Crown, efforts have, at the same time, been made to secure, in ever-increasing measure, the co-operation of non-official Indians in local self-government and in imperial and provincial administration through the municipalities, District Boards, and Legislative Councils. The Local Self-Government scheme, introduced during Lord Ripon's viceroyalty, has not been so successful as was hoped in securing the co-operation of the classes whose co-operation is essential. This is due partly to the inertia of the people, but mainly to the nature of the electoral franchise which was created under the scheme. The constituencies resulting from that franchise were not such as to secure the best representation of important interests, or to induce some of the natural and most desirable leaders of the people to offer themselves for election. This was not the fault of the scheme, but rather of the thoughtless and injudicious manner in which some Local Governments applied it.

Bengal has, in my opinion, suffered most in this respect. Remedies are now under consideration. They were placed before the Government of India during my tenure of office; but the consideration of them was, perhaps unfortunately, postponed owing to the measures which were under consideration for the alteration of the Constitution of the Imperial and Provincial Legislative Councils. The ridiculously low qualification for the exercise of the franchise is one of the sad illustrations of the evils of thoughtlessly introducing Western methods into India, without full consideration of the circumstances, and without that gradual and steady progress in political history which has characterised our own country. The principle of Lord Ripon's policy was sound; the details of its application in certain Provinces were not.

An effort was, indeed, made to safeguard the interests of the people generally, by giving perhaps too great a representation to official classes in the district and Municipal local bodies and also by nominating a number of members selected as fit representatives of the interests which it was felt must be represented. These could not be secured by election by the vast numbers of really inferior and indifferent men who, without any real stake in the country or intelligent appreciation of public affairs, formed the electoral constituency. These nominated members were, for the most part, very suitable representatives of the interests and classes which they were nominated to represent; but they had this grave disqualification, that they were nominated. They were open to the reproach, in the great majority of cases entirely undeserved, of having sold themselves to the Government which nominated them.

It is clearly necessary to secure the presence on the local bodies of such men, men with an intelligent appreciation of the needs of their neighbourhood and of the interests of the people generally, by election instead of by nomination. That is to say, where an interest or a class clearly requires to be represented on the local body, a constituency of persons sharing that interest, or belonging to that class, ought to be formed to elect the representative. In this way the co-operation of all classes, and especially of those who have an important stake in the country, may be effectively secured. It can be secured in no other way. Of course, we cannot disfranchise the people upon whom the franchise has been conferred; but we may break up the electoral constituencies into sections, which will secure the representation of the interests and classes which justice and sound policy alike demand to have represented. If we can secure this, we shall not only feel more confidence in the advice which the local bodies give us; but we shall also be able to put much larger powers into their hands, and to get rid, by decentralisation, of much of the burden of administration, which in these days of progress is becoming intolerable.

The principle which I have set forth above in regard to local bodies has been applied to the Legislative Councils in the scheme submitted by the Government of India, and adopted with modifications by Lord Morley as Secretary of State. In the main that scheme has my entire approval; and I look forward with interest and hope to its working. But this is not enough. The principles which I have indicated must be applied to local self-government throughout the country. I am inclined to think, indeed, that to apply them to Legislative Councils before they had been applied to local bodies was to begin at the wrong end of the matter. The explanation is that though the need was great, there was no loud demand, for reform of the local bodies. The demand for political power was louder and more effective.

Tradition and ancient usage in India have given the people no small share in local affairs, and that was a fact of which much use had long been made. In some Provinces Lord Ripon's scheme was so applied that the old system was utilised and developed. But in Bengal and elsewhere it suffered a reverse because a franchise system was introduced which disgusted many of the best men and most natural leaders, and deprived the local bodies of their services. These natural leaders have been to a large extent replaced partly by nominated members, and partly by unsuitable men who represent little beyond their own interests. It is of urgent necessity that this error should be corrected, not by disfranchising men who have enjoyed the franchise, but by subdividing the electorate so as to secure the representation of different classes and interests by suitable representatives, somewhat on the lines of the scheme which has been adopted for the Legislative Councils.

As to these recent reforms in the Imperial and Provincial

Legislative Councils, I believe that their general effect will be to bring the central governments of India generally, and of the Provinces in particular, into more perfect touch with the natives of the country; and they will tend to further developments which the progress of civilisation and of political enlightenment entitle us to expect and desire. I believe also that they have given great satisfaction to moderate men of all classes. I have received from many of my Indian correspondents strong expressions of approval both of the spirit which has animated these reforms, and of the manner in which they have been carried out. On the other hand, I certainly do not believe that the adoption of this scheme will be the end of our difficulties in Indian administration. We have great difficulties to face. This in itself is a great difficulty, that principles of Government are being taught to the educated classes for which the vast body of the people are yet altogether unfit. We must make up our minds to associate the people of the country more and more in its government in accordance with the royal promise to which I have referred; but we must never forget that we are in India for the sake of the just and righteous government, not of small classes, but of the whole body of the people; and when I say this, I am speaking of the many nations and peoples and tongues, in all stages of political and social development, which have been committed to our charge in that great Empire.

The task of governing India has never been easy. I believe that it will probably grow increasingly more difficult. Certainly the problems with which those who are concerned with the government of India in the future, and especially the members of the Indian Civil Service, will have to deal will differ in many respects from those which have occupied attention in the past. It will be at least necessary in the future to take pains not only to do the best thing we can for the people, which has generally been our sole aim in the past, but also to vindicate our action before, and secure the concurrence of, an increasingly powerful public opinion. This will call for the exercise of gifts and qualifications which we have not so much required in the past.

We may reasonably hope, however, that it will be found that the best and most moderate of the Indians will be thrown more closely than ever into sympathetic co-operation with those of more liberal mind and sounder judgment among ourselves, to work together for the public good. If we continue to be animated by the spirit of the great past, the difficulties may be bravely and cheerfully faced; for there is privilege as well as responsibility in the burden of Empire.

CHAPTER XXI

INDIAN UNREST: ITS LIMITATIONS

To return to the unrest, we must not allow ourselves to take too pessimistic a view of the situation. We must endeavour to realise the limitations of unrest. In this connection it is necessary to bear in mind that the peoples of India are not a homogeneous mass, so that what is true of one part of India must necessarily be true of another. Nothing could be further from the real facts. A man in one part of India may have no conception of what is going on in another, or of the precise difficulties which have there to be faced. There has been an amount of mischief working for a long time in Bengal, which led to a distinguished European officer saying to me before I went there, "We have lost Bengal"—an altogether exaggerated statement. In Bombay there has been mischief brewing for a quarter of a century at least, and the earliest repression of any importance had to be effected there. In Madras, on the other hand, where there is more of enlightenment than in any part of India, there is apparently less cause to think of sedition. In the Central Provinces there was nothing but loyalty until some Beraris, tainted with the discontent of Poona, began to work in Nagpur, and the colleges were infected with the poisonous stuff which a section of the Bengal and Bombay Press had been too long allowed to circulate. There was fortunately there a strong man to deal with it, a man who knew the people of the Province well. In the north of India, despite occasional trouble given by people on whose religious feelings mischievous statements had been working, there was practically nothing of what we ordinarily know as sedition. The people there are not likely to be led by Press writers in Bombay and Calcutta. They require to be carefully guarded rather against irritation and discontent arising from misunderstanding and misrepresentation of the action of the Government in particular measures, than against any foolish aim to supplant British rule in favour of some vague dream with which they have no sympathy. They understand the officers who go in and out among them, and are amenable to kindly advice.

A fine Indian gentleman once told me how one of his boys went all wrong at a local college, and began to air sentiments which he could not bear to hear, and to take in the "Amrita Bazar Patrika" and other papers even more unwholesome. He determined to send him to Allahabad. The lad came back within a short time quite cured. The strong air of Allahabad had restored his mind and dispelled the poison. "He found," said his father, "that the people there laughed at what he had begun to believe to be manly and patriotic."

In estimating the limitations of unrest, I must speak mainly of the part of India that I know best, that is, of Bengal. The first limitation lies in the fact that India is an agricultural country. It is clear therefore that while the economic changes to which I have referred have undoubtedly pressed hard on certain sections of the community, they have been fraught with benefit to the great bulk of the population. The high prices of grain have been greatly to the advantage of the cultivating classes, which form the vast majority of the people; and they have brought with them a higher standard of living, greater comfort and much prosperity, as anyone who has moved about among the people will be able to testify. Similarly, the trouble that has fallen on some of the industrial classes is due to a reduction in price on wearing apparel and certain other necessaries of life, which has benefited the people generally. This consideration leads naturally to the conclusion that, while there is unrest among certain sections of the community, the great mass are unaffected by it, and are as loyal as ever.

The mass of the people are naturally loyal to the *de facto* government. They are averse to change; and if we do justly and do not seek to tax them too heavily, they cheerfully accept our rule. It often seems as though they were especially loyal to the British Government. They appear generally to regard it as more in accordance with the fitness of things that the supreme Government should be in the hands of a power easily distinguished from themselves, less known to them than their own people, and not subject to the same impulses and moods. However that may be, there is no doubt about this, that the people have a great belief in the impartiality and justice of the British Government and a very loyal personal devotion to the officers who come among them, except where there is some serious defect of character in any individual officer which tends to make him unpopular. While the loyalty of the great mass of the community in every Province may be, as I think, still accepted as a fact, there is always this at the same time to be borne in mind, that the people are generally ignorant, superstitious, and excitable. A baseless rumour, a mischievous misrepresentation, or a suggestion of interference with what they hold dearest, may create a panic which may develop into very serious mischief. This does not, however, alter the fact referred to above, that the economic causes of unrest affect only a very small portion of the community.

As to the unrest amongst the educated classes, it is necessary to look at the facts and not to be misled by vague impressions or disproportionate clamour. I have already indicated that I consider it necessary to pay full attention to the reasonable claims of the educated classes; but it is at least equally necessary to bear in mind how small a proportion of the community are educated at all, and that the educated classes are not all affected with unrest. Bengal is often spoken of as a Province in which a fairly high standard of education has been reached by a large proportion of the population. Education is comparatively widespread in Bengal, though in my opinion the teaching in most of its educational institutions is undoubtedly less efficient than in some other Provinces. This is a matter which is engaging the earnest attention of Government, of the educational authorities, and of the best leaders of thought among the people themselves; and its importance cannot be overrated. It is not necessary, however, to dwell on it here. What is to be pointed out here is, that, even in Bengal where education is comparatively widespread, it is only a very small proportion of the people that can be regarded as educated.

Statistics are not all important and do not always convey an accurate impression; but a few figures on this point may tend to correct misapprehension. When we hear of the educated classes as being animated with such and such a feeling, or as desiring such and such a measure, those who think of the matter in the light of conditions prevailing in this country are very apt to believe that practically the whole population of India share this feeling or demand this measure. This is very far from being the case. The census figures of 1901 for the most advanced division of Bengal showed as "literate" a total in the Presidency Division of 15·64 per cent. of males, and 1·52 of females, or 8·9 of both classes, while for the Bardwan Division the percentages were 18·82, ·82 and 9·8 respectively. For the whole of Bengal the percentages of "literates" were 11·06 for males, ·57 for females, and 5.77 for both classes.* Let it be borne in mind that to be included under the term "literate" in the census figures requires no more than to be able to read and write. The term includes any one who is able to sign his name in any one language. Education is not very widespread, when under this definition the highest proportion of "literate" males in any District was 20 per cent.

The last Quinquennial Report on education in Bengal throws further light on these figures. It shows that the percentage of school-going children among those of a school-going age is somewhat higher than the percentage of "literate" among the whole population. This is partly due to the steady though

* The percentages for the province in the census of 1911 are 11·36 for males, ·83 for females, und 6·27 for both classes.

slow progress of education, but also to the fact that some who have acquired in early youth a small amount of education lose it from disuse in later years. At the same time the Report shows how small a proportion of the children in the primary schools go on to higher education. In the primary schools of Bengal the figures show 27·8 boys and 3·1 girls, per cent. of the population of school-going age, as under public instruction. But while there were 1,027,377 pupils in primary schools there were only 156,958 in secondary schools, and 7,253 in the arts and professional colleges combined. These figures indicate how far we are from being able to say that education is really widespread in Bengal.

Something has been done during the last fifty years; but the task before the Government is still enormous and demands its utmost efforts, supported by the earnest co-operation of all who have the welfare of the country at heart. For the present purpose I quote these figures to show how necessary it is carefully to guard against the mistake of considering the interests of the educated classes as necessarily identical with those of the vast communities committed to our charge, or the demands of the former as necessarily expressing the requirements of the latter. As a fact, the educated classes are, to a large extent, to be found gathered together in the cities; and they are, generally speaking, altogether out of touch with the great mass of the community. They can make themselves heard; but they cannot safely be accepted as giving voice to the feelings of the people generally.

Again it must be borne in mind that it is not all the educated classes that are affected by unrest. Few in number as the educated classes are, we have still to make a very considerable deduction for those who are in no way affected by the unrest which, perhaps, characterises the majority. There are many well-educated chiefs, noblemen, bankers, merchants, and officials, and not a few highly educated professional gentlemen, who have no sympathy whatever with the unrest of which we have recently heard so much. Indeed, they think and speak of it with a greater intolerance than will be found among Europeans or among what are called the ruling classes. The stake that they have in the country, and their intelligent grasp of the real facts of the situation, combined with their lack of personal ambition in regard to offices under the Crown, separate them in interest altogether from agitation. They have not, until quite recently, considered it necessary to make themselves heard on this matter; for their Oriental sentiment has led them to leave it entirely to be dealt with by the Government. But now that unrest has begun to be associated too much with sedition, anarchy, and crime, their attitude has very greatly changed; and it may be hoped that the worst features of the unrest will pass away under the influence of repression by the Government and the loyal co-operation of the more moderate men amongst our Indian fellow-subjects.

Intellectual unrest in India is undoubtedly to be expected. We have ourselves sought to bring before the people our Western civilisation, our industrial methods, our education, and even our political ideas. We have sought to awaken the intellectual powers of the people; and at the same time we have aimed at securing their assistance in bearing the burden of public administration which becomes ever heavier and heavier. We are bound to expect that there will be an awakening from the sleep of centuries, that political thought and ambition, desire after progress and reform, a sense of national life and energy, will be awakened in the minds of the peoples of India. This change is taking place among all the non-Christian nations with which the West has been brought into contact; and it would be a strange thing, and scarcely creditable to us, if it did not take place among the nations of India, with which we have been brought into very intimate and close connection. These nations are demanding, and they are acquiring, our education, our industrial methods, and our civilisation. These we could not withhold if we would, and we certainly would not if we could. If we can at the same time imbue them with the ethical principles of our religion, we need not fear the consequences.

I have said enough to show that the unrest to which attention has been so much drawn of late is distinctly limited in its area and scope; and it is necessary for us to bear this well in mind, not only that we may not be unduly despondent regarding the future, but also that we may realise that the measures to be taken in view of this unrest ought not to be such as will meet the demands which are clamorously made, without due regard to the very often conflicting interests of the vast, though more silent, multitudes under our care. The demand for employment in the administration of the State made by the educated classes is one which is distinctly reasonable and entirely in accordance with principles with which we have ourselves imbued these classes and which cannot righteously be neglected. At the same time we have to bear in mind that, in giving to the Indians, that is to the educated classes of Indians, a share in the Government of the country, we must consider not the interests of the educated classes alone, but the interests of the whole community. In other words, we must see to it that in accordance with the language of Queen Victoria's proclamation those only are appointed to office who "may be qualified by their education, ability, and integrity duly to discharge," the duties of that office.

Here I desire again to emphasise more clearly the distinction to be drawn between appointment to Executive office and appointment to a local body, or a Legislative Council. In the latter case, what is ordinarily wanted is a man to represent a particular class or interest, and to press, within reasonable limits, the interests of the section of the community which he represents. Therefore, a man may reasonably and very properly be appointed to a local body or a Legislative Council because he is a Hindu, or a Muhammadan, or a landowner, or a banker. He will represent the interest of his own section of the community; and that is what is desired. It is the very opposite with a man who is to be appointed to responsible Executive office. He is not qualified merely because he represents a particular interest. That fact may, indeed, be a serious disqualification. What is required of him is capacity to rule justly, the power of considering all interests and balancing one against another, a training in impartiality and in administration. He ought not to be appointed because he is a Hindu or a Muhammadan or a member of a particular class, but only because he has, as far as can be ascertained, proved himself fit for the office in question. No man ought to be excluded from Executive office on account of any racial or religious consideration; but on the other hand, he ought not to be appointed to it merely on account of any such consideration. For example, it is a right thing to put a man into a Legislative Council because he is a Hindu; it is not a right thing to put him into an Executive Council for that reason. In the former he is to represent a particular interest, in the latter he is to hold a portfolio and administer a department in the interests of all. The recent appointment of the Hon. Mr. Sinha, to the Viceroy's Executive Council as Legal Member had my hearty approval, not because Mr. Sinha is a Hindu, but because he had proved himself in his past history to be fitted for that high office. I heard with great regret of his having made up his mind to retire. His successor, Mr. Ali Imam, is an old Behari friend of mine. He also is a barrister. I believe him fit; and therefore I am able to rejoice in the appointment of my friend. It is no disqualification that he is a Muhammadan, though I hope that this was not the ground for his appointment. The first and almost the only considerations are education (or training), ability, and integrity.

I do not intend to dwell upon the sad features of the unrest, which have tended to lead people to identify it with anarchy and crime. I believe that the anarchical conspiracies, the existence of which has been discovered, are very limited in their extent. Mischievous wire-pullers, some of whom are well known to the police, though they cannot be brought before the courts, have been able to exercise an influence over a limited number of the young, which has led some of the latter to give their lives, without reserve, to the practice of assassination. Some of these wire-pullers themselves are known to have a strain of insanity in their blood; they are also sometimes stirred by personal grievance and desire for revenge, as much as by anything approaching a patriotic motive; and the wretched lads whom they have influenced are frequently found to be of unstable character, unsuccessful in their prosecution of education, and liable to that form of moral weakness which makes in India the half-brained and fanatical fakir or *sanyasi*.

Undoubtedly the soil has been prepared by an irresponsible and ill-conditioned section of the Press; but the direct cause of anarchy is education in political crime received abroad and applied in India. Nothing will save the country from this, except severe repression by the Government and cordial co-operation in that repression on the part of the Indian community. Anarchy is fraught with danger to the landlord, to the money-lender, even to the teacher, against whom the spirit of lawlessness may instigate a discontented tenant, client, or pupil to turn the hand of crime; and the interests of the people and the safety of society are involved as much as the interests of Government. The evil is not yet widespread. There may, indeed, be many more acts of violence. A score or two of even weedy youths, guided by one or two able and unscrupulous men and determined to devote their own lives to violence, may succeed in committing a few deplorable crimes. Even this would not show that the evil was widespread or deep-seated. I believe that it is not. I do not by any means believe that we have seen the end of it; but I do think that the Government and the people combining together may well prevail to eradicate the evil.

I think that I can best illustrate this point by briefly describing one of the last incidents of my life in India, to which reference has already been made in a former chapter. On the 7th November, 1908, less than a month before I gave over charge of the office of Lieutenant-Governor of Bengal and left India for good, I was invited to preside at the Overtoun Hall in Calcutta at a lecture to be delivered by Professor Burton, of Chicago, on "University education in the United States." The Overtoun Hall is a fine building, in charge of the Young Men's Christian Association (College Branch) in Calcutta. The lecture was to be delivered to students and graduates of the Calcutta University. My young friend, the Maharajadhiraja Bahadur of Bardwan, who is deeply interested in education and in all good work, drove with me to the lecture. We arrived punctually at the appointed hour, to find that the lecturer, whose carriage had broken down on the way, had not yet arrived. On the landing at the top of the stairs outside the platform door of the hall, I was met by Mr. Barber, an American gentleman, who is secretary of the Young Men's Christian Association. We entered the hall and stopped just inside the door, while Mr. Barber informed me that the lecturer had not arrived, and asked me whether I would await him on the platform or in the waiting-room. Before I could reply, a student, who was seated in the chair next the door on my right, clad in the white chaddar (or shawl) often worn by Bengalis, stepped quietly past Mr. Barber and standing in front of me presented his revolver at my breast.

It happened that, at that time, I was engaged in filling up vacancies in the Provincial Service of Bengal; and the thought occurred to my mind that this might be a student who was taking advantage of this opportunity to press his claims to an appointment. I did not notice the revolver. Looking him in the face, I asked him what he wanted. At the same moment, I heard the click of the falling trigger, which had been pulled without effect, owing to causes afterwards ascertained. All the other chambers of the revolver were loaded and exploded readily when tried subsequently by the authorities. Mr. Barber, who was standing on my right, with great presence of mind seized the hand of the assassin which contained the revolver. The web of Mr. Barber's hand, between the thumb and index finger, came under the trigger, and so prevented the next barrel from exploding.

Simultaneously the Maharajadhiraja, who is a very stalwart man and was standing behind me, suddenly threw one arm round my neck and another round my arms, and thus pinioning me turned me round so that his own body came between me and the would-be assassin. At my request the Maharajadhiraja released me; but meanwhile the student had been knocked down by his own fellow-students and others, and Mr. Barber was in possession of the revolver, of which he had not let go his hold. The young man was handed over to the police, and was subsequently tried and sentenced by the High Court. The lecturer arrived very soon after the lad had been handed over to the police. There were some who urged that the lecture should be postponed or abandoned; but I knew the audience better than that; and we ascended the platform. The large audience of students and graduates accorded me a most enthusiastic reception; and the lecture was delivered. An hour later I passed with the Maharajadhiraja through the streets on our way home. All the way home I was engaged in acknowledging the cheers of the crowd who gathered under every lamp-post to see us pass.

These are the facts. I think that they are very instructive. The following points demand special attention. The miserable young man, at the direct or indirect instigation of some one who had obtained influence over him, but who remained concealed, had undoubtedly determined to take my life, from no personal enmity against me, but, as he pompously said, "to encourage Bengal by showing that even the Lieutenant-Governor was vulnerable and mortal." He had clearly also made up his mind to sacrifice his own life in the attempt; for he had no chance of escape. The police were powerless to prevent the crime. Apart from the protection of Divine Providence which was universally recognised, there was no safety against such an attack, unless the Lieutenant-Governor of Bengal had been ready to abdicate his functions and abstain from meeting with the people, which is unthinkable. The accusation of remissness made in some quarters against the police was unjust and unwarrantable; and, on the contrary, it should be remembered that the existence of these anarchical conspiracies would not have been discovered but for the great improvement in police administration effected during recent years. The audience and the outside public were wholly out of sympathy with the assassin and hailed my escape from peril with great enthusiasm. Finally, an Indian nobleman, the senior Hindu nobleman of Bengal, animated by loyalty to our Sovereign and devotion to his own friend, was willing to give his life to save mine. It has been a great pleasure to me that the devotion of the Maharajah and the promptness and courage of Mr. Barber were recognised by His Majesty King Edward VII., who was graciously pleased to bestow on them distinguished marks of favour, appointing the Maharajah to be a Knight Commander of the Most Eminent Order of the Indian Empire, and bestowing on Mr. Barber the Kaisir-i-Hind medal of the first-class.

The main facts in this case, I repeat, are these: that a young man of unbalanced mind, with no personal grudge against me, was willing to give his life in attempting to take mine; that a brave Indian gentleman was at the same moment offering his life to save mine; that the would-be assassin was knocked down and arrested with the active assistance of some of his own fellow-students; that the whole meeting was against him; and that the people everywhere rejoiced in my escape without injury. These facts are well worthy of special attention. They seem to me to illustrate the true state of things in regard to recent unrest in Bengal, and, I believe, in India generally. Anarchists and men inclined to such deeds of violence are very few; but they are implacable, and ready to make any sacrifices to achieve their objects. The mass of the people are loyal; and the loyalty of some of them is devoted and ready for any sacrifice. The people generally must not be condemned for the crimes of the few; and officers of Government must take care that these crimes are not allowed to prevent them from free intercourse with the people, or to make their sympathy and touch with them less real and effective. The incitement to, or commission of, such crimes ought to be dealt with in the sternest manner; and all measures of repression that are necessary ought unhesitatingly to be adopted. But, at the same time, a strong Government will not allow itself to be turned aside from a righteous and large-hearted policy by such incidents as these.

CHAPTER XXII

MEASURES OF REPRESSION AND REFORM

THERE is one cause of unrest in its worst forms that demands notice, that is the writings of a section of the Indian Press. Several of those who have recently committed crimes of violence with a political object have mentioned these writings as having incited them to these offences. There was an excellent article published by the late editor of the "Indian Nation" not long before his death. He was a Bengali gentleman, highly esteemed among his own fellow-countrymen, of sound education, robust character, and self-sacrificing patriotism. Though duly qualified as a barrister-at-law, he had given up what would have been a most lucrative practice to devote himself to the instruction of youth. In this article he pointed out that the Press is not in India an indigenous institution, but that it has there developed peculiarities of its own. A portion of the Press is conducted by men of ability and character, who aim at maintaining the best traditions of the English Press. But there is another portion of the Press, he said, written in English or vernacular, which seems "only to keep itself going by things sensational." The most sensational thing in writing is piquant abuse. Therefore the stock-in-trade of some journalists comes to be abuse either of the Government or of individuals. He characterised these journalists as "worthless, characterless men, unable to turn an honest penny," who think that a newspaper offers them a livelihood and a certain status, and who do not hesitate to indulge freely in falsehoods and to devote themselves to abuse. "It is these wretched pests of society," he added, "that are responsible for the present state of public feeling. They pose as authorities with the ill-educated." It is useless, in his view, to hope that the law can wholly eradicate a curse of this kind; there must be improvement in the tone of society itself. This writer, however, was clearly of opinion that all that the law can do to suppress such writings should be done, in the interests of the public and especially of youth.

We found in Bengal that the criminal law as reasonably interpreted was adequate for dealing with the offender when he could be distinctly indicated. Section 124A of the Penal Code provides for the punishment of any person who by words, either spoken or written, or by signs or otherwise, brings or attempts to bring into hatred or contempt, or excites or attempts to excite disaffection towards, the Sovereign or the Government established by law in British India. Section 153A of the same Code similarly provides for the punishment of any person who by such means promotes or attempts to promote feelings of enmity or hatred between different classes of His Majesty's subjects. Besides these, there is Section 505, dealing with persons who make or circulate statements, rumours or reports conducing to mutiny in the Army or Navy, or to the commission of offences by any person. These provisions seemed to deal adequately with seditious and mischievous writing, provided that responsibility for the offence can be fixed, and that these provisions are reasonably interpreted by the courts. Both of these points, especially the former, presented difficulty.

It was with this fixing of responsibility that the Government of Bengal had particularly to deal. This is a matter of great moment. We had a number of prosecutions; and they may at first sight be regarded as successful. They invariably ended in convictions; no sensational speeches were delivered in the courts; and the cases attracted little or no interest. Further consideration, however, shows that it would be a very great mistake, for these reasons only, to regard the prosecutions as successful. They did not reach the persons really responsible. This was due to a manifest defect in the law: proprietors and editors of newspapers are not registered under the law as it at present stands, and they are therefore able to evade responsibility. It is only the printer or publisher that is registered. Any person may appear and declare himself printer or publisher of a newspaper. He may be merely a compositor, and have no interest in the paper at all. He gets a high salary for the kind of man he is, to compensate him for any risks he runs. In 1907, in the case of the notorious "Yugantar" newspaper, the seriously mischievous consequences of this were exemplified. Convictions were obtained; but they were against uneducated compositors. Surely it might be enacted that the person registered as printer shall be the actual printer, and actually in possession of the press, the magistrate having power to inquire into the truth of the allegations made. This would prevent the law from being manifestly and ludicrously ineffective in this respect.

Then again, as I have said, editors and proprietors of newspapers are not registered at all. The first prosecution of an editor that we undertook in Calcutta was successful; but the second was frustrated by the accused taking advantage of this defect of the law. In that case, which the Government took up against the "Bande Mataram" paper, Arabinda Ghose, whose name had been mentioned as editor in the paper itself, and who was generally accepted as the editor, denied that he occupied that position, and left a so-called printer, who was nothing but an uneducated coolie, to bear the brunt of the prosecution. Witnesses from among the Press establishment came forward to give evidence that there was no editor, and that contributors merely laid down their articles on the table and left them to be taken up and printed. The magistrate felt compelled to regard the evidence against Arabinda Ghose as inconclusive. His judgment showed that he had little doubt that Arabinda Ghose was the editor, but that the prosecution, "contending against a policy of silence and suppression," had failed to establish this legally to his satisfaction. In disposing of the so-called printer's appeal, two Judges of the High Court said, "It is unfortunate that the person or persons really responsible for these seditious utterances remain undetected. . . . It is evident that, if the law cannot reach the more guilty persons, it should be, and we have little doubt it will be, amended." This defect of the law was at once brought to the notice of the Government of India. But it is not yet amended.

The difficulty has been met, for the present at least, by the law giving power of confiscation of presses and suppression of papers. But no Act should be allowed to remain so ineffective in itself as this law of registration of 1867 has been proved to be. The Government is responsible for taking the necessary measures to prevent ignorant people from being incited to crimes which must tend to convert wise and gracious government into a series of acts of repression which may involve, and have involved, bloodshed, loss of property, and serious injury to innocent and irresponsible persons, not to speak of the possibility of the temporary subversion of government altogether in certain tracts. It is not severer measures against the Press that are necessary: the existing law is adequate in that respect. What is required is to fix responsibility on the right persons. It is most undesirable to make the law more strict than is necessary, for it is very important to India to have the means of ventilating grievances, exposing abuses, and giving expression to the opinions even of small sections of the community. But it is, on the other hand, as experience has now fully shown, absolutely essential to restrain the licentious section of the Press from the dissemination of such literature as has poisoned the minds of not a few, and brought about a state of things which tends to separate the officers of Government from the people, and make effective administration hardly possible. The best way to do this is not by devising exceptional procedure, but by making men realise their responsibility under the ordinary law. The men really responsible should have their responsibility fixed; and the lesson of responsibility should be taught in a way that will make it clear to everybody.

I am of opinion that wise statesmanship demands in India at the present time, and indeed always, a firm and consistent policy. The experience of the last few years seems specially to indicate the necessity for firmness in the suppression of incitements to race-feeling and sedition. It is true that undue severity and repression are never necessary or desirable. Measures of undue severity are not the mark of calm and plucky statesmanship; they are rather the sign of panic and unwisdom. What the true statesman will aim at is the least amount of severity and repression which will adequately meet the case. There can be no doubt whatever of the full importance of putting an end to the anarchy and crimes of violence which are an incalculable evil in the administration of the country, and tend to a deplorable state of feeling, not only between the people and the Government, but between different races and classes. For the preservation of society and the efficiency of Government, it is incumbent to take whatever steps may be necessary for their repression; and in doing this the Government will undoubtedly have the support of all well-disposed and reasonable persons, even though some of these may, from causes not difficult to surmise, not give their support in a very active or public manner. But on the other hand, the Government must approach this task with a sense of grave responsibility, and must make up its mind to limit its repressive measures to what the case clearly and undoubtedly requires.

While holding that more severe measures than are required should not be adopted, I am at the same time most strongly of opinion that anything like want of firmness in carrying out the measures decided on, or anything like want of continuity of policy in respect of repression, is most unwise and deplorable. I do not profess to be now behind the scenes in regard to the administration of India; but there are two things which have struck me recently as seeming to indicate a tendency to dangerous weakness in this respect. One of these was the sudden release of all the men who were deported in the cold weather of 1908-9. There was in my mind, when I demitted office, no doubt of the wisdom of deporting certain persons, in regard to whom there was good reason to believe that they were a source of great mischief in the community, and that they were largely responsible for the miserable outrages which have cast a stain on the Indian people, without in any way advancing their interests. I have no intention of discussing the propriety of the order of the deportation in each individual case. The orders were passed after I left. I accept all the responsibility that a Local Government can have regarding the measure of deportation itself, though I cannot now say whether in every case the order was an accurate one. That is a matter for which my successor must share the responsibility with the Government of India and the Secretary of State. I say this, not because I desire to indicate any doubt in any of the cases, but because no one has a right to assume responsibility in such a matter who is not at the time that it occurs the responsible adviser or officer of the Government.

The power of deportation is a special one which is entrusted to the Government for the preservation of peace and order by the country, which relies on the Government using the power with discretion when necessary. The very use of the power indicates that the grounds on which it is used in any particular case are of a strictly confidential nature. It is essential not only that the Local Government should be thoroughly satisfied in each particular case, but also that it should be able to place the case before the Government of India in a way that will thoroughly satisfy that Government also, and will enable the Secretary of State to inform the House of Commons that he, as a responsible officer of the Crown, has been fully persuaded of the necessity for the order. When a case is thus complete, and not otherwise, the order of deportation may be passed under circumstances which demand it; and an order of deportation so passed should not be rescinded until the state of things in the country clearly indicates that the necessity has passed away.

When certain proposals for deportation were submitted to the Government of India, just before I left the country, I was strongly of opinion that, while these proposals were rendered necessary by the circumstances of the case, they should not be accepted unless it was distinctly determined that the deportation should last for some considerable time. The object of deportation is to remove a man from the scene of his mischievous activities, and to obviate his influence for evil. At first there is some feeling of sympathy for him on the part especially of foolish, misguided, or irresponsible persons; but that passes away; and if he is kept out of mischief for some time, it may be hoped that he will return, shorn of his influence for evil, to a state of things where he may be safely trusted to do no harm. But if he is away only for a short time, and if he returns under circumstances which give clearly the impression that a concession in his favour has been wrung from the Government, either by him or by others on his behalf, the result is only unfortunate. He comes back to pose as a martyr and as a successful worker in the evil cause which he has adopted as his own. He comes back with greater bitterness on his own part and with enhanced influence among those whom he desires to lead. Deportation is a good weapon only if it is used under circumstances of clear necessity and with a firm and unfaltering decision.

Another instance which seemed to me to indicate a regrettable want of sense of the necessity for continuity in policy, was the temporary character given to the legislation against seditious meetings. The necessity for that legislation was clearly established. The measures adopted were certainly reasonable and not more than the circumstances required. These circumstances had not changed. What could show more clearly that the legislation was still required than the discussion which took place in August, 1910? Yet it was proposed to continue the Act only up to March, 1911, a matter of about eight months. It was indeed hoped that this extremely mild proposal to continue this legislation for so short a period, so as to allow the measure to come up before the Government of the new Viceroy, would be accepted without discussion. It was not so accepted; speeches were made by certain members of the Council which represented the state of things in India as so altered in character as to show that such a measure was no longer required. These speeches led to statements by the responsible members of the Government of India which clearly indicated the absolute necessity for continuing repression. There are those who believe that the state of things in India is as bad as ever it was, if not worse. I am not myself of that opinion. With my knowledge of what occurred while I was still in India, I am of opinion that the crimes which are now being brought to light, and the arrests which are now being made, are merely the result of the continued activity of the police in respect of matters of which they had more or less information and evidence at the time when the Seditious Meetings Act of 1907 was passed into law. But of this there can be no doubt, after what has been said by the responsible members of the Government of India, that the state of things at present is not such as to justify the removal of the restrictions on seditious meetings which were then considered necessary. It is therefore, in my opinion, distinctly unfortunate that discussion of this question should again and again be renewed, and that there should appear to be any want of determination to keep this measure in force as long as there is any necessity for it whatsoever.

The condition of things in India has undoubtedly changed for the better. There is the fullest evidence of it in the Press and in private letters from men of all classes in India. It may be attributed, as one of my Hindu correspondents says, to the "gracious measures of reform," or as another Hindu says, to the "vigorous prosecution of seditious persons." It is also attributable to a revulsion of feeling caused by the outburst of outrage and crime which has recently characterised the operations of the extremist section of Indian politicians. Murder and dacoity, even when political, are not yet popular in India. And many who were indifferent, or sitting on the fence, have in view of recent events stepped down with vigorous intention on the right side. For myself, I think that the principal cause of the diminution of political crime is the repressive legislation.

Local Governments were greatly handicapped in their action against sedition and anarchy by the utterly ineffective weapons of repression which they possessed. It took a great deal of pressure from below, and a great deal of sad experience and anxious consideration, to induce the Government of India to pass adequate measures. The necessity for the Indian Explosive Substances Act and Summary Justice Act of 1908, and the Press Acts of 1908 and 1910, was clearly established. There is no doubt that the credit for the subsidence of crime and lawlessness is due mainly, if not exclusively, to the operation of these Acts. These Acts gave both precision and promptness to the courts in dealing with the offences to which they refer. Both the uncertainty and the delay which had characterised the action of the courts had been deplorable. And I am bound to say that the administration of justice in India demands that measures should be taken to enable the courts to deal more promptly with criminal work. The delays that are at present allowed to occur are often scandalous.

To return to the Acts, I do not mean that the improved feeling in India is due mainly to them, but merely the diminution in crime and lawlessness. The reforms do not touch or influence those who are given to murder and political dacoity. Murders are still attempted and dacoities committed. But those who are connected with these crimes run now a far greater risk of being brought to justice; and the incitement to these crimes is, to a large extent, prevented by this repressive legislation. It must not be supposed that the minds and sentiments of anarchists and political criminals have in any way altered. They never directed their violence against particularly unpopular officers: the instructions were distinctly to aim rather at the more popular and influential officers; for the object was to render government difficult by preventing friendly relations between the officers of Government and the people. Therefore there should be no change of policy. India is "as quiet as gunpowder"; but mischievous and irresponsible persons should not be allowed again to scatter sparks.

At the same time, there can be no doubt that, so far as the results are up to the present apparent, the measures of reform adopted by the Government of India, with the sanction of the Secretary of State, have been of great benefit. I am proud of the Government of India, in that it was able to persevere with its wise and liberal measures of reform, in spite of the existence of anarchy and of the anxiety and work involved in dealing with it. I always urged that the Government should persevere; and the reforms have given satisfaction to thoughtful and moderate men throughout India, and have so far been fully justified by their successful working.

In a sense it is a mistake to talk of this policy as having been initiated either by Lord Minto or Lord Morley. I do not propose to touch the unfortunate controversy as to whether the Viceroy or the Secretary of State is primarily responsible for the precise character and shape of the reforms. But I think that it is not accurate to speak of the policy of these reforms as having been initiated by either. The policy is old. The reforms constitute a step forward—an important step—in a policy which has been in operation for many decades. They go further than the Government had ever gone before; but that is of the nature of all progress. A new policy might have been dangerous: it might have been unwise. It was experience which justified men in believing that this advance was wise and safe. The step that has been taken is a great step; it alters the position of things in India in some important respects; it will make it more difficult in some respects, but more simple in others, to deal with Indian questions. I believe that, under the altered conditions, the dignity and interest of the work of administration in India will remain; it will be as worthy of the best men as ever; and if the old principles of rectitude, firmness, and sympathy prevail, it will be as full of hope and of reward.

CHAPTER XXIII

THE "PARTITION OF BENGAL"

Some have attributed recent unrest in Bengal mainly, if not exclusively, to the partition. I am decidedly of opinion that this is a mistake. The records of the Government of India will show that the Local Governments of more Provinces than one had drawn the attention of several successive Viceroys to existing unrest. In Bengal there had been for years a conspiracy for the promotion of sedition and anarchy, of which documentary evidence came into the hands of the police. We found that lads had been under training in the manufacture and employment of explosives for years, and that the worst crimes had been planned long before partition was heard of. The agitation against partition was mainly due to causes which can easily be pointed out; and the comparative success of that agitation was really an indication or symptom of the existing spirit of unrest of which the partition was certainly neither the origin nor the cause. I do not think that it is necessary or desirable to revive this controversy; but I do think that the whole story of the agitation against the partition is illustrative of certain features of Indian life and work which it is worth while to mark and to remember.

In the first place, let us see what was the object of the "partition," as it is called. It was a readjustment of the boundaries of the Province of Bengal. It consisted of three different parts. Two of these have little or no connection with the agitation against partition. The first part was the constitution of a large Uriya Division by the addition to the existing Orissa

Division in Bengal of the District of Sambalpur and five Feudatory States from the Central Provinces. This was a measure of great importance, though it attracted but little attention. Sambalpur and these five Feudatory States had been connected with the Central Provinces from the formation of that Province half a century ago. The Feudatory States were governed by their own chiefs under the general supervision, in more recent years, of the political agent for the Chhattisgarh Feudatories. The Sambalpur District was under a Deputy Commissioner, who was subordinate to the Commissioner of the Chhattisgarh Division, with his headquarters at Raipur. The language of that District is Uriya, and it was the only Uriya District in the Central Provinces. The difficulty of administering it properly was immense. Any officer transferred to that District from any other part of the Central Provinces had to acquire the Uriya language. The Police, Revenue, and other departments had to be manned either by men belonging to the District itself, or by Uriyas imported from the Orissa Division in Bengal, or by men unacquainted with the language and traditions of the Uriya people.

This in itself was manifestly an evil. The District did not produce its own staff of all grades; the men brought from Bengal were generally very inferior in capacity or character, or they would not have moved from home for anything that Sambalpur could offer; and the men of other races regarded Sambalpur as a penal settlement, being altogether out of touch and out of sympathy with its people. Worse than that was the fact that it was almost impossible to transfer men from Sambalpur to any other part of the Province. The separate services had therefore a tendency to become exceedingly lax in their work and in their morale. The evil was so great that one of the Chief Commissioners of the Central Provinces obtained the sanction of the Government of India to make Hindi the court language of Sambalpur, as it was the court language of the rest of Chhattisgarh. A beginning was made in teaching Hindi as the District vernacular in the village schools. The

Revenue and Police Records were kept in Hindi; and the work of the courts was done in that language. Immediately after these orders were given effect to, showers of petitions came in protesting against the practical abolition of the true language of the people; and soon after this I had, in the course of my first tour as Chief Commissioner, to visit the Sambalpur District. I found the state of things exceedingly distressing.

I found cases of men who had been summoned to court forty or fifty miles. They could not themselves read the summons, nor could they find any one in their village to read it. They were merely told by the illiterate officer that brought it that it necessitated their appearance at the court. Fearful of the consequences of absenting themselves, they went to the court, and there inquired what it was that was wanted. Then they had to apply for an adjournment to enable them to bring up their papers or their evidence; and they had to take their weary journey back again—perhaps fifty miles on foot or in a country cart—to obtain these. Or again, a man went up to the police-station and laid information before the police regarding some offence which it was his duty to report. This report, which he gave in Uriya, was taken down in Hindi and read over to him in that language. He was called on to sign it, without being able to read it for himself or understand it when it was read to him. Or again, in regard to that which interests the people most, the Patwari (or Village Accountant) kept the village records in Hindi. The cultivator or tenant went to look at the entry, or received the Parcha (or paper containing details of his holding), and found it in Hindi, which neither he nor any of his friends could read; and it was of little or no use to him. Again, his children were beginning to learn to read Hindi; but they could not read anything to him of all that he had been accustomed to regard as of sacred or pleasant association. He could not afford to teach them two languages; and his own beloved vernacular—and Uriya is a very pleasant language to hear or to see in writing—was lost to him. No wonder that the people were grievously stirred.

An attempt was made by some officers to produce the impression that after all Hindi was fairly well understood by the people generally. Fortunately, however, we had very clear proof that this was not the case. At that very time preparations were being made for a census, and the Census Commissioner found that he could not get men to do the work in Hindi, although there was a great rush for employment on census work at the liberal terms offered by the Government. He had of necessity to get almost the whole of the work done in the Uriya language and then translate it into Hindi for abstracting. Finding things in this condition, I obtained the sanction of the Government of India to restore the Uriya language to the District; and at that time I urged that the true remedy for the difficulties of administering the District was to hand it over to the neighbouring Division of Orissa in the Bengal Province. This suggestion was the official initiation of the "partition" movement.

Some time after this, I had again to visit the Sambalpur District; and it was a most touching thing to see how the people turned out, at every village through which I passed with my camp, and at every railway station where my train halted, to return thanks for the restoration of their language. One of the striking features of the case was that the priests of all the temples everywhere, who rarely if ever come to take part in any public function, were found in the forefront of these crowds, singing some of their sacred songs and pronouncing upon me their blessings. The deep and universal distress of the people at the attempt to deprive them of their vernacular, the incalculable and far-reaching vexation and inconvenience caused by the substitution of Hindi for Uriya, and the rejoicing with which the restoration of the latter was hailed, formed a valuable lesson on the importance of working among the people in their own vernacular.

When I reached the headquarters, I was met in the usual way by the Deputy Commissioner, who was an Indian, and the European and Indian officers and members of the local bodies, and had a formal reception from them. The Deputy Commissioner warned me that about half a mile farther on, on the outskirts of the town, I should meet a large crowd who desired specially to return thanks for the restoration of their vernacular. When I came to this crowd I stopped my carriage. I was received with enthusiasm, which arose to a degree which I could not approve. I had great difficulty in restraining the people, who came with sacred fire and offerings, from paying me something of the nature of divine worship. I explained to them why I could not receive this, but that I greatly appreciated and sympathised with their sentiments of joy in that the Government of India had fully considered and rightly dealt with their case; and so we parted.

During the years that I was in the Central Provinces, the enthusiasm of these people lasted, and when the Sambalpur District was added to Bengal, at the time of the partition, and I visited it as Lieutenant-Governor of the latter Province, I found that that enthusiasm had not abated. We cannot too highly estimate the regard that the people have for their own language and their own traditions, and the enormous advantage that is to be derived from going about among them and knowing them intimately. The correct solution of the language difficulty was found in adding Sambalpur to the Orissa Division of Bengal. This was not because the people objected to be a part of the Central Provinces: if anything, they much preferred the Central Provinces Government to that of Bengal. But they could not tolerate the loss of their mother tongue; and as they could not retain it and remain part of the Central Provinces, they much preferred to go over to Bengal.

The second part of the partition scheme which may be briefly noticed was the transfer to Bengal of the five Uriya Feudatory States above referred to, and the transfer from Bengal to the Central Provinces of five Hindi States, on the other side of the Province. This measure was dictated by something of the same feeling as led to the transfer of the Sambalpur District to the Orissa Division. By being transferred to Bengal, the five Uriya

Feudatory states were brought into association with the adjoining Uriya States of Bengal, a change which greatly improved the chances of their efficient administration. On the other hand, the five Hindi States were added to adjacent Hindi States in the Central Provinces, the result being that the political agent of Chhattisgarh had under his control a more compact body of Feudatory States, the official language of all of which was Hindi.

A very interesting incident occurred in regard to the transfer of the five Uriya States to Bengal. The chiefs of these States had known me as the Chief Commissioner of the Central Provinces. They came to me as a friend and presented to me a petition in which they stated that they had three objections to the proposed transfer to Bengal. The first was that their powers and status as Feudatory chiefs were higher than those of the Feudatory States of Bengal, and that they feared that they might be reduced to the same level. The second was that Orissa had twice been under the charge of an Indian officer as Commissioner, and that it was the only Division in Bengal of which, up to that time, an Indian officer had been Commissioner. They strongly urged that they preferred very much to be under the supervision and control of a European officer. The third reason was that they had had for years in Chhattisgarh a Political Agent, who had been their kindly adviser, and had often assisted them in difficulty and saved them from trouble with their people or with the Government. They looked upon him as their friend. There was no such officer in Bengal; and they would prefer therefore to remain as they were.

It was easy for me to assure them that their powers and privileges and status would be clearly and fully defined and recorded, and that no reduction of any of them would occur; that there was a European Commissioner in Orissa now, and that there was neither more nor less chance of an Indian Commissioner being in future appointed there than in Chhattisgarh. I also assured them that I would ask the Government of India to give me a Political Agent for the Orissa Feudatories. This promise I kept, to the great satisfaction of all the chiefs of that large Agency, and to the great advantage of the administration of the States in smoothness and efficiency. It is interesting and important to observe the desire of these chiefs to be under European supervision and control, and the personal regard and attachment that they had for their European Political Agent.

As I have said, neither of these items of the partition scheme was in any way connected with the unrest. I pass now to the partition as it affected the Bengali portion of the Bengal Province. I regard the adjustment of the boundaries between the old Provinces of Bengal and Assam as a wise and statesman-like measure. It was passed after the fullest consideration, after public and private discussion with representatives of all the interests concerned, and from no other motive than the real and permanent benefit of the people of the two Provinces. I have never known any administrative step taken after fuller discussion and more careful consideration. It is not accurate to describe the change as "the partition of Bengal," inasmuch as there had already, many years before, been handed over to the Assam Province one or two of the Districts of Eastern Bengal. Eastern Bengal is a tract well known in the history of the Province, and of that tract part already belonged to the Assam Province. The transfer of the rest of it to that Province was, in my opinion, exceedingly desirable, if not absolutely necessary.

In Bengal, as it was constituted before the partition, there was an area of nearly two hundred thousand square miles, with seventy-eight and a half millions of people. It had been growing increasingly difficult, until it had become practically impossible, to conduct efficiently the administration of this great Province. It was not a matter only of the burden of work laid on the Lieutenant-Governor, but rather of the impossibility of efficient working of the various departments of the Government. No head of a department was able efficiently to deal with the great charge committed to him. The result of this was that many of the Districts of Eastern Bengal had been practically neglected. There were many reasons which led the ordinary head of a department, when he found that he could not overtake efficiently his whole charge, to give to Orissa and Western Bengal such time as he had at his disposal; and the Districts of Eastern Bengal suffered most from the undue pressure of work.

On the other hand, the neighbouring Province of Assam was too small for efficient administration. It was impossible to have an adequate body of officers permanently settled in the Province, and the consequences were that discipline was weak, and that the officers did not take that interest in their work which an officer ordinarily does in the work of his own Province. I fully concur in the statement made by the Government of India that "the evils which these proposals seek to cure, the congestion of work in Bengal and the arrested development of Assam, are of the gravest kind; and every branch of the administration in these important Provinces suffers from them in an increasing degree." It is gratifying to find that after very few years' experience the local officers and the Government of India were able to point to vastly improved administration of the transferred Districts, and that many of the people of these Districts who formerly opposed the partition had by that time given it their hearty approval.

The opposition to the transfer was mainly engineered from Calcutta; and a consideration of the character and methods of that opposition cannot fail to be in some measure both interesting and instructive. There were undoubtedly many Bengalis who were at first honestly opposed to the partition of Bengal, with whose views one could not but feel full sympathy. Their objections were patiently heard and fully considered. In most cases they were entirely removed. Among these objections were such as the following.

Some thought that when the Districts of Eastern Bengal were transferred to the Province of Assam, they would cease to be under the jurisdiction of the High Court of Calcutta, and would come under that of a Judicial Commissioner such as had existed in the Central Provinces when that Province was small and somewhat remote. They had been taught to regard the High Court, a certain proportion of whose Judges come from home, as a security of their liberty, and of their civil rights. The strength of this feeling was great. It influenced some men of the highest intelligence in all walks of life. It was a great relief when the Government of India gave the fullest assurance which a Government can give, that the jurisdiction of the Calcutta High Court would remain as long as possible, and that if in the future it should ever become necessary to give the new Province a separate Supreme Court of its own, that court would be a High Court and not a Chief Court. A similar objection was the fear that the Board of Revenue in Bengal would be abolished so far as the transferred Districts were concerned, and that they would be left in revenue matters to a final appeal either to the Head of the Province or to a Finance Commissioner. The Government of India met them on this ground also and gave a Board of Revenue to the new Province. A third objection was that they would have to go with their appeals to the remote and comparatively inaccessible hill station of Shillong, which was the sole head-quarters of the Assam Chief Commissioner. They were reassured on this point also; for they were to have a Lieutenant-Governor in the new Province, and his head-quarters were to be at Dacca, the historic capital of Eastern Bengal.

I well remember how, when I summoned a conference of all who felt that they were in any way interested in this matter, many attended who raised these objections. On finding that these difficulties were removed, they generally expressed their satisfaction. The result, however, was that some of the native papers urged the people not to attend these conferences at Belvedere, on the ground that in doing so they simply "showed their hand," and enabled us to meet their objections without giving up the project of partition. The fact was that the opposition of these particular papers to the partition was due to motives and reasons altogether different from such as I have indicated. It is worth while looking at the character and features of their opposition. It casts light on the methods which are sometimes adopted in Indian politics, and affords a lesson which ought not to be forgotten.

The character of the permanent opposition to the partition may be judged from the fact that those who publicly expressed their approval of the partition were often pilloried in the Press and boycotted so that they were practically ruined. I recall the case of a member of my own Council, who was a native of one of the Districts of Eastern Bengal which had long belonged to the Assam Province, and who represented, as a High Court practitioner, one of the Bengal constituencies sending up a member for nomination to the Bengal Council. He prepared a confidential memorandum for me, setting forth the advantages of the partition as they appeared to him, and to those who thought with him. Unfortunately, when the papers were published by the Government of India, that memorandum was published with them. He was immediately boycotted by the majority of the Bengali Bar; and his practice before the High Court fell to about one-third of what it had originally been, that one-third being mainly supplied by others than Bengalees. He had been a respected and successful practitioner; but, so far as these members of the Bengali Bar could, they deliberately ruined him, because he had differed from them in opinion on this question. It is easy to understand how difficult it is, in such circumstances, to induce men to speak out their views publicly: we must be ready to make allowance for this.

There is no doubt that there were some, among the professional classes especially, but also among the non-resident Zamindars, belonging to the transferred Districts, who did not like the separation from Calcutta; but even their feeling on the subject, which was certainly not wholly unselfish, was not very strong, until they were stirred from Calcutta into vehement opposition. Among the common people generally there was absolute, complete and universal indifference, until agitators coming from Calcutta circulated misleading statements and roused certain sections of them. It is instructive to note this fact. The strength of the opposition lay in the excitability of the people, the imputation of bad motives to the Government, and the raising of scares among the ignorant. The history of this agitation indicates a general danger to India which ought not to be overlooked or forgotten. We have in the masses ignorant and excitable peoples to deal with; and mischievous men have only to go among them with false stories to produce dangerous disquiet and to rouse them to violence.

The opposition was mainly confined to two great parties whose interests were, not unreasonably, regarded as to some extent threatened by this scheme, and whose voice is a very powerful voice in India. One of these is the Calcutta Bar I do not intend to bring any railing accusation against the Bar. I am myself a barrister, and am free, I think, of the prejudice which not a few Executive officers sometimes show against that profession. But there is no doubt that it is only natural that members of the Bar, and especially those of second-rate character and practice, should be very jealous of anything that seems to interfere with their professional prospects. Now it is clear that the transfer of a certain number of Districts to a new Province, whose head-quarters would no longer be Calcutta, would tend to diminish the business of the Calcutta Bar. They felt this, and their voice was raised with no uncertain sound against the measure. They adopted exaggerated language in regard to it, ignored the advantages which it was intended to produce, and did all they could to prejudice the people against it. They engineered with great skill, through the agency of the local Bars which had been long connected with the central Bar in Calcutta, a violent opposition to the scheme throughout the transferred Districts and throughout the Bengali Districts which were not transferred.

The other strong agency in engineering the opposition was a section of the Native Press. There are some native newspapers which have a high aim and a good tone; but the Native Press as a whole is not characterised by either good tone or high purpose. It has become to a large extent truculent and offensive. It is well known that a certain section of it exercises its influence and maintains itself partly by what it regards as spicy writing, and partly by a deliberate or perhaps occasionally unconscious terrorism. An officer on whose conduct the Government is bound to keep its eye, or a Zamindar who cannot but live a public life, is compelled to support the Press lest it should attack him. I have myself seen the following letter, which was addressed by the editor of a newspaper to a prominent public man: "As you are much before the public, it is our intention to write an article about you on such and such a date. Perhaps you would like to become a subscriber to our paper so that you may see that article when it appears?" The recipient of this letter, rightly or wrongly, believed that the character and tone of the article would be greatly influenced by his decision in regard to becoming a subscriber. Whatever the intention of such letters may be, there is no doubt that among Indian officials and gentlemen in the interior there is an impression that any attack made on them in a public newspaper tends to injure them with the Government. Now in the transferred districts the Government would no longer be the Government of Bengal, with its headquarters at Calcutta, where the newspaper was to be published. It would be a Government at Dacca, in another Province, where these newspapers were not read. The loss of influence and prestige, and the loss of clientèle was one of the causes which led some at least of the native Press to oppose the partition scheme. Others were led into it by their normal inclination to oppose anything which the Government advocated. In the usual way they misrepresented the motives and intentions of Government, and poured forth vituperation upon the measure it was carrying out. Only one or two were honest in their opposition.

The opposition was largely characterised by absolute want of principle. False stories were circulated to rouse the fears and indignation of the people. The Government, which only desired effective administration of the two Provinces concerned, was abused as being animated by a determination to break up and so destroy the influence of "the Bengali nation." All sorts of false statements were made in speeches delivered and in leaflets scattered throughout the country. There was, for example, maliciously and falsely attributed to the Government, in leaflets scattered among the common people throughout the villages of the transferred Districts, the outrageous motive of wishing to place the cultivating and labouring classes of these Districts at the disposal of the Government of Eastern Bengal and Assam, so that that Government might be able to remove them against their will from their own homesteads to a position of practical slavery in the tea-gardens of Assam. The mercantile classes were told in public speeches that the object was to injure the Port of Calcutta, a statement the ridiculous character of which may be seen from the fact that the Bengal Chamber of Commerce supported the partition scheme. Furthermore, inasmuch as the Districts transferred to the new Province had all of them a majority of Muhammadans in the population, a wicked attempt was made, by insinuations of an intention to place the Hindus under the heel of the Muhammadans, to set the professors of these two religions against each other, and to produce those religious animosities which are so real and constant a danger in India.

By such means, a violent opposition was raised against a measure, the administrative value of which was so abundantly established that the agitation against it rapidly died out in Bengal. Unfortunately, that agitation was again and again stirred into new vigour by incitements from the floor of the British Parliament. It was satisfactory to find these evil influences weakening, as the people really concerned began to see the advantages which they had derived from the measure and to be convinced of the good intention of the Government in carrying it out.

I cannot but recall a conversation which I had with a highly esteemed Indian friend, who was one of my colleagues on the Bengal Council. He was an Indian merchant of considerable distinction, and had had an honourable connection with public affairs. He made a public attack on the partition scheme, based mainly on the impression as to the intentions of the Government in regard to the High Court to which I have referred. I asked him to come and see me, and explained to him his mistake. He expressed himself fully satisfied on the point; and I suggested to him that perhaps he might withdraw his remarks. He replied that he could not do so, as he was in full sympathy with the opposition to the partition. I asked him what were his grounds for his opposition. He said that he was perfectly sure that one result of the partition would be very much to develop the Port of Chittagong, and that this could not be done without injuring the Port of Calcutta. I asked him whether he really believed that the drawing of an imaginary line between the two Provinces, and the declaration that the Districts on the one side of that line were under the government of one Province and those on the other side under that of another, would really divert the course of trade? "No," he said, "but Chittagong will be under the government of the new Province; efforts will be made to improve it; the natural communications between the transferred Districts and Chittagong will be developed, and trade will therefore take its course to Chittagong which is the natural port for that part of the country." I pointed out that this surely meant that trade would be benefited by the change; and I asked him whether he would not state that view in public. He said he would not; because he was a Calcutta man and he himself would be injured. I pointed out to him that Government must take a higher view than that, and must consider the general interests of the country. His reply was characteristically honest, but at the same time very discouraging. He said, "I do not blame you for supporting a measure which undoubtedly appears to be to the advantage of the Districts concerned; but I am bound to fight for my own interest."

The whole history of this agitation indicates some of the difficulties of Indian administration. A measure may be sound; but it may be influentially opposed by those who believe that their own private interests are at stake. That opposition may be easily exposed as regards its character; but it is not on that account overcome. Sometimes again the opposition adopts measures most dangerous to the interests of sound administration. These consist of the circulation of misrepresentations in regard to motive and intention, and of stories which an ignorant people too readily receive. In time, the motives of Government, if they are pure, will undoubtedly be vindicated; but that time may be delayed and the injury to sound administration may be great. It may also be intensified by thoughtless or malignant encouragement given to the opposition by those who are animated too often by a desire to embarrass the Government. Such encouragement is sometimes given, more or less innocently, and more or less effectively, by Members of Parliament.

I remember the late Sir Curzon Wyllie telling me that he was on one occasion walking, at the Indian Civil Service garden party in London, with a nobleman of considerable standing and distinction in India. One of the so-called "Indian members" of the House of Commons came up to this nobleman and claimed acquaintance with him. He said to him, "I hope that you have come to throw your weight into the scale on behalf of the cause of India to which we are devoted?" The nobleman replied that he did not quite understand what he meant. The Member of Parliament entered into a brief explanation. The nobleman replied, "I do not quite understand your position and your objects; but there is one thing that I do understand, namely, that you are drawing a pension of £1,000 a year from the Government of India, and you are doing all that you can to make the government of India impossible. That does not commend itself to my Oriental ideas." The Member of Parliament did not seem to have ready on his tongue an adequate rejoinder to this remark; and they parted. The view expressed is a thoroughly Indian one: the high-toned Oriental does not understand that disloyalty to the salt which seems to be indicated by persistent and unfailing opposition and cavilling criticism; and there are not a few men of Western birth and education who share this feeling.

For the sake of the lessons which it teaches, it has seemed to me well worth while to record the whole history of this measure and of the agitation against it, although it has already been greatly modified in detail by the administrative changes announced by His Majesty the King at the Delhi Durbar on the 12th of December, 1911. I do not propose fully to discuss these changes here, as they have taken place after the severance of my connection with India. Perhaps the greatest objection that can be taken to them is the manner in which the Government brought them about. None of the Local Governments or responsible officers concerned appear to have been consulted by the Government of India or the Secretary of State, nor were the public in any way taken into confidence in the matter. Under all the circumstances, however, there is much justification for this. Public discussion before the announcement of the scheme would have been surrounded with difficulties; and the scheme itself would probably not have been accepted without bitter opposition in many quarters had it not been announced by the King; and such an announcement could not have been made after prolonged public discussion. The circumstances, therefore, may be held to justify the particular procedure which would otherwise form a most dangerous precedent.

There is no doubt that the weight of public opinion is in favour of the removal of the Indian capital from Calcutta to Delhi. With my experience as Lieutenant Governor of Bengal for five years, I have no hesitation in saying that the presence of the Government of India in Calcutta rendered the administration of the Province of Bengal very much more difficult than it otherwise would have been, and was no source of strength to the Government of India itself. As to the selection of Delhi, I have no strong views; but I most certainly consider it of great advantage that the headquarters of the Government of India should not be placed alongside of the headquarters of any Local Government.

In respect of the modification of the partition of 1905, as regards the boundaries of Provinces, it may be briefly stated thus: (1) The old Province of Assam is restored precisely where it was before that partition. (2) All the eastern districts of Bengal have been restored to their connection with the western districts; and all of them, forming the five Bengali divisions, have been constituted the Presidency of Bengal under a Governor-in-Council. (3) The three sub-provinces of Patna, Chota Nagpore and Orissa have been severed from the old Province of Bengal and constituted a new Province by themselves. I do not intend to enter into a full discussion of these changes. It is clear that the object of the old partition in respect of Assam has been abandoned. The Government of Lord Curzon aimed at curing "the arrested development of Assam"; and there is no doubt that the measure they proposed was calculated to accomplish that object. The Government of Lord Hardinge, however, have proposed to sacrifice any advantage in this respect for the sake of having a small frontier Province on the north-east of India, similar to the frontier Province which Lord Curzon considered it necessary to form on the north-west, for the purpose of dealing more satisfactorily with troubles on our Indian border. The Government of India are entitled to have their view on this matter received with respect and consideration; and I do not think that there is ground to believe that any serious mistake has been made in this respect.

The propriety of this change being granted, the other changes almost follow of necessity. The need for reducing the area of the old Province of Bengal had been so clearly established, that it could not possibly be restored. Some division had to be made; and that adopted is in the main as good as any other that is at all possible. The newly constituted Province of Bengal will, in regard to the climate of its districts, be somewhat undesirable; but it will have the great advantage that there will only be one vernacular language to acquire. The three sub-provinces which have been formed into the second Province are just precisely such tracts of country as may well be administered together. The great object of Lord Curzon's partition (apart from its relation to Assam) was to divide the Province of Bengal into two manageable Provinces. This object has not been abandoned; but it has been carried out on a different method from that adopted then because of the change of view in regard to the political necessity for having a small Province on the north-east frontier. Whatever difference of opinion may exist in regard to these changes, it is, at all events, a satisfactory thing that they have been made in a way which has commanded their acceptance on all hands and has prevented undesirable agitation in regard to them. It is to be hoped that all the three new Provinces will be left undisturbed to work out their own destiny, and that they will make steady advance in prosperity and enlightenment.

CHAPTER XXIV

THE AMEER OF AFGHANISTAN

I CANNOT close these reminiscences of my Indian life without reference to the visit of the Ameer of Afghanistan to India in the beginning of 1907, which was an event of great interest. It was not a political visit, and the subject of politics was, I believe, avoided throughout the whole period. We were all enjoined, indeed, to remember that the Ameer is a sovereign ruler of a friendly State, that he was to be addressed as "His Majesty," and that he was everywhere to receive royal honour. But his visit was that of a friendly neighbour coming to see India, to make the acquaintance of some of the principal officers of the British Government, and to study the manners and customs of the country. The Ameer was a most intelligent observer, and was evidently inclined to enter on those frank and friendly relations with the people whom he met which would facilitate his obtaining some insight into the things which he wished to know.

I did not see His Majesty until he came to Calcutta. My first opportunity of talking to him was on Wednesday, 30th January (1907), when I met him at a dinner given in his honour by Lord Kitchener, the Commander-in-Chief. It was not a large or formal dinner, being given to him on the very day of his arrival in Calcutta. He was evidently on the best of terms with Lord Kitchener, whom he had met in the north of India. He spoke of him to me after dinner in terms of the deepest admiration, having been fascinated evidently, not only by the strength, but also by the courtesy and friendliness, of the Commander-in-Chief.

At this dinner, to which the mess dress uniform of all the officers present gave a very bright appearance, the Ameer sat on Lord Kitchener's right and I on his left. On my left was one of the sirdars who accompanied the Ameer, Brigadier Muhammad Nasir Khan. The latter conducted his conversation with me mainly in Hindustani, though he was far from ignorant of English. He showed himself deeply interested in all that the party were seeing of India and its administration. My conversation with the Ameer himself was partly conducted in Hindustani. He was, however, rapidly acquiring a colloquial knowledge of English, and quite liked to use that tongue.

His Majesty's determination to acquire English, and the manner in which he used what he knew of it very much impressed me. He had got hold of some very colloquial phrases as the following incident shows. I overheard him talking to Lord Kitchener about the British Nation. The Commander-in-Chief was explaining to him that there are three great divisions of the British Isles, and that the inhabitants differed in many respects from each other, but yet were equally devoted to and eligible for the service of His Majesty the King. By way of illustration he pointed to Sir Henry M'Mahon, a fine Persian scholar, who was the Political Officer in attendance on the Ameer, and was seated on the Ameer's right so as to render him any assistance that might be required in conversation. Lord Kitchener remarked that Sir Henry was an Irishman. "I myself," he said, "am an Englishman; and the Lieutenant-Governor, who is on my left, is a Scotsman. The Scots have a dress of their own. Probably," he added, as he noticed that I was listening, "because it is economical, they only wear a cloth twisted round their loins which they call a kilt."

The Ameer looked across at me with a smile; and I said, "I think that Your Majesty has seen some of our Scottish regiments in the north of India." He replied, "Yes, I have seen them. I like Scottish regiments, and" (turning to Lord Kitchener) "they do not wear kilts because they cannot afford trousers, but because the kilt leaves the legs freer and stronger for going up

Photo by *Bourne & Shepherd*

THE AMIR OF AFGHANISTAN

His signature is in the corner of the illustration

and down the hills." I remarked, "Your Majesty and I being hill men understand one another." The Ameer laughed heartily and, with a very humorous glance at Lord Kitchener, added, "Wrong box, Your Excellency!"

The next time we met was when the Ameer dined with us at Belvedere on Friday, the 1st of February. When his carriage drove up at the door I received him at the bottom of the steps, and taking his hand in mine, according to Oriental custom, I conducted him into the drawing-room. The company were standing about the room. As we entered, the Viennese band played the Afghan National Anthem, of which the music had been obtained through the military authorities of the Punjab. As the first chord was struck His Majesty stood fast; and, with his hand to his hat, he took the salute. When the Anthem was over he turned round and courteously thanked me. He and I then led the way to dinner, hand in hand in Oriental manner, Lady Fraser being taken by a member of my staff to her place next to His Majesty, and the lady whom I ought to have brought to dinner being taken to her place by the Private Secretary. I placed Col. Sir Henry M'Mahon on the other side of the Ameer so that he might act as interpreter for His Majesty when required; but there was also an Afghan interpreter standing behind his chair. Three sirdars of his staff were at table; and two pages who had accompanied him were given their dinner elsewhere.

The Ameer was most cheery throughout the dinner. He talked to Lady Fraser partly in English and partly through the interpreter in Persian, breaking out now and again into Hindustani, of which he has some little knowledge, so as to see how far she could speak the language, a matter in which he appeared to be considerably interested. His conversation was of the frankest character, and every now and again he broke into jest and laughter. His face is a very difficult one to photograph, because it is so very different when it is at rest from what it is when lighted up and animated in conversation. He expressed very freely his views on the different dishes that were served to him, and was much interested in all our cooking. We had been careful, of course, and he knew that we were careful, to avoid having any forbidden food placed on the table, so that he was quite able to partake of everything without asking any questions for conscience' sake. He did not take any wine; nor was any wine passed round the table in front of any of the guests. He and his sirdars had decanters of water and non-alcoholic drinks placed for their use; and all wine to the other guests was served from behind.

When at the end of the dinner I proposed His Majesty the King-Emperor's health, the Ameer stood and drank to it in soda-water. When we had resumed our seats, he leaned forward and said to me across the table, "Your King is very kind. He has issued the order that his health may be drunk in water. But for this I could not drink it; for I cannot touch wine. But I drink it very gladly in water with your King's royal permission." I replied that His Majesty's order had been prompted also by a desire not to force on any of his own subjects, many of whom do not approve of the use of wine except medicinally, the alternative of using wine or forbearing from this particular form of expression of their loyalty. Immediately after this I proposed that we should drink the Ameer's health, and assure His Majesty of the warm welcome which we gave him to Bengal, and to Calcutta, a compliment which he courteously acknowledged.

Immediately after this toast, the ladies left the room, and I went over and took my place where Lady Fraser had been seated between the Ameer and the then Foreign Secretary, Sir Louis Dane. I asked His Majesty whether he would like to smoke or join the ladies at once. He said he would prefer to smoke one or two cigarettes first. In the course of conversation he alluded to several matters which had struck him in the course of his present visit. One was the immense number of objects of interest which were to be seen in Calcutta; and he gave expression to the wonder that filled his mind as he drove round the city and saw its teeming population and its busy life, with its varied forms both of activity and of pleasure. He declared that he had not seen half of what he wanted to see, and stated strongly his inclination to postpone for a few days his departure from Calcutta, which had been fixed for the following Monday. This, he said, would involve giving up an arrangement which had been kindly made to show him some tiger shooting in the Sohagpur jungles of the Central Provinces; but, much as he would have liked to see such sport, he felt more deeply interested in the great shops and depots of Calcutta. He told me that the Army and Navy Stores and other large shops had greatly fascinated him, and that he was purchasing a number of things which would be most useful to him in Afghanistan, and of the very existence of which he had up to then been ignorant.

He was much struck with the magnificence of the military displays which he had seen in the north of India; but he said that he was at least as much struck with the fact that in ordinary life the troops are kept entirely in the background, and have no manifest connection with the preservation of the public peace or with the maintenance of His Majesty's authority in India. The police arrangements, the regulation of the city traffic, and the order that prevails, had made a great impression on him. He mentioned also several of our customs which he had observed. Amongst these was the custom of standing at attention and uncovering the head at the National Anthem, indicating our constant respect for, and loyalty to, the throne, though we were so far away on the other side of the world. Another custom which he incidentally mentioned was that of giving photographs to friends with autograph signatures; and he told me that he had volunteered to give one to Lady Fraser, and that he would, as soon as possible, have a good one taken for the purpose. All his conversation was courteous. There was nothing in it inconsistent with his dignity; yet it was bright and lively and often jocular.

When we went to the drawing-room he was greatly delighted to hear English music and songs from some of our guests. M. Bastin, the Belgian Consul, sang one or two French songs which greatly interested him; then one or two English songs were sung; and he asked Lady Fraser to let him hear one of the songs of her own country. To each singer he courteously returned thanks; and after the Scottish song had been sung he himself sat down at the piano and played on that instrument with both hands, but in unison, some Persian and Afghan airs, one of which was a national dance. He explained to us how this dance was performed. It required seven dancers. The band was in the middle, and the dancers were outside and swayed their bodies to and fro, and moved backwards and forwards from and to the band, in a manner which he indicated. He then asked for some Scotch music, which my wife played, and four of our guests showed him a portion of a Scotch Reel. After another Scottish song, he again sat down at the piano, and, playing his own accompaniment in unison, he sang an Afghan song in the quaint tones of the hill music. He entered into it with his whole soul, and sang with great vigour. Leaving the piano, he stepped up to my wife and me and spoke of his love for the hills of his own country and how he missed them on the plains of India. I told him that I believed all hill men have the hills of their native land near their hearts; and he stretched out his hand, with Oriental enthusiasm but an English gesture, and said, "Shake hands." He added, "I have much enjoyed myself, Lady Fraser, I have felt as though I were in my own country among my own friends."

He laughingly told us that although Hastings House, which the Government of India had placed at his disposal, was so close to Belvedere, the escort had in the dark misled his carriage on the way to dinner, and had taken him round to the Kachahri (or Magistrates' Court House), which he said was fortunately closed, or he did not know when he might have arrived at dinner. He hoped that he would get home without any such mishap. As a matter of fact, however, the escort, who were strangers, led him out of the Belvedere grounds by the wrong gate, and took him out to Tollygunge, so that he was about half an hour in reaching Hastings House, which was not more than five minutes' drive from Belvedere. I am told that he took this misadventure in the best of humour, having been engaged in pleasant conversation with Sir Henry M'Mahon, for whom he evidently has a great regard.

I saw a good deal of the Ameer after this; but I shall not allow myself to recall many of the incidents of his visit. I may, however, say that he did postpone his departure from Calcutta; and on Tuesday, the 5th, he suddenly sent to inquire whether I should be able that afternoon to fulfil a promise I had made to show him the Industrial Exhibition which had been opened just a short time before in Calcutta. I at once agreed and started off. I observed that the Ameer did not fall in with the European habit very generally adopted by advanced Indians of shaking hands. With perfect courtesy, but with equally perfect determination, he declined, as though not observing them, the hands held out to him by the Exhibition officials. He told me that he thought it was better rigidly to observe that rule with strangers. He noticed also that I was not returning the salutes of the people, and suggested that I should do so. I said, "They are meant for your Majesty." He replied, "No. You are the Governor. I am here only as your guest. You must take them." And he insisted on this.

He spent well over an hour looking at jewels and goldsmiths' work, educational exhibits, machinery, and cloths of cotton and silk. His conversation was addressed at least as much to the exhibitors as to me; and his remarks indicated the great interest which he took in everything which he saw. It was amusing to see the emphasis with which he declined to purchase any of the gold and jewelled ornaments for men. He was shown some of these, and said they were more suitable for women. He was told, however, that they were much worn by rajahs; and he suddenly broke out into a remark more plain and less courteous than usual. He said, "Are, then, your rajahs women?" He immediately recovered, however, and turned the matter into a jest.

It was interesting to see the useful objects on which he fixed his attention and spent some of his money, and the business-like care with which he insisted upon price lists being sent over to him accompanied by samples and indicated the way in which he desired these price lists and samples to be prepared. As he was leaving he was offered one or two presents. He very courteously thanked those who offered them; but touching the presents in Oriental manner with his hand he added, "I do not accept. It is not my custom." He interrupted the proceedings at one time to offer prayer at the prescribed hour. He asked one of the *maulvis* on his staff to find out a suitable place, and declined to use a room in which there were some pictures hung. A suitable place having been found, he had a prayer-carpet spread, and proceeded with his devotion, without paying any regard to those who were looking at him from a respectful distance.

The Ameer visited the Medical College Hospital in Calcutta. He was deeply interested in all he saw; and his questions to Col. Lukis, then Principal of the College and Superintendent of the Hospital, evinced great intelligence and much sympathy with the objects of the Hospital. As he was leaving, he stood for some time talking to Col. Lukis at the door of the Principal's house. A large number of crows were making a great chattering in the tree under which he was standing. He moved away to a little distance from the noise, saying, "The Calcutta crows are like many people whom I know. Their chattering prevents reasonable conversation."

He spoke very happily to me about his visit to India. He said, "While the door is shut you cannot tell whether the man within is a jeweller or only a worker in glass; even so I did not know my neighbours in India until the door was opened and I was able to pay this visit." He added that many of his people had very erroneous impressions about the English; that he himself had feared when he came that he would always have to watch every word lest he should commit himself on any political question; but that he had found nothing but friendship, brotherliness, and hospitality. No one had desired to get anything out of him or to make him commit himself to anything. He had been simply welcomed in the heartiest and frankest manner as a friend, and he would be able to tell his people, when he went home, of the great kindness which he had received.

On one occasion at Belvedere after dinner, he showed a little irritation with a servant who was attracting attention and disturbing conversation by carrying round cheroots. He turned to him and said in an undertone, "Go." The man did not understand English, and did not carry out the order. The Ameer, quite quietly and with no roughness of manner, took the box from him, placed it on the table, pointed to the door, and said "Go." The man understood the gesture and went. The incident had only taken a moment, and there was no time to have interfered. The Ameer turned round to me and said half apologetically, "You do not mind? I did not like him dancing round us like a crow among the peacocks."

On two other interesting occasions I met the Ameer. One was at the Viceroy's State Ball, a scene of great brilliancy, and the other was at the Calcutta races, where the crowd was, I suppose, greater than anything the Ameer had ever seen. His interest was untiring, and he spoke freely of all that he thought about both. I need not, however, dwell further on such subjects. A farewell dinner was given to him by Lord Kitchener on Friday, 8th February, and he left Calcutta by special train that night. After dinner he spoke again very strongly about the great advantage which he had derived from his visit to India, in having set right the vague and erroneous impressions the reports brought to him had produced on his mind. He said, "In a certain city there dwelt a people who had never seen an elephant. It was felt that their ignorance was great, so arrangements were made that a deputation of them should go and see an elephant and report. They went, and in a somewhat dark place an elephant was pointed out to them. They could not see the elephant clearly, but they felt that they could not tell their people so. They went up to it and touched it with their hands that they might carry to their people some report of what it was like. One man felt its legs, another felt its trunk, and a third felt its ear. They went back and reported to their people: one that the elephant was like a great pillar on which a house might rest, another that it was like a great serpent or sea-monster, and the third that it was like a great sheet with which a man might cover himself and keep warm." Even so, he said, erroneous reports had been brought to him by persons of imperfect observation; but now he had come to see for himself. He was very glad he had come, but sorry that he would have to part from the many friends he had found in India. He did, indeed, seem greatly to feel his departure.

In the beginning of March, just before leaving India, the Ameer was received at the Islamia College at Lahore and laid the foundation stone of the new building. He received an address from his co-religionists, the authorities of the College. When he rose to reply, the whole audience, of course, also rose. He waved to them to resume their seats, and standing alone before them he delivered an impressive extempore oration in sonorous and musical Persian. His utterance is worth recording.

He said, "First thanks to God, praise to His prophet. My brothers, I speak to you, the Muhammadans of the Punjab in India, who are present here to-day. You have read me your address. I have understood your thoughts. This is my reply. Mark it: it closely concerns your welfare. Before all else I want, at the outset, to say how deeply I appreciate the tolerance and the beneficence of the Government of India in allowing my innumerable Muhammadan brethren in this great country perfect liberty to perform their religious duties where and when and how they desire. That acknowledgment being paid, which lies foremost on my conscience, I come to the pith and marrow of my message to you and to the millions of Muhammadans whom you represent.

"In a single sentence I give you my whole exhortation. Acquire knowledge. Do you hear me? Acquire knowledge.

I say it a third time! Acquire knowledge. Oh, my brothers, remain not ignorant, and, what is worse, remain not ignorant of your ignorance. There are those who utter solemn warnings in your ears, who urge that Muhammadans have nothing to do with modern philosophy, who declaim against western sciences as though they were evil. I am not among them. I am not among those who ask you to shut your ears and your eyes. On the contrary I say, pursue knowledge wherever it is to be found; but this also I declare with all the emphasis at my command, science is the superstructure. Do not mistake it for the foundation. The foundation is, and must always be, religion. Begin, then, at the beginning. Ground your children, before everything else, in the eternal principles of their glorious faith. Start with the heart. When that is secure go on to the head.

"Some would like to finish with the heart, they are afraid of the head. They are wrong. I must speak plainly to you. You cannot earn your bread by religion alone. Religion will not give you raiment. It will not build a roof over your head. If you turn away from education, you turn away from the means of raising yourself to prosperity and power. I will be more plain still. Pinch your head and you will feel the pain in your belly. But do not lose sight of my other injunction. It is your duty to infuse into the hearts of your children, when they are young and impressionable, such a love for their holy faith that nothing can ever eradicate it. You must so bind their hearts to it, that neither the influences of other religions, nor those new influences which are antagonistic to all religions, can weaken their loyal adherence to the tenets of Islam. Do not think that my two injunctions are incompatible. I tell you that if you place your feet firmly on the sublime teachings of your holy prophet, you may let your mind wander over the other forms of knowledge in the world without losing your balance. If the light of religion be truly entered into a man's inner being, it will never afterwards leave."

After referring to the work of the College, to the interest of the Government of the Punjab in Muhammadans, and especially in Oriental education, he made a gift to the College, and concluded by saying, "Now I pray God that He may keep Islam in good countenance before the eyes of the whole world, and that we and our faith may retain the respect of the nations." The Muhammadans of India have shown a good example in their efforts to teach the young the elements of their faith and to train them in the practice of religion; but, in their too general suspicion and even rejection of modern science and education, they have greatly injured their position and influence. They have fallen behind the Hindus in the march of progress, and it will be well for them if they take to heart the earnest exhortation of the Ameer.

CHAPTER XXV

THE HUMOURS OF ADMINISTRATION

I do not think that there has been any time in my service when I have found my work light except, perhaps, when, many years ago, I was Excise Commissioner of the Central Provinces, before that office was amalgamated with several other miscellaneous departments, and before Berar came under the Central Provinces administration; but though our work has generally been quite sufficient for each day, it has been varied work; and as a great deal of it had to be done outside the office, in the town or among the villages, it has been both interesting and healthy. There have also been incidents occurring every now and again, which have been of a more or less humorous character and have relieved the monotony of our work. Many such incidents crowd on my memory now. But I shall only relate a few of them. The homely character of our life in the Central Provinces led to many private little jests which were pleasant at the time, but would seem almost silly if set down in print. I shall therefore confine myself to a few incidents more or less connected with work.

On one occasion, when I was a District Magistrate, I exposed myself to severe censure from the European ladies of the station on account of the version which got about of a decision in my court. I was reported to have judicially ruled that, according to the law prevailing in India, a husband had a right to beat his wife, and that she had no remedy in such a case. It will be understood that this was not a very popular decision with the ladies. The facts of the case were a little interesting. There had been a long-standing feud between two small Zamindars (or landowners) in a certain village; and they had been in the habit for some time of taking all manner of means to annoy one another. At last one of them got an opportunity of which he promptly availed himself. His rival Ramparshad was heard speaking in strong terms to his wife in the verandah of their house; and the sound of a slap was heard. Gangaparshad either heard the quarrel or was told of it; and he got hold of a friend to take a document to Ramparshad's wife on which she was asked to make a mark, and was informed that by doing so she would receive considerable benefit. Trusting to the friendliness of Gangaparshad's messenger she made the mark.

The document stated that Ramparshad very frequently assaulted her, entered in detail into an exaggerated recital of the events of the quarrel above referred to, and ended by asking the protection of the Magistrate. There is no doubt that Gangaparshad thought that Ramparshad would suffer very much in dignity by this attack on his character, and by the necessity for having his wife called as a witness in court; and Gangaparshad being a relative of the lady was able to appear as her friend and quasi guardian in the case. A very careful inquiry on the spot showed the triviality of the incident, and the enmity which lay at the bottom of the complaint.

The case came up for hearing when I was in camp near the village where the parties resided. Ramparshad was advised by his counsel to allow his wife to appear, closely veiled, as a witness for the prosecution. She admitted that her husband had spoken roughly to her and had given her a slap in a fit of temper, for which she proceeded to make an elaborate apology. In cross-examination by the accused she spoke of the excellent terms on which she lived with her husband; and I allowed villagers to appear to corroborate her evidence. I was entitled under the law to compel Gangaparshad to make compensation to Ramparshad for a frivolous and vexatious complaint; and I did so. The effect was not unsatisfactory. It did not indeed make Gangaparshad more friendly to his rival; but it made him a little more cautious in his conduct. It is very curious how much we see, even in very serious cases, of the use of the courts for purpose of private enmity. Cases have been well known in which even a charge of murder has been trumped up by a man against his enemy.

Another matter which, though very serious, has its more or less humorous side, is the practice of trial by jury, as we not infrequently find it in India. Every country has experience of the difficulty of persuading men to find a verdict against the accused in certain cases where political or faction feeling is involved; and this, of course, is found in India as elsewhere. There is, however, a case peculiar to India which is of very common occurrence, that is, the difficulty of persuading jurors or assessors to find a verdict against a Brahman, especially in cases involving capital punishment. Assessors differ from jurors in that their opinion has not the weight of the verdict of a jury. Assessors are there to advise the Judge, not to decide with any finality even questions of fact; and in the more backward tracts we have much more of trial with assessors than trial by jury.

As a young officer, I was once called on to inquire into a case of murder and to prosecute it before the Court of Session. It was as clear a case as ever had been. The murder was cruel; and the eye-witnesses were beyond suspicion. There were two assessors; and both of them returned a verdict of "not guilty." The Judge, differing from the assessors, sentenced the Brahman accused to death, and he paid the penalty. Some time afterwards, one of the assessors came to visit me. He was a fairly influential landowner, and himself a Brahman, well educated in the vernacular, but without knowledge of English. I asked him how he could find a verdict so contrary to the evidence; and he frankly said to me in the most friendly way, "I could not possibly find a verdict that would lead to the death of a Brahman. You know that it is grievous sin for any Hindu to cause the death of a Brahman; and it does not matter whether you do it with your own hand or indirectly by the hand of another." "But," I said, "it is a serious thing for you to violate the trust which is reposed in you by the Government on behalf of the public; and you cannot help regarding this as most blameworthy failure of duty." He replied with some emotion, "It is you really who are to blame. You are not ignorant of our views in this matter. Why, then, should you put us in a position where we might be called upon, as I was on that occasion, to choose between the sin of saying what I believed to be untrue, and the infinitely awful sin of causing the death of a Brahman?" The strong feeling with which the old man spoke to me on the subject made a great impression on my mind; and I have often thought that we do not know, or at all events do not fully consider, what grievous injury we inflict on the people of India by forcing on them customs and duties which are altogether inconsistent with their traditions and beliefs.

I remember another case in which an Honorary Magistrate tried a Hindu belonging to a religious order for habitually receiving stolen property. As in this country so in India, the receiver of stolen property ought to be severely dealt with because of the demoralising effect of his occupation on the community. The evidence was clear and conclusive; and the Magistrate felt himself bound to convict; but there is a provision of the law whereby the period of police custody after conviction is included in the period of imprisonment. The worthy Magistrate therefore set himself to calculate how long it would take to march the prisoner, from one police station to another, to the head-quarters of the District where the jail was situated. He calculated that it would take a week; and he sentenced the sacred receiver to a week's imprisonment. I well remember how he could not conceal from me afterwards his disappointment that he had forgotten that there was an indirect road to head-quarters which included a considerable stretch of newly made railway line; and the prisoner arrived at the jail in time to undergo three days' imprisonment. The washing off of the sacred ashes and filth which he had, perhaps for years, allowed to accumulate, was a terrible blow to the criminal; and he very vigorously cursed the Magistrate.

Another curious case may be recorded. When I was Commissioner of Chhattisgarh I had appellate jurisdiction over certain civil courts. In one of these subordinate courts a certain plaintiff had brought a suit against a debtor. The debtor's plea was that he had certainly incurred the debt, but that he had also repaid it; and he challenged the plaintiff to take an oath to the effect that he had not been paid. The law allows a case to be decided in this way with the consent of parties. The party agreeing must take an oath which he regards as most certainly binding upon him, and the obligation of which on him the opposite party is also prepared to admit. The parties in this case agreed that the plaintiff should take his oath with his hand on the tail of the sacred cow at the great temple of the goddess Samlai in Sambalpur—an oath of great solemnity in these parts. The plaintiff took the oath and declared that he had not been paid; and decree was accordingly passed in his favour. That night the plaintiff died; and the ground of appeal to me was that the gods had manifested their displeasure at the false affirmation by taking the plaintiff's life, and that therefore the decree ought to be reversed. I have very little doubt that the plaintiff's oath was false; but I was, of course, unable to alter the decision; for the law makes such an oath, when taken by consent of parties, final in the case.

A more amusing decision in a civil case came to my notice. A certain officer was trying a case in which the facts were very similar to the above. The plaintiff was a usurer well versed in the law. The defendant was a Gond, a member of a jungle tribe, improvident in habits, but well versed in jungle work. The plaintiff sued for a debt of Rs. 100. The defendant stated that he had only received Rs. 10. The usurer produced a book entry showing payment of Rs. 100, and called two witnesses, who in cross-examination admitted that they were employed habitually by the usurer to witness payments to his clients who could not read nor write; and that they had seen a payment made to the defendant, but could not precisely say how much had been paid. The Judge, who was trying the case in camp (as was not uncommon in those days), pointed to two trees in front of his tent and said that whoever should first reach the top of either of these trees would obtain a decree, and that the plaintiff should have his choice of trees. Of course, the plaintiff, poor man, after toiling violently for a time, gave up the enterprise to find that the Gond had been to the top of his tree and down again, and was awaiting the decision. The judge gave the decree for the plaintiff for Rs. 10 only. The plaintiff, however, told him that he would appeal from that decision, as it was entirely contrary to law. When he came to ask for a copy of the judgment to append to his memorandum of appeal, he found that it was a reasonable and well-stated discussion of the evidence, showing that the plaintiff had failed to establish the payment of more than the sum awarded. The Judge, who was, on the whole, a very sound and fairly popular officer, received in connection with this case an admonition with which he was more or less familiar, that such humorous treatment was to be deprecated as leading ignorant people to suppose that the courts of justice depended for their decisions on something else than legal evidence.

I remember accompanying a distinguished officer in an inspection of plague hospitals in a city which I was visiting. Some of these plague hospitals were supported entirely by private charity. The inspecting officer was walking round one of these private and temporary hospitals with the promoters. I was behind with an officer who was largely responsible for plague work. We passed through a ward in which we were shown a number of convalescents. One man attracted my attention from his clear eye and healthy appearance. I drew the attention of my companion to his condition; for I had never before seen a man who had so thoroughly recovered in apparently so short a time from the terrible effects usually resulting from a case of plague. I happened to know the vernacular of this town, though it was in a different Province

Photo by *Johnston & Hoffmann, Calcutta*

KINCHINJANGA FROM DARJEELING

from my own. I asked the man how long he had been ill; and in the simplest way he told me that he had never been ill, but had been ordered to lie in bed quietly while the distinguished inspecting officer was going his round. He also said that all the malis* and other servants had been similarly put to bed for that morning.

This is an illustration of two things against which one has very carefully to guard in Indian inspection. The one is what we know as "eye wash," that is, a regular preparation for the inspection by arranging places and things as one would like the inspecting officer to find them. The other is the tendency that some Indians have to strengthen a really strong case by false evidence. There could be no doubt whatever that this private and temporary hospital was meeting a real need and doing good work; and yet its promoters were not above putting healthy men into the beds of a selected convalescent ward for the purpose of strengthening the impression of the usefulness of the institution.

In this same institution there occurred that morning an incident which gave me really a thrill of horror. The inspecting officer, who was deservedly beloved for his deep interest in the people, and for the courage and devotion with which he fought the terrible battle he had to fight against the plague, was passing through a ward in which some plague patients were lying in more or less serious condition. One of these was requested by the chief promoter of the institution to place a garland of flowers round the neck of the inspecting officer. The patient rose from his bed and, standing beside it, placed the garland as requested. The inspecting officer, with surely a reckless courage, bowed his head and received it. The promoters were fatalistic in their faith, and gave no consideration to the possible consequences of their act.

The fatalism of Muhammadans and Hindus alike, militates, to a very large extent, against sound sanitary arrangements throughout the country. When I was Commissioner of Chhattisgarh, we had a series of lectures on Saturday evenings in the

* *Mālī* is a gardener.

Raipur Town Hall on social, sanitary, educational, and moral subjects. The Civil Surgeon was lecturing one evening on "sanitation," and delivered a very clear and popular address which, some of us thought, must have made a great impression. What was our surprise when we found a member of the Bar, an orthodox Hindu but very fairly versed in English, rising and delivering an English speech in defence of the opposition or indifference of the people to sanitary measures. I remember that one point which he made was this, "The Civil Surgeon has spoken to us strongly of the insanitary condition of the great tank in the middle of the city, and of the impurities which analysis has found in its waters. We could see that he even shuddered as he spoke of people drinking that water. Now I and my family have drunk that water for years and have never drunk anything else. On the other hand, I have no doubt that the Civil Surgeon sometimes eats beef at his dinner. As for me, on account of the traditions of my people, and my hereditary views in regard to the cow, I cannot think of eating beef without shuddering in a similar way. It is all a matter of tradition and training. The Civil Surgeon has no more right to call upon me to give up the water which I have been in the habit of drinking, than I have to call on him to give up the beef of which his religion allows him to partake."

Somewhat different from this was the case, a very exceptional one indeed, of an officer well up in the Service, under whom I had once to serve. He was a man by no means wanting in courage or in pluck; and he had often faced unmoved great danger in the jungle; but there was one thing of which he was always in deadly fear: that was cholera. When there was any cholera visitation that required the personal attention of a Magistrate, he always sent out one of his subordinates. In sending me out on one occasion he said to me quite frankly, "I send you out because I really feel absolutely unfit to go myself. I recognise that with reasonable precautions, which I know you will take, the risks of infection are minimised; but I cannot reason about cholera. I can only feel." I had too much respect for his character to consider him a coward on account of this idiosyncrasy; and I went willingly to my duty to save him. The fatalism of the Hindu or Muhammadan very often saves him from such fear; but on the other hand, there is nothing more awful than the panic which a severe visitation of cholera sometimes brings to the country villages. I have already described an experience of this kind. When such a panic seizes the people, they cannot reason, they can only feel.

Talking of sanitation reminds me of an amusing incident which I once met with in a certain town in the Madras Presidency. The Sanitary Commissioner had just been round inspecting, and had prepared a note on the sanitary conditions of the town. One copy of this note was in the usual way sent first of all to the Indian Deputy Magistrate in direct charge of local sanitation, that he might make any remarks or suggestions in regard to the criticisms of the Sanitary Commissioner. A brief paragraph in the Sanitary Commissioner's note contained the words, "I have specially noticed the absence of any cesspool near any house in the parts of the town that I have been able to visit." The Deputy Magistrate apparently regarded it as the sole function of an inspecting officer to point out faults; and as the Sanitary Commissioner had added no comment to this statement, he wrote in the margin, "One can easily be supplied." As the cesspool is one of the most dangerous of insanitary conditions, this remark indicated a strange ignorance of the subject on the part of an Indian officer more or less directly responsible for sanitary work. The incident illustrates the fact that sanitary science is still a thing which we have to teach the natives of India.

I remember an amusing but somewhat instructive incident illustrative of the simplicity and superstition of the jungle peoples. The Government had ordered certain selected fields of defined area to be sown with certain crops, so that the out-turn might be carefully ascertained. An officer responsible for these crop experiments was going round inspecting. He came to a field which had been selected. The crop was all on the ground, and a number of Gond women had been gathered together to cut it as soon as he gave the order. A certain practical joker, who had much local influence, was present. Out of thoughtless mischief he said to the reapers, "This man," (referring to the inspecting officer) "is a magician; you will see that he will first of all take a chain in his hand; he will then stride all round the field dragging the chain after him; and when he has completed this movement he will turn round suddenly and cry, 'Abhi kato!'* If he does so, do not cut; for, if you do, there will be no children in your houses." The inspecting officer acted exactly as was anticipated; and as soon as the two fatal words were uttered, the reapers fled into the jungle; and the experiment was held in abeyance. This ill-timed jest indicates the danger that may be caused by foolish and mischievous statements made to ignorant and credulous villagers, a danger which can hardly be overestimated.

In this connection there occurs to my mind a strange petition which was solemnly presented to me by a large number of the inhabitants of the Bhandara District during a great cholera epidemic. The cruel amusement of cock-fighting was illegal. This petition informed me that the great goddess, under whose orders cholera was sent, demanded blood. If but a little blood could fall to the earth, the cholera would abate: therefore they besought me to suspend temporarily the operation of the law. I formally passed order that no action could be taken on this petition. At the same time I privately gave orders that if a cock-fight took place, to soothe the feelings of the people and put heart into them, the police were not to take proceedings. There is no doubt that there are many among the ignorant and superstitious residents both of town and country who believe that the abolition of some even of the horrid cruelties of olden days has evoked the wrath of the gods.

I have noticed elsewhere how the Khonds in Bastar revived all the formalities of human sacrifice in their attack on the Kultas, so as to appease the goddess of the soil. I remember

* "Now cut!"

also being present at the great observances of the Dassara festival in the Raipur District and seeing self-immolation practised in a manner which greatly shocked me. Amongst other observances there were men who danced the whole length of the route of the procession with steel spits thrust through their protruded tongues. I was told that they did this in accordance with vows that they had made to the gods when asking for special favours. There is clear evidence to show that, though our legislation for the suppression of murder and of cruelty in the name of religion has commended itself to the intelligence of Indians and to the acceptance of the people generally, there are times of distress and panic when the people are very much inclined to revive them.

On one occasion when Commissioner of Chhattisgarh I was travelling through certain very jungly districts, preparing the minds of the people for the coming of the new railway. The jungle people were a little disturbed at rumours of the unknown power that was coming among them; and, as I knew them well, I went out to soothe them and to win their confidence. Rails had been lightly laid down along the track for the carriage of materials and a light engine with a first-class carriage was placed at my disposal. I ran down to the end of the line to meet the Chiefs, whom I had often met before in the course of my tours. I had a talk with them on the evening on which I arrived; and we then retired to rest. I was awakened in the night by the weird sound of jungle music. I knew that the tribes were at worship. Next morning I asked the local Chief where the shrine was at which they had been worshipping. After some hesitation he told me that there was no shrine, but that his people had been offering a goat to my engine. He apologised for having disturbed me, and hoped that I would not mind this liberty having been taken with the engine by these simple people. I found the engine sprinkled with blood, and beside it the signs of the sacrificial feast which had been held. These superstitious people had wished to conciliate the unknown power; and I was thankful that their ignorance prompted that desire, and not the smashing of the engine to pieces and vengeance on all connected with it, as it might have done.

To return to lighter subjects, I remember an old Feudatory Chief who was very punctilious about all forms of ceremonial. When as Commissioner I entered his State, he always met me on the border. During the marches to his capital he sometimes asked me to sit with him in the howdah of his elephant and discuss the business of his State as we went along. I occasionally accepted his invitation for a part at least of the march. He always placed me, as a distinguished guest, on his right hand. At the same time he was strongly of the opinion that neither he nor I should descend first from the elephant; for whoever should first reach the ground and stand awaiting the other was, in his view, to be regarded as distinctly occupying the position of the inferior. He recognised the feudal superiority of the British Government, but he regarded the Commissioner rather as his guest and friend than as his superior. Accordingly he always had two ladders placed on the near side of the elephant. With some difficulty he scrambled to the farther away ladder, leaving the nearer ladder to me. We descended our ladders *pari passu*; and we paused for a moment on the last rung of the ladder, balancing ourselves each on the one foot, with the other ready to place on the ground. We stepped to the ground simultaneously, and thus succeeded in avoiding any question of precedence.

A quaint correspondence came to my notice when I was in the Central Provinces Secretariate. An officer, able but of a somewhat peculiar style of humour, and holding the position of head of a department, was once encamped within a cantonment. There is a rule that tents may not be pitched in certain parts of a cantonment without the consent of the officer commanding. The officer in command in this case was a Brigadier-General, who was well known to be somewhat of a martinet. As he rode round with his Brigade-Major (as it was in those days) he noticed the tents, and asked that officer whose they were, and whether his sanction had been obtained for pitching them.

The Brigade-Major replied in the negative, and was ordered to find out whose the tents were. Galloping up to the tents he found out that the officer in question was absent. He reported that he was the head of a certain department. The General said, "Then tell him that he has no right to pitch his tents in cantonments without my permission, and that I cannot have this rule broken. He must either strike his tents or obtain my permission." The Brigade-Major carried out the order too literally, and wrote a letter in almost these very words. The head of the department replied as follows:—

"My dear Sir,—I am in receipt of your letter of this date. You ought to have known that I could not be aware of the order requiring the General's consent to pitch my tents in the cantonment; or I should have asked for it.

"2. As the matter now stands I shall neither ask for that consent nor strike my tents; for they are already pitched at a place called Ganeshpur, seventeen miles off.

"3. I propose to bring out a new edition of a useful publication known as the 'Polite Letter-writer'; and I am indebted to your courtesy for a gem.

"I am, yours faithfully,

"A.B."

The General sent the correspondence to the Chief Commissioner. The latter directed the civil officer to withdraw the third paragraph of his letter as needlessly offensive, and forwarded a copy of that order to the General Officer commanding the cantonment, with the remark that he thought the Brigade-Major's letter to the civil officer was scarcely courteous to a man of his official position. We heard nothing of the matter for some time. After a few weeks the civil officer wrote to me, "I daresay you will like to know the end of the correspondence between the General and me, which was submitted to the Chief Commissioner for orders. Immediately on receipt of the Secretariate letter, I wrote to the Brigade-Major saying that I had received an order from the Chief Commissioner to withdraw the third paragraph of my letter to him; that as the letter was of no importance I had kept no copy; that I was very anxious to carry out the orders promptly; and that I should therefore be much obliged to him if he would send me a copy of my letter that I might withdraw the third paragraph. I have received no reply."

I conclude this chapter with an account of a very curious case which I had to decide early in my service. One of the officers of the station, who was exercising the powers of a civil court, had a sweeper in his employment. This sweeper had a quarrel with his fellow-craftsmen in Jubbulpore. It appeared that this class, which is generally regarded as altogether without caste, has still, or had then at least, some caste feeling. The sweeper to whom I refer had been guilty of some breach of caste law, and his fellow-craftsmen turned him out of the caste. They managed, however, to patch up a peace, and they agreed to receive him back into fellowship. This was to be done, as usual, by his giving a feast and their partaking of it, so as to show practically that the caste barrier in his case had been removed.

The sweeper prepared the feast; and the members of the caste came together. Unfortunately, however, they renewed their quarrel before they had sat down to the feast provided; and the guests refused to partake of it at all. He sued them for the cost of the provision he had made. His master reported to superior authority his relation to the plaintiff, and recommended that some other judge should be appointed to hear the case. I was accordingly solemnly gazetted with special civil powers of a subordinate court, for the trial of this case of Jangi Mihtar vs. Bhangi Mihtar and others.

It was an extraordinary experience to have a court full of sweepers. My Sharistadar (or Clerk of the Court) was a Brahman; so was my Court orderly. Their feelings at being brought into close contact for a whole day with a large number of members of this untouchable community were such as it is difficult for a European to realize. They seemed to shrivel with horror and try to sink through the wall or floor. Papers had to be handed to the Court containing statements of the parties. My Brahman Sharistadar would not touch them with his fingers. I doubt if he would have picked them up with a pair of tongs. I had to take them with my own hands, and then to peruse them with my own eyes: he would not even look at them.

It was curious to hear these people telling, in their quaint way, of their controversy, of their would-be reconciliation, and of the manner in which that reconciliation came to nought. Then it was curious to have to decide that such caste disputes were hardly for the intervention of the Government or the courts, and that while a man was fully justified in preparing a feast for his friends if he chose, he had hardly a claim at law for the expense of that feast if they failed to partake of it. It was also experience of some value to see, on the one hand, the terrible antipathy and aloofness of the high caste Brahman from these unfortunate outcasts, and, on the other hand, the fact that the European's want of any share in or sympathy with these feelings did not in any way injure his prestige with his Brahman fellow-workers.

CHAPTER XXVI

THE LAST

In the course of these reminiscences I have only very occasionally referred to other Services than my own, or to any other matters concerning that Service than its relations with the people of the country. This is because my intention has been to deal chiefly with that which is peculiar to India and not with that which is easily imagined by residents in this country. For the same reason I have not had much to say of European society, or of the life of the European except where it comes into contact with his Indian fellow-subjects. It is not that I have not most pleasant memories of my relations with non-official Europeans or with European officers of all Services, but merely that these memories do not form part of those impressions of Indian life that I desire to convey.

I have, of course, been much brought into contact with officers of the Army in India. I had some most interesting work with Lord Kitchener immediately after his arrival, when he was working out his scheme of more scientific disposal of the troops under his command. I was then President of the Police Commission; and we had to discuss together personally how best to employ the police for the maintenance of the peace, which is surely their legitimate work, when troops were removed from some of the places where they had been scattered abroad over India. I found him, as might have been expected, a delightful man to work with.

I have had to work with military officers of all ranks: rarely has there been anything but pleasure in so doing. But of all my experiences in this respect, the best was that of co-operation with them in famine work. I confess that I was surprised beyond measure to find dashing young fellows caring, with all a woman's tenderness and care, for the cholera-stricken man or the poor emaciated famine baby. I could have foretold with confidence the energy and courage which these officers displayed; but I could not have imagined the depth of their tenderness and sympathy with distress. It was a fine experience of the peculiar gentleness which often characterises the brave and manly.

With the Medical Service I was brought much into contact in the ordinary work of the Province. This service has much improved during the last forty years. When I went to India, it had in its ranks some splendid men, worthy in every way of the great traditions of the profession to which they belonged, men of zeal and capacity and kindliness which endeared them to Europeans and Indians alike. But the Indian Medical Service, as a whole, is higher now than formerly in its appreciation of the opportunities of usefulness in India, and in the sense of responsibility for the discharge of its duties. I have often been struck with the devotion to professional study and medical work shown under very trying circumstances.

We have some stations in which the Civil Surgeon leads a lonely and weary life. In the early morning he spends hours in the work of the local jail, of which he is the Superintendent, enforcing discipline, working like a shopkeeper among the jail stores, dealing with the sick or the malingering, and often weary with the drudgery of his clerical work. He passes on to the Dispensary and Hospital, and gives to the poor of other races than his own the best of his skill and attention. And then, when the long round of morning work in small and sometimes crowded rooms, or within the hot enclosures of the prison walls under the Indian sun, might reasonably have been pleaded as an excuse for rest, he has turned to reading intended to keep him abreast of modern science, or to research as to the causes and cure of tropical disease.

THE LAST CHAPTER

I have been filled with admiration sometimes to see a man in a remote station, with a laboratory and instruments of his own, working steadily, with no sympathetic colleague to encourage him, doing his duty as best he could, not with eye-service but from devotion to the cause of suffering humanity. The Civil Surgeon has his reward. Not only is there intense interest in his professional work; but he wins, more fully than perhaps any other, the love of his fellow-men. His help comes when we need it most; and we cannot forget it.

The Forest Officer has a delightful sphere of activity. For myself, I have enjoyed no part of life in India more than the life in the jungles. Nature is so rich and beautiful. The air is generally so cool and fresh. The people are so simple and primitive. I do not wonder at the love of his profession which I have seen in almost every Forest Officer I have known. I shall never forget the pleasure it was to have a short tour through his forests with Colonel Doveton, the first Conservator with whom I was well acquainted. It was amusing to see his indignation when a tree, in the forest or out of it, was ruthlessly lopped, or prematurely cut down. It was the cruelty of the deed that galled him. The tree was to him a living thing, whose beauty had been marred or limbs injured by the pitiless act of a wicked or thoughtless person. He lived in the forests for months together; he knew the trees individually, and watched them with kindly interest; he knew the wild beasts, and could lead you to them without fail; and, more than all, he understood the simple forest folk, and could get work out of them as no other could, for they trusted him and regarded him with respectful affection. The one thing that the Forest Officer generally has especially to guard against is the danger of not giving adequate consideration to the requirements of the neighbouring villages in regard to jungle produce. He seldom knows these villages as he knows the forests; but the best Forest Officers do what they can to acquire the necessary knowledge; and the Revenue officer will help to keep them mindful of this part of their duty.

THE LAST CHAPTER

It would be a strange thing if I were to forget my years of co-operation with the Public Works Department. The Chief Engineer of a Province is also Secretary to the Local Government in that department. When I was Chief Secretary in the Central Provinces, my colleague was my old friend James Glass, C.I.E., whom I had known intimately during nearly all my service, a man who made his mark throughout the Province, and left behind him many monuments of his skill and energy, among which the water works in Jubbulpore hold, perhaps, the first place. I cannot even now recall without emotion the unselfish and unsparing devotion to duty which wrecked the health of one of the best officers I ever knew, Edmund Penny, whose health was shattered by his labours in the great Central Provinces famine, and who has not yet fully recovered what he freely sacrificed.

Memories arise of many others who have left their permanent mark in the Provinces in which they served. The Public Works officers have this great advantage over us all, that their mark does remain. We may think we have done some service—they can point to material evidence of their work. If they have a defect, it is that they seem sometimes to forget that they are building for time and not for eternity: they are sometimes too solid, too slow, and too expensive. It seems to me also that sometimes they are engaged on matters too small for them and on works which, though great enough, might be as well and more cheaply carried out by non-official agency. Where private contractors exist they should be utilised.

There is one fact about the Public Works Department that may be mentioned as very encouraging, viz., the considerable number of exceptionally good men that have been produced by Indian Schools of Engineering. I regard it as of the utmost importance to utilise in such departments as Engineering, Medicine, and Law, as far as possible, the men who have been trained in Indian schools, and to make these schools so efficient that they will produce men with the necessary training, capacity, and integrity.

THE LAST CHAPTER

Non-official Europeans are apt to be forgotten when talking of Indian work. Yet they do some of the most important work. They are bringing capital into the country; and they are engaged in developing its resources. Some of them are selfish enough; but many of them are animated by a high sense of duty. There is a good deal of ill spoken of the men "of the dispersion," the Europeans scattered abroad over India, sometimes in lonely places, as merchants, planters, or mechanics. This is, to a great extent, due to misunderstanding and to exaggeration. Of course they are not all what they ought to be. They do not all live as we should like to see Europeans live in the presence of the peoples of India. But even if they were not as good as their brethren of the same position and occupation at home, some allowance would have to be made for the different character of their surroundings, and for the great neglect of them by the Churches at home, and by many of the servants of the Church in India. My experience is that most of them appreciate fully any efforts to help them to maintain in India the traditions of the fatherland, by providing them with religious ordinances and their children with education.

Sometimes, when they come home, they talk a good deal of nonsense about work in India in which they have taken little interest while there. This comes of a too natural inclination to talk without any knowledge about things with which one feels that he is expected to have some acquaintance. This should be discounted. It is not a very difficult thing to guage the value of a witness and his capacity to speak with authority. Ascertain what opportunities he had of knowing that whereof he affirms, and how far he was likely to use these opportunities well. As for the men themselves, I need only say, in a word, that some of my best friends in India were non-officials, and that I have always found such men willing to co-operate in any enterprise which they saw to be for the good of the people.

The domiciled community, partly European, but mainly Eurasian, has been too much neglected in the past. One does not realise the importance of this community, nor the serious consequences of this neglect, until he comes to live in a city like Calcutta. We owe much to America for its co-operation in educational and missionary work in India. We owe much to that country also for its work among the domiciled community. There are some earnest British clergymen and laymen who have devoted themselves to such work ; but the Methodist Episcopal Church of America has done very special service in this respect. Its servants have laboured hard and successfully. I am glad to find of recent years a great increase of the sense of responsibility for the intellectual and moral training of the children of this community. And I earnestly trust that the scheme which is now being inaugurated by zealous men in all the Churches largely through the influence of Sir Robert Laidlaw, a wealthy and benevolent business man in Calcutta, will be successful throughout India. It is of the utmost importance to save this community from a position which would make it a scandal in the country.

What I have aimed at in these reminiscences has been to convey some idea to the ordinary British imagination of the life we live in India, and of the peoples among whom that life is spent. I have not aimed at giving either a scientific or statistical account of India and its affairs, but merely at communicating in a simple way some impressions of life and work. I hope that I have made it clear that India is not a mere "land of exile." It is the scene in which a man finds his life-work—work honourable and delightful, the place where he has friends whom he loves and ties which it is hard to sever. Its peoples and its ways become very dear to him. At the same time, he must not forget that, though his life is there, he belongs all the time to that little Island in the far-off Northern Seas whose life in its great essentials he has to bring with him to his work. He must not forget the traditions and principles of his fatherland. He does not adopt the ways and customs of the peoples to whom he goes. In a sense he remains apart: he is not of them. He must maintain touch with the Home-land. He must take the best books, magazines, and papers that he can afford to get, so as not to fall out of sympathy with its life and thought. To this end he must keep up constant correspondence with his friends at home; and the arrival of the English mail, though a weekly event, can never lose interest.

The man who sinks to the level of the East is not the man for India, where he is expected to help to benefit and elevate its peoples. He ought to aim at fellowship with the people of his own race, and to join with them in every effort to make life brighter and better. Though he may be months among the people of the country without seeing a fellow-countryman or talking a word of English, and though he enjoys such life among them, he is glad to get back among his own people, every now and again at least, to talk of the things, the scenes, and the friends that they have in common. He never can forget—he never ought to forget—his fatherland.

Yet he must come among the people without haughtiness or aloofness. He will soon learn, if he cares to know them, that they are not to be despised, that they are worthy of his respect and of his most kindly feeling. The Government officer must specially remember that he is there in their interest, that he has been entrusted, by their Sovereign and his, with work to be done for them, that if he can win their trust and affection he has done the highest part of that work. He will, as far as possible, live among them, and he will find the deepest pleasure in that life. He may be fortunate enough in time to find true friends among them; and he will then know their worth—not till then.

There are men—fortunately very few—who never care for India. They are constantly looking out for leave and impatiently counting the years that must elapse before their service is completed. We have no use for such men. It is well to keep in touch with the life and thought of the mother-country; and men wisely take leave for this purpose, as well as to preserve or restore health. But the man who despises his life-work, especially when it is work such as the officer of Government has to do in India, is a fool and an unworthy servant of the Crown.

He is a fool, for he loses the happiness of his life: he is unworthy, for he crushes out of his heart the true motive for earnest and efficient work. The Government wants officers of whom the people may say, as they said of the old Roman centurion, "He loveth our nation": men whose work is a delight to them. I can hardly believe that any man that gives himself with a broad mind and kindly heart to his work in India, will fail to merit that description, whatever men may say of him, and however they may misrepresent him. And I believe that we shall always have such men; for the people win affection, and the work is fascinating.

I once had the pleasure of receiving in India a friend from Scotland, who was a great authority on agriculture. I was on tour in the Nerbudda Division of the Central Provinces. He joined my camp for several days. He rode the march every morning either with me, or with one of my staff, who acted as interpreter for him. He talked to the people about their agricultural methods; and he watched with the greatest interest all our work among them. One day he said to me, "Is it true that you were thinking of retiring from the service?" I replied that, a year or two before, my health had rather broken down, and I did think then of retiring. He said, with strong feeling, "Man, if I were in your position, I would never retire; you are a king!" Yes, one's power and influence are great, and the work is worth doing.

I went to India in 1871 with a good deal of British enthusiasm for the work which lay before me; but I confess that my feelings of love to the country and its peoples, and my pride and pleasure in my work, have intensified year by year. I know more of the country probably than most men. I have not only served for many years in one Province, and for five years in another; but I have also visited every Province in India twice, on Government Commissions, and seen almost every important Native State. I cannot tell of the depth of interest with which I have studied the manners and customs of the people, the various forms of their faith and practice, and the characteristics of their life in town and country. I have had experiences which are practically impossible for any man outside of India: experiences sometimes of difficulty, sometimes of anxiety and even distress, but almost always experiences such as ought to tend to elevate the mind, to strengthen the character, and to enlarge the belief in human nature. I have found among the people of India multitudes who have elicited my kindliest feelings, and who have shown the kindliest feeling towards myself, and I have found not a few whom I value as among the worthiest of my friends.

I am very proud of India. My imagination is enthralled by her lofty mountains, her mighty rivers, her historic cities, and her sacred groves. I love the virgin forests and the primitive villages where my happiest days have been spent. I am proud of her possibilities and of the great opportunities she gives of work and influence. I am proud of her people, whose patience in suffering and response to kindness have won my love: excitable they sometimes are, and too easily misled; but their instinct is the instinct of loyalty, and their gratitude is far more than for favours to come.

Not long after our arrival in Calcutta, my wife and I went to see the place where lies my old friend and chief, Sir John Woodburn; and my wife took with her some flowers to lay on his grave. We found the grave covered with beautiful flowers. I inquired who had placed them there. It was an Indian gentleman who still came, week after week, to show his gratitude to one who had been his friend, though it was then more than a year since that kind heart had ceased to beat and that willing hand was powerless to help. This incident read me a lesson worth the learning. Courtesy, justice, and freedom from caprice, are among the qualities that win the love and gratitude of our Indian fellow-subjects.

He is a poor man who comes to India without a deep feeling of pride in the mother-country, and of loyalty to the King that reigns there; and there is no more worthy object of ambition for a man, who is animated by such sentiments, than to maintain the high traditions of British rule in all his dealings with the people of India. If the life is worthy, it is also unspeakably pleasurable. To call it up before one's memory is itself a delight; and I can hardly tear myself away from these reminiscences, so interesting to me, whatever they may be to others.

> "Still o'er these scenes my memory wakes,
> And fondly broods with miser care!
> Time but the impression deeper makes,
> As streams their channels deeper wear."

INDEX

INDEX

INDEX

INDEX

INDEX

BILLING AND SONS, LTD., PRINTERS, GUILDFORD